WALL STREET'S PICKS FOR

1999

KIRK KAZANJIAN

Dearborn
Financial Publishing, Inc.®

This publication is designed to provide accurate and authoritative information in regard to the subject matter covered. It is sold with the understanding that the publisher is not engaged in rendering legal, accounting or other professional services. If legal advice or other expert assistance is required, the services of a competent professional person should be sought.

Editorial Director: Cynthia A. Zigmund
Managing Editor: Jack Kiburz
Interior Design: Professional Resources & Communications, Inc.
Cover Design: Design Alliance, Inc.

Charts and some financial data reprinted with permission of IDD Information Services. All information contained in this book was gathered from sources believed to be reliable, but accuracy is not guaranteed.

Published by Dearborn Financial Publishing, Inc.®

Printed in the United States of America

98 99 10 9 8 7 6 5 4 3 2 1

ISBN 0-7931-2733-5

DEDICATION

To my dad, John R. Kazanjian, with thanks for supporting my many adventures in life. May this book help keep you on the road to a prosperous future.

CONTENTS

PREFACE

It's not easy gaining access to Wall Street's top minds. After all, most manage multibillion dollar portfolios and won't even consider taking you on as a private client unless you have $1 million or more to invest. It's even harder to convince these folks to let you pick their brains for a while, maybe over lunch or dinner, to learn their investment secrets and favorite stock or fund ideas for the coming months.

Fortunately, I have come to know many of the investment world's biggest stars personally. I'm privileged to enjoy the kind of access to these luminaries that few have. And now, for the fourth year in a row, I'm pleased to let you in on their investment insights and strategies for the year ahead in *Wall Street's Picks for 1999.*

This is by far the most timely and user-friendly investment guide on the market today. Instead of focusing on a bunch of abstract theories or listing hundreds of possible investment choices (like many other publications), *Wall Street's Picks for 1999* cuts through the financial jargon to bring you specific and current recommendations from the very best minds in the business.

In Part 1 of this new edition, you will learn the number one favorite stock ideas for the year ahead, according to such gurus as Fred Kobrick, the late Philip Carret, Elizabeth Dater, Louis Navellier, Seth Glickenhaus, Ronald Muhlenkamp, James O'Shaughnessy, L. Roy Papp, Robert Sanborn, Martin Whitman, Michael DiCarlo, Alan Bond, and many more. These are all successful investment managers who are at the top of their profession and consistently generate outstanding returns for their clients.

In essence, I asked each panelist to name the single stock they would own in 1999 if they could only choose one. The answers are revealed in the form of in-depth reports on each selection, including a background on the company, reason for the recommendation, financial figures and charts, and a discussion of what kind of performance to expect as the year unfolds.

Because many readers are more interested in mutual funds, I have interviewed some of the country's leading fund analysts for Part 2. Following a general discussion about how funds work and why they are such great investment vehicles, you will find promising recommendations in various categories from such renowned fund authorities as Sheldon Jacobs, Stephen Savage, Michael Hirsch, Paul Merriman, Larry Chin, Janet Brown, and Bob Markman.

As I've said before, the idea behind this book is to bring together an investment dream team to help you develop a first-rate portfolio. It's the kind of inside information that used to be reserved exclusively for Wall Street's heavy hitters. This knowledge can't be found in any other book or magazine on the market today.

Of course, no pick is guaranteed to go up, and some may fall dramatically in price, despite my panel's optimistic expectations. That's all part of the risk you take when you become part-owner of a company through purchasing stock. However, judging from the past performance of those featured on my panel, most of these choices should be very rewarding in 1999. They certainly have been over the past few years.

As usual, Part 3 features a complete biography of each adviser, describing his or her background, investment philosophy, market outlook, and other bits of advice you can use to make more money in the market. I want to thank nationally syndicated personal finance columnist, Humberto Cruz, for calling *Wall Street's Picks* one of only three investment books available today that survives the marketing hype. Humberto agreed with me that Part 3 is perhaps the most valuable part of the book, because the insights these living investment legends share can help make you richer for many years to come.

Additionally, even though this book is written in reader-friendly language, if you're ever confused by any financial verbiage that seems like a bunch of gobbledygook, simply turn to the back where you'll find a glossary full of definitions for some of the more commonly used investment terms and phrases you will encounter in the pages that follow.

If you're a regular reader of this series, you know that my list of panelists and picks changes dramatically from year to year. In fact, this time around the only stock making a repeat appearance from previous editions is Intel. (It was a featured selection in both 1996 and 1997.) By the way, if you want to know how last year's contributors feel about the prospects for their investment ideas going into 1999, their latest buy, sell, and hold ratings can be found at the end of Part 3.

For now, sit back, relax, and enjoy what I hope will be a very prosperous journey into the world of Wall Street's best advice on how to invest your money over the next 12 months.

—Kirk Kazanjian

part

1

THE TOP STOCKS FOR 1999

STOCK PICKS —
AN INTRODUCTION

Before we discuss this year's stock selections, it makes sense to review some of the important principles that should guide all of your investment decisions. To begin with, as all smart investors know, basing portfolio decisions solely on the economy, specific items in the news, or the direction of the Dow is a recipe for disaster. In fact, the richest and most successful investors understand the key to great profits is finding individual companies with stories and valuations so compelling, their share prices are bound to go up, regardless of what happens with the overall economy or underlying indexes.

Those who try to time the market usually end up making the least amount of money. That's because no one has created a foolproof system for predicting where stocks are headed. Though some look back and boast about how accurate they were at calling certain tops, bottoms, and crashes, they rarely mention the number of times their advice was wrong.

Investors versus Traders

It has often been said that *investors*, those who buy quality companies and stay in the market regardless of outside influences, drive Cadillacs, while *traders*, people who jump in and out on a regular basis, ride around in Chevys. History suggests this is true. Statistics show the majority of all market gains come on only a handful of trading sessions each year. Therefore, if you are out on those days, you can expect nothing more than mediocre returns, or even losses.

An often-cited study shows that during the 1980s, the Standard & Poor's 500 index produced an average annual return of 17.6 percent. However, if you were in cash on the top ten trading days during that period, the figure dropped to 12.6 percent. Had you been on the sidelines for the 20 best days, you would have earned a mere 9.3 percent. And, if you missed the 30 biggest advancing sessions, your return would have plummeted to just 6.5 percent, less than what you would have earned in a money market fund. Clearly, not being fully invested is costly, since stocks tend to move in lumps. They rise or fall, and then remain stagnant for awhile, before rallying up or down again.

This is further proof that market timing rarely makes sense. Sure, it would be great to avoid every correction and bear market. But that's impossible to do. Those who make the right calls often owe their success more to luck than anything else. It's a point driven home by the great investor Sir John Templeton. When I asked for his market outlook a few years ago, he replied, "In the 52 years I was in the investment industry, I was never able to answer that question. I just searched for those stocks whose prices were lowest in relation to earnings."

In other words, he had a strategy and stuck with it, regardless of what was happening with the "market."

Take it from Sir John: The secret to investment riches is finding the right stocks to be in at any given time. After all, though the major indexes may fall or go nowhere, some individual issues always manage to skyrocket. For example, back in 1994, the S&P 500 and Nasdaq each squeezed out a mere 1 percent gain, including dividends. Yet Microtouch Systems soared 555 percent, Cooper Companies leaped 227 percent, LSI Logic rose 154 percent, and Rock Bottom Restaurants jumped a full 128 percent for the year, proving that even though the overall market may be stagnant, it's possible to make a lot of money through superior stock selection.

Uncle Sam Likes Investors Too

Another reason to avoid running in and out of stocks is that you'll save on the amount of profits you have to share with the government. As part of the Taxpayers Relief Act of 1997, Congress decided to cap all long-term capital gains for positions held more than 18 months at a maximum rate of 20 percent. This compares to the 30 percent-plus rate you could be forced to pay for short-term trades.

Building Wealth with Equities

By now you've figured out that creating wealth with stocks requires you to construct a stable of spectacular companies with bright future prospects. But how can you, as an individual investor far removed from the inner-workings of Wall Street, find these jewels for yourself? That's what Part 1 of this book is all about.

Over the past several months, I personally spoke with dozens of the world's top investment experts and asked, "If you could only choose one stock to hold in 1999, what would it be and why?" The panelists represent leading portfolio managers, investment advisers, newsletter editors, and market strategists, all of whom have a slightly different style or area of expertise, giving you a truly diversified list of potential holdings.

Next, I followed up on these responses by doing further analysis on the selections, such as culling through annual reports, financial statements, and historical price charts. This provided some perspective as to where the stocks have been, and where they might be going. Additional insight came from talking with corporate officers about any developments that might make the picks either more or less compelling.

All of this revealing information was then put together in the form of an easy-to-read research report. There are a total of 25 different companies, which are listed in alphabetical order. Be aware that this isn't a beauty contest to see who can pick the best performer, nor are these stocks you should buy in January and sell in December. Instead, they are quality companies that each expert considers to have great prospects for 1999 and beyond.

Dissecting the Information

Each discussion starts off with a table showing the company's ticker symbol, trading exchange, and business industry, along with such data as current price, PE ratio, book value, and earnings per share. Next is a profile of the company that includes specific reasons why it was selected. You'll also find IDD/Tradeline graphs showing the stock's daily price patterns for the past 12 months, total return versus the S&P 500, and performance compared to its peer index. There's even a box containing important balance sheet numbers (like current assets, liabilities, and shareholder's equity) going back two years. You should also pay attention to each stock's estimated beta factor, which is included in the statistical box at the bottom of every profile. This measures its price volatility compared to the S&P 500, which has a beta of 1. Simply put, a stock with a beta of 0.6 is less volatile than the market overall, while a stock with a rating of 1.6 is much riskier. At the end of each profile, you'll find the address and phone number you can use to request more information from the company. In addition, I have also included each company's Internet address, if applicable.

Please understand that these reports present predominately positive comments about the various companies. This stands to reason, because the recommending advisers are very upbeat about these stocks and their future prospects. However, there are always negatives to every story, and I have taken care to bring some of them to your attention. Make sure you evaluate the potential downfalls of each idea before investing. Remember, not every optimistic expectation by my panel of experts will come to fruition.

When choosing equities, it usually makes sense to stick with companies reporting steady annual earnings growth, a characteristic shared by most of the stocks in this book. In addition, generally speaking, the lower the current percentage of institutional ownership in a stock, the better. That's because institutions account for more than 70 percent of all daily trading activity. If they own only a small amount of stock, it shows the potential for them to buy more; and unless institutions are gobbling up shares in large quantities, it will be difficult for the price to substantially rise. High ownership by inside management is another bullish sign. It indicates that those in the know have enough faith in the firm to put their own money on the line. You'll learn much more about many different successful stock-picking strategies by reading the biographies in Part 3. In many respects, this is one of the most important sections of the book, since the insights and advice these market masters provide are invaluable.

Stock Selection

It should be noted that each stock has been selected for a different reason, from low valuation to high future earnings potential, based on the adviser's particular style. In fact, every panelist has a unique process for selecting stocks. This information is spelled out for you in every discussion and should be an important consideration as you decide which ideas make the most sense for you, given your risk tolerance and overall objectives.

You'll notice the recommendations once again cover the gamut in terms of market capitalizations, industry groups, and geographic locations. There are some very big blue chips, namely Chubb and State Street; smaller high-tech outfits with more risk, like Western Digital and Vitesse; and international concerns, among them APT Satellite and Alcatel.

Asset Allocation

As you stroll through these pages, keep several things in mind, including asset allocation. You need to consider whether you even belong in stocks and, if so, to what extent.

Let me first make it clear that only *investment capital* should be put into the market. In essence, this is money above and beyond what you need to live on. Think of it as funds you could afford to lose without dramatically altering your lifestyle. Granted, no one invests to lose. But, because the stock market is inherently risky, this is a good attitude to have. That way you won't be scared out just when you should be jumping in.

After you've identified your investment capital, you must outline your goals. If you're saving for retirement, or a similar long-term objective that's at least five to ten years away, stocks should comprise a significant amount of your portfolio. They are the only investment class to consistently stay ahead of inflation, while providing the highest rates of return throughout history. (We'll delve deeper into the subject of asset allocation in Parts 2 and 3.)

Once you determine what percentage to devote to stocks, you should understand that smaller and international issues generally carry more risk than those that are larger and better known. Keep this in mind as you evaluate which companies to purchase. If you consider yourself to be conservative, you might want to stick with only blue chips. If you're more moderate, perhaps several large companies sprinkled with a few small-caps and an international issue or two make sense. The brave, those shooting for huge gains and willing to take a potential roller-coaster ride in this pursuit, could concentrate almost entirely on smaller names with big prospects.

How many stocks do you need in your portfolio? Ask ten different people and you'll get ten different answers. An important rule of thumb is you should never put more than 5 percent of your total assets into any single investment. Therefore, to really reduce your downside exposure, you need at least 20 different issues. On the other hand, Warren Buffett, who is among the greatest investors ever, only holds a handful of stocks and has racked up enormous gains by concentrating on a select group of companies he knows well.

Just make sure you don't buy too many stocks in the same sector. If you simply own 30 high-technology stocks, your diversification is virtually nil. Spread your choices over many different areas, so when one is out of favor, you can profit from another. Fortunately, the selections in this book are highly diversified in terms of size, industry, and even geographic location.

A good technique for developing a nice mix involves constructing your portfolio around a core. In other words, you choose a handful of great, mostly blue chip, companies that you plan to hold for the long haul, and build some more speculative names around them.

Remember, you will have to pay a commission for each stock you buy or sell. These charges can add up quickly and eat into your profits. You can save money by using a quality discount broker. Some brokers will now execute trades for as little as $5, especially on the Internet, so be certain to shop around. I'm sure you'll agree there's no use paying those high full-service brokerage fees when you're acting on your own investment advice (with the help of a few well-connected friends).

Limit or Market Orders?

Another decision you will face is whether to place market or limit orders for your stock selections. When you place a market order, you agree to pay whatever the prevailing price is at the time your order is executed, which may be more or less than the amount quoted by your broker.

On the other hand, limit orders allow you to set the terms. Here's why: All stocks trade at a spread, which is the difference between the bid and offer price. If a stock is trading at a bid of 15 and offered at 15 1/2, the spread is 50 cents. With a limit order, you can specify that you will only buy the stock at 15. Otherwise, it would likely clear at market, or 15 1/2. Be advised, however, that while limit orders can save you money, they may take longer to execute, especially for thinly traded issues.

Limit orders are also used to set much lower price targets. For example, if you like a stock today that trades at 20, but only want to get in if it drops to 16, you can place a good-till-canceled (GTC) limit order for 16, which means the trade won't clear unless the issue hits your price point of 16. This may not ever happen, so be realistic if you place such an order.

Conversely, you can set stop-loss limit orders once you've purchased a stock on the New York or American Stock Exchanges to cushion your potential loss. Let's say you buy a stock for 20 and want to sell if it falls more than 10 percent. You can place a stop-loss order for 18, which means the stock will automatically be sold if it reaches that level. (This technique should be used with caution, given that the market is highly volatile today and many stocks tend to bounce around by several points during each trading session. If you're not careful, you could be sold out of a position, even though the stock closes the day at a much higher price.)

When You Should Buy or Sell

Unfortunately, when writing about the stock market, be it for a book such as this or a daily Internet site, information and valuations can change dramatically in a matter of seconds. That's why I have tried to include each analyst's 1999 price target in every profile. If a stock has already reached this target by the time you read about it, you may want to determine whether this enthusiasm is sustainable, or simply move on to another pick that appears to be a better bargain. If the company has just introduced a new product or acquisition that will make a significant contribution to earnings, it may merit the higher valuation. (As I mentioned earlier, it's wise to favor companies with rapidly growing earnings.) If nothing has changed, perhaps the price has moved ahead of itself or reached full value. On the other hand, if a stock is trading well-below its target price, it may be an even more compelling buy, assuming nothing catastrophic or scandalous has happened to change the fundamentals in the interim.

The question of when to sell is more difficult. Some feel you should never get rid of a quality company. Others suggest you let go when the price appreciates or depreciates to some arbitrary level, such as 20 or 30 percent above or below cost. You'll find plenty of advice on this subject in Part 3.

Needless to say, if something happens to cloud both the company's future prospects and your reasons for buying in the first place, this too may be a good reason to get out.

Before You Begin

A few final notes: Please don't invest in any stock just because a person you admire likes it. Simply use this validation as a starting point. Then call or write the company (the location, phone numbers, and addresses are provided for each stock), request an annual report and form 10-K, check out available research reports at your library or broker's office, talk with an investor relations representative, check out the company's Internet site, and ultimately make a decision as to whether the recommendation makes sense for *you*. Just because it's right for Marty Whitman, Louis Navellier, Elizabeth Dater, Michael DiCarlo, or anyone else doesn't necessarily mean it belongs in your portfolio. Use these suggestions as a launching pad, but do a little legwork to confirm everything in your own mind and, for heaven's sake, make sure you understand what you're buying. If a company is engaged in some exotic technology, and you have no clue as to what it does, stay away. Keep an eye on how your ultimate stock selections perform, and remain informed about any new positive and negative developments surrounding them.

Be sure to read the quarterly and annual reports, and keep good records. This will make your life easier when it comes time to pay Uncle Sam for capital gains and dividend interest. It's also smart to periodically examine and calculate your total return figures to see how you're doing, especially compared to the S&P 500, which is the industry's standard benchmark. In essence, you should run your investment portfolio like a business. Once you make a purchase, you become a part-owner in the company and have a duty to run your affairs accordingly.

Finally, always remember: There are no guarantees. While the following stocks truly represent the best ideas of some wonderful investors, the market never goes straight up. All equities carry a significant amount of risk. Also be aware that the various experts may own positions in the equities they recommend, either in personal and/or managed accounts. This is not necessarily a bad thing, it's just something you should know. With that in mind, let's begin naming names of which companies could make you rich in 1999.

AIRBORNE EXPRESS

Louis Navellier

Navellier & Associates

Company Profile

When UPS delivery drivers went on strike in August 1997, effectively shutting the company down, businesses around the world were left crippled, unable to get their time-sensitive documents and packages delivered without turning to another shipper. Among the biggest beneficiaries of this strike were UPS's three major competitors: the U.S. Postal Service, FedEx, and Airborne Express. What many former UPS customers learned is that it doesn't make sense to rely on just one shipper. Therefore, many who temporarily switched from UPS in desperation have never returned. "The strike made many businesses mad, and they're diversifying away to avoid being disrupted by an event like this again," surmises Louis Navellier of Navellier & Associates.

Navellier believes Airborne Express has gained the most from this trend. "Airborne was a good company to begin with, but sales and earnings really took off after UPS went on strike," he says. "Before the strike, UPS had 63 percent of the U.S. shipping market. That has now decreased significantly. The reason it especially helped Airborne is because the company is getting a lot of the second-day air blue label shipping that used to go to UPS." FedEx is better known for its overnight service, which is more expensive. The U.S. Postal Service offers a priority mail option. But delivery in two days isn't guaranteed and there is no way to track a shipment. "FedEx does everything and is always trying to break into new markets," Navellier observes. "I have nothing against FedEx. I think it's a great company too. My only criticism is that Airborne seems to do it cheaper and more efficiently."

Navellier notes that Airborne has taken advantage of the situation by wooing businesses with special contract rates to get them locked in as long-term customers. The strategy has clearly been successful. Earnings tripled from 1996 to 1997, making for the most financially successful 12 months in the company's 52-year history. "During 1997, various events occurred in the first three quarters that enhanced operating results," Airborne's chief financial officer Roy Liljebeck points out. "In the first quarter, the Federal Aviation [Administration] excise tax was not in effect from January 1 through March 7, 1997, and we commenced a fuel surcharge in mid-February that was in effect until July 1, 1997. In the third quarter, the strike at United Parcel Service in August added significantly to our business. We estimate that the cumulative effect of these items added 95 cents to $1 per share on a diluted basis. However, even without the benefit of those items, the company would have experienced a record year."

Airborne Express is the nation's third largest express package shipment company. It delivers time-sensitive documents, letters, small packages, and freight to virtually every location in the U.S. and in more than 200 countries. Delivery options include same-day, next-morning, next-afternoon and second-day. While the company's recent success cannot be disputed, the question is: Will it continue? Navellier concludes the answer is yes. "The economy is very healthy, and there are plenty of things to ship," he maintains. "Airborne's operating margins continue to expand, sales are strong, and analysts keep revising earnings estimates higher. I grade my stocks on a variety of fundamental criteria, and Airborne is one of my highest rated companies."

Reason for Recommendation

This brings us to Navellier's reason for recommending this stock. In addition to believing that Airborne will keep benefiting from disgruntled businesses seeking new shippers, he notes that the company has many other things in its favor. Among them are lower fuel prices, which means it costs less to operate its fleet of planes and vans. Then you have the stock itself, which Navellier contends has the precise characteristics Wall Street is enamored of right now. "Investors love what I call companies with good present value of growth, or growth at a reasonable price," he says. "Airborne's growth PE ratio is very reasonable, and the fundamentals keep going higher and higher. This stock is under a lot of institutional accumulation, which is another positive factor. When I first bought it, it was a small-cap stock. Today it's a mid-cap. As long as it continues to have smooth, steady growth, Airborne is going to become even more of an institutional darling."

Navellier maintains he doesn't have a specific price target in mind for the stock. He just plans to ride it as long as the company's prospects remain favorable. "I see continued smooth sales growth for Airborne, with margin expansion and the chance to capture more of the two-day air shipping market that UPS still dominates," he predicts. But what about the World Wide Web? Aren't people shipping overnight documents less frequently, since they can simply e-mail them instead? "I don't think that has any relevance, because you can't send signed documents or glossy brochures over the Internet," Navellier counters. "That's the same argument everyone used when they said we'd have a paperless society one day. Instead, we now use more paper than ever before."

Contact Information: Robert Cline, Chairman and CEO
Airborne Freight Corporation
P.O. Box 662
Seattle, WA 98111
(206) 285-4600
www.airborne-express.com

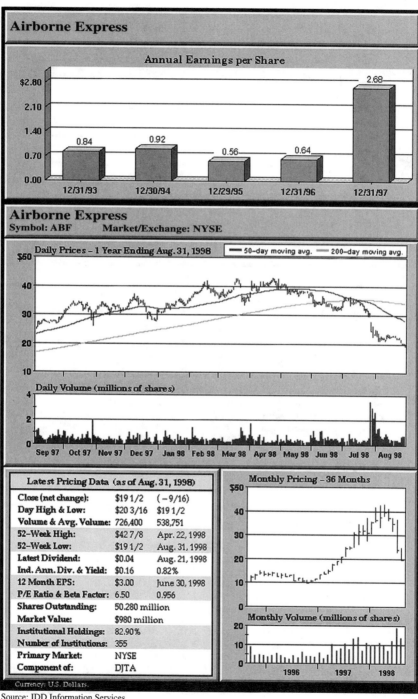

Airborne Express

Annual Earnings per Share

Date	EPS
12/31/93	0.84
12/30/94	0.92
12/29/95	0.56
12/31/96	0.64
12/31/97	2.68

Airborne Express
Symbol: ABF   Market/Exchange: NYSE

Daily Prices – 1 Year Ending Aug. 31, 1998   ▬ 50-day moving avg.   ▬ 200-day moving avg.

Daily Volume (millions of shares)

Sep 97 Oct 97 Nov 97 Dec 97 Jan 98 Feb 98 Mar 98 Apr 98 May 98 Jun 98 Jul 98 Aug 98

Latest Pricing Data (as of Aug. 31, 1998)

Close (net change):	$19 1/2	(–9/16)
Day High & Low:	$20 3/16	$19 1/2
Volume & Avg. Volume:	726,400	538,751
52–Week High:	$42 7/8	Apr. 22, 1998
52–Week Low:	$19 1/2	Aug. 31, 1998
Latest Dividend:	$0.04	Aug. 21, 1998
Ind. Ann. Div. & Yield:	$0.16	0.82%
12 Month EPS:	$3.00	June 30, 1998
P/E Ratio & Beta Factor:	6.50	0.956
Shares Outstanding:	50.280 million	
Market Value:	$980 million	
Institutional Holdings:	82.90%	
Number of Institutions:	355	
Primary Market:	NYSE	
Component of:	DJTA	

Monthly Pricing – 36 Months

Monthly Volume (millions of shares)

1996   1997   1998

Currency: U.S. Dollars.

Source: IDD Information Services

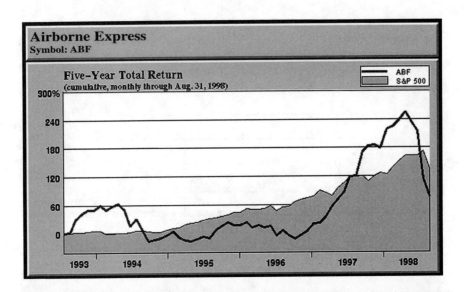

Airborne Express
Symbol: ABF

Five-Year Total Return
(cumulative, monthly through Aug. 31, 1998)

Legend: ABF, S&P 500

SELECTED INCOME STATEMENT AND BALANCE SHEET ITEMS

INCOME STATEMENT	12/31/93	12/30/94	12/29/95	12/31/96	12/31/97	1 Year
Sales/Revenues	26,456	31,400	32,709	31,269	30,854	30,854
Cost of Goods Sold	18,782	23,627	26,013	24,908	24,099	N.A.
Pre-tax Margin (%)	5.80	2.40	(15.20)	2.10	3.20	N.A.
Operating Income	2,235.7	780.80	(2,616.0)	131.40	939.90	N.A.
Net Income before Extras	1,195.1	678.00	(5,216.3)	525.70	774.40	774.40
Reported Net Income	1,195.1	678.00	(5,216.3)	525.70	774.40	774.40
Depreciation & Amortization	1,460.1	1,788.7	4,186.7	1,653.0	1,512.3	N.A.
EPS from Net Income (Primary)	1.680	0.950	(0.710)	0.670	0.990	0.820
EPS from Net Income (Fully Diluted)	1.680	0.980	(0.650)	0.700	0.970	0.810
Dividend per Common Share	0.359	0.414	0.470	0.239	0.289	0.289
Dividend Yield (%)	1.25	2.44	2.68	1.49	1.14	N.A.
Payout Ratio	0.21	0.44	N.A.	0.36	0.29	0.35
BALANCE SHEET						
ASSETS						
Cash & Cash Equivalents	5,217.9	7,409.2	7,124.3	5,657.9	4,618.0	
Inventories	7,670.2	8,454.5	9,317.2	9,579.0	7,242.1	
Total Current Assets	29,143	32,909	34,855	32,516	28,364	
Total Assets	44,012	51,309	52,132	47,890	41,794	
LIABILITIES & EQUITY						
Short Term Debt	4,098.4	3,083.7	5,734.7	4,518.1	2,955.6	
Long Term Debt	4,199.1	6,594.3	5,465.3	3,675.7	3,638.1	
Total Liabilities	34,216	40,112	45,159	40,022	34,498	
Shares Outstanding	717.300	732.725	752.740	782.135	815.995	
Common Stockholder Equity	9,795.7	11,198	6,972.8	7,868.0	7,296.4	
Total Stockholder Equity	9,795.7	11,198	6,972.8	7,868.0	7,296.4	

Note: Figures in Millions of $ except: per share items, margins, yields, and ratios.

Source: IDD Information Services

ALCATEL ALSTHOM

David Williams
U.S. Trust

Company Profile

Alcatel Alsthom is the largest industrial company in Europe. It is a leading international supplier of telecommunications equipment, systems, and services. You might think of it as the Lucent Technologies of France. While based in Paris, you can buy shares of this company in the form of American Depositary Receipts on the New York Stock Exchange. "Alcatel is in all the right areas," says U.S. Trust portfolio manager David Williams. "For one thing, it's involved in the area of cable. This division is the largest supplier to Cisco Systems in Europe. Cisco's really growing like a weed there. The company recently entered into a huge contract to build an underground cable linkup between China and the United States. Alcatel also makes mobile phones and switching equipment. It's even in the wireless communications business."

At one point, Alcatel had its fingers in many diverse areas, making trains, for example. In recent years, however, the company has been shedding its noncore businesses and really focusing on what it does best. "That's the main reason I'm recommending this stock," Williams admits. "I like this restructuring. A couple of years ago, the company had a big loss. It's still not earning much money. But every year, the situation gets a little better. Management is becoming more focused by shedding off the slow growth businesses."

Let's take a look at each major division within Alcatel in greater depth. To begin with, the telecom unit designs and markets complete telecommunications systems. These include public switching systems, mobile communications, corporate networks, submarine cable systems, and space and defense systems. This group is active in more than 130 countries, with a large market share in the emerging markets. Next, there's the cable and components division. This unit manufactures telecommunications cables, power cables, batteries, metallurgy (such as conductors and enameled wire), and components (like electric motors and vacuum pumps). One major project for this division is the advancement of battery technology for electric vehicles.

Alcatel's engineering and systems division works to expand the company's large-scale turnkey contract markets. Alcatel's customers increasingly are demanding turnkey systems that can easily be put to work. The engineering and systems group creates systems especially tailored to the needs of each client. Finally, the research division focuses on software, energy, optical systems, radio communications, network accesses, private networks, and network architectures. It operates research and development centers in both Europe and the U.S.

Incidentally, another division, GEC Alsthom, is now listed on the stock exchange as a separate company. GEC Alsthom designs a wide range of high-performance, environmentally-friendly power generation systems. It also manufacturers high-speed trains, locomotives, metros, and the associated control and signaling systems.

Reason for Recommendation

Williams runs a mutual fund called Excelsior Value & Restructuring. As you might guess from that name, he is always on the lookout for value-oriented restructuring plays. You already know about the restructuring story at Alcatel. But another positive is the fact that Europe is moving to deregulate the telecommunications industry, which should be a further benefit to Alcatel. "What's more, this company is going from a negative to [a] positive cash flow position and will likely buy back a lot of stock in the future," Williams predicts. "When that happens in any company, it's like magic." In terms of price, Alcatel is no real bargain. It trades at about a market multiple, which is kind of high for Williams. However, it sells for much less than Lucent. So, on a relative basis, it's attractively priced. "Don't get me wrong, this company isn't as good as Lucent," Williams cautions. "There are some uncertainties. The company's R&D needs to be improved. Management is only in the early stages of refocusing the business, and it's too early to know whether it is going to be successful. There is also a lot of competition from companies that are better positioned than Alcatel. As a result, this stock is clearly not going to trade at the same multiple as Lucent overnight. But it has the potential to get there in the future. That's why I like it."

One more potential danger, in William's estimation, is that investing in Europe in general now is risky. "Yes, they are restructuring, but the politics aren't quite right," he observes. "The government still has too much control. On the other hand, so much of Alcatel's business is outside of France that I think this is less of a problem than it might be otherwise."

Williams insists this is a stock you should buy and ignore for awhile, until all of these changes kick in. He's convinced patient investors will be rewarded. He forecasts earnings for Alcatel will grow by 20 percent a year, once all of the cost-cutting measures are in place. "There has been no predictability from this company in the past whatsoever," he adds. "That's finally starting to change. Management is refocusing on sales growth, and earnings are definitely beginning to come back."

Contact Information: Serge Tchuruk, Chairman and CEO
Alcatel Alsthom
54, rue La Boétie
75008 Paris - France
011 331 4076 1068
www.alcatel.com

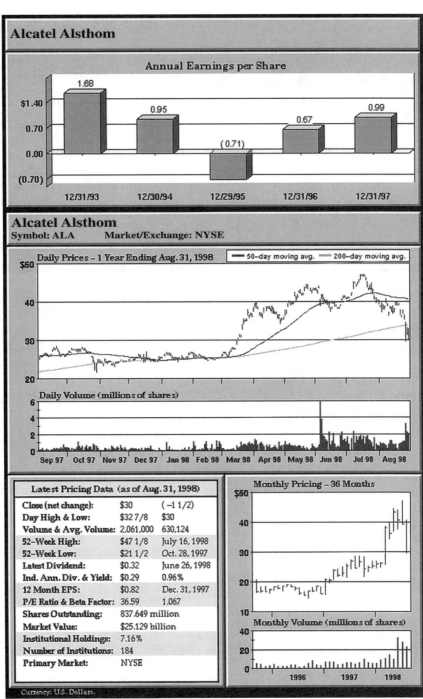

Alcatel Alsthom

Annual Earnings per Share

12/31/93	12/30/94	12/29/95	12/31/96	12/31/97
1.68	0.95	(0.71)	0.67	0.99

Alcatel Alsthom
Symbol: ALA　　　**Market/Exchange: NYSE**

Daily Prices – 1 Year Ending Aug. 31, 1998　　━ 50-day moving avg.　━ 200-day moving avg.

Daily Volume (millions of shares)

Sep 97　Oct 97　Nov 97　Dec 97　Jan 98　Feb 98　Mar 98　Apr 98　May 98　Jun 98　Jul 98　Aug 98

Latest Pricing Data (as of Aug. 31, 1998)

Close (net change):	$30	(–1 1/2)
Day High & Low:	$32 7/8	$30
Volume & Avg. Volume:	2,061,000	630,124
52–Week High:	$47 1/8	July 16, 1998
52–Week Low:	$21 1/2	Oct. 28, 1997
Latest Dividend:	$0.32	June 26, 1998
Ind. Ann. Div. & Yield:	$0.29	0.96%
12 Month EPS:	$0.82	Dec. 31, 1997
P/E Ratio & Beta Factor:	36.59	1.067
Shares Outstanding:	837.649 million	
Market Value:	$25.129 billion	
Institutional Holdings:	7.16%	
Number of Institutions:	184	
Primary Market:	NYSE	

Monthly Pricing – 36 Months

Monthly Volume (millions of shares)

1996　　1997　　1998

Currency: U.S. Dollars.

Source: IDD Information Services

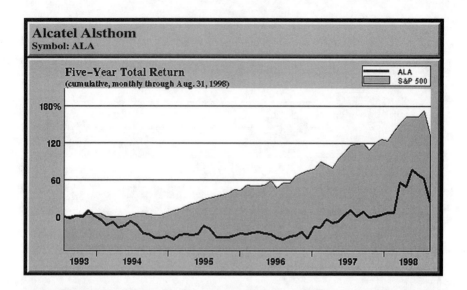

Alcatel Alsthom
Symbol: ALA

Five-Year Total Return
(cumulative, monthly through Aug. 31, 1998)

ALA
S&P 500

SELECTED INCOME STATEMENT AND BALANCE SHEET ITEMS

INCOME STATEMENT	12/31/93	12/30/94	12/29/95	12/31/96	12/31/97	1 Year
Sales/Revenues	26,456	31,400	32,709	31,269	30,854	30,854
Cost of Goods Sold	18,782	23,627	26,013	24,908	24,099	N.A.
Pre-tax Margin (%)	5.80	2.40	(15.20)	2.10	3.20	N.A.
Operating Income	2,235.7	780.80	(2,616.0)	131.40	939.90	N.A.
Net Income before Extras	1,195.1	678.00	(5,216.3)	525.70	774.40	774.40
Reported Net Income	1,195.1	678.00	(5,216.3)	525.70	774.40	774.40
Depreciation & Amortization	1,460.1	1,788.7	4,186.7	1,653.0	1,512.3	N.A.
EPS from Net Income (Primary)	1.680	0.950	(0.710)	0.670	0.990	0.820
EPS from Net Income (Fully Diluted)	1.680	0.980	(0.650)	0.700	0.970	0.810
Dividend per Common Share	0.359	0.414	0.470	0.239	0.289	0.289
Dividend Yield (%)	1.25	2.44	2.68	1.49	1.14	N.A.
Payout Ratio	0.21	0.44	N.A.	0.36	0.29	0.35
BALANCE SHEET						
ASSETS						
Cash & Cash Equivalents	5,217.9	7,409.2	7,124.3	5,657.9	4,618.0	
Inventories	7,670.2	8,454.5	9,317.2	9,579.0	7,242.1	
Total Current Assets	29,143	32,909	34,855	32,516	28,364	
Total Assets	44,012	51,309	52,132	47,890	41,794	
LIABILITIES & EQUITY						
Short Term Debt	4,098.4	3,083.7	5,734.7	4,518.1	2,955.6	
Long Term Debt	4,199.1	6,594.3	5,465.3	3,675.7	3,638.1	
Total Liabilities	34,216	40,112	45,159	40,022	34,498	
Shares Outstanding	717.300	732.725	752.740	782.135	815.995	
Common Stockholder Equity	9,795.7	11,198	6,972.8	7,868.0	7,296.4	
Total Stockholder Equity	9,795.7	11,198	6,972.8	7,868.0	7,296.4	

Note: Figures in Millions of $ except: per share items, margins, yields, and ratios.

Source: IDD Information Services

APT SATELLITE

Seth Glickenhaus
Glickenhaus & Co.

Company Profile

The skies over Asia are increasingly becoming populated with products produced by APT Satellite. This Hong Kong-based company provides high-quality satellite transponder services for broadcasting and telecommunication companies worldwide, although the bulk of its business currently comes from the Asia-Pacific region. The company is traded as an American Depositary Receipt on the New York Stock Exchange.

"APT buys or leases satellites and sells transponder space to big corporations," notes Seth Glickenhaus, president of Glickenhaus & Co. "I believe it will eventually be the major satellite company in China. That's important because, in my opinion, China will be the world's most dominant industrial country within ten years."

Demand for satellite transponders in APT's target area has been on a steady rise in recent years. "As the telecommunication and broadcasting business in the Asia-Pacific region grows, and the general living standard of the region improves, the demand for satellite transponders shall maintain at a higher level towards the turn of the century," predicts APT chairman Xie Gao Jue. "In order to become a leading satellite transponder services provider, the company will continue to pursue its business development strategies by focusing on the Asia-Pacific market and by leveraging its relationship with shareholders to establish a competitive edge."

APT's first satellite was launched into orbit in 1994 from Xichang, People's Republic of China. The company now has several more in active service. At last check, more than 90 percent of APT's total transponder capacity had been leased out on its two oldest satellites, APSTAR-I and APSTAR-IA. During the summer of 1997, APT was in charge of broadcasting by satellite the handover ceremony of Hong Kong to China, and various other activities surrounding that event. APT has an agreement with the China Broadcasting Film Television Co., under the Ministry of Radio, Film, and Television in the People's Republic of China, to lease two transponders for broadcasting programs on several television stations in the country. It is also currently conducting discussions with the Chinese government, which owns part of the company, about ways to further increase its satellite direct-to-home television broadcasting business.

Furthermore, Chairman Jue is optimistic about APT's latest satellite, APSTAR-IIR, which was scheduled to be launched sometime in the fourth quarter of 1998. "Following the successful launch of APSTAR-IIR into orbit and the commencement of its commercial operations, the company will be able to set up a comprehensive and advanced satellite system to provide satellite broadcasting and telecommunication services with its high output power transponders for more than 100 countries, servicing approximately 75 percent of the world's population," Jue says. "At the same time, the company has started planning for the launch of a high output power satellite with C-band and Ku-band coverage by the end of 2000 to satisfy the expected market demand."

But it's not just the ability to beam TV shows around the globe that has Glickenhaus excited about this company. "You can't set up phones in China the way you can here, by putting telephone poles all over the place," he points out. "It has to be done using wireless technology, and you need APT's satellites to make that process work. China has about 1.2 billion people now. Eventually it will have 1.6 billion. The country is just now coming into the 20th century, 100 years late. However, it will enter the 21st century at a very fast rate. I'm convinced of that."

Reason for Recommendation

Unfortunately, because APT's operations are overseas, it's not easy for American investors to do a lot of hands-on research on this company, although you can get an annual report written in both English and Chinese. But Glickenhaus was so intrigued by this business, he sent his son to China for a personal inspection (His son is a fellow portfolio manager at his firm). "He was very impressed with them," Glickenhaus reports. "I have also talked to company management. I don't speak Chinese, but they have interpreters who speak English very fluently. I keep up with what's going on over there."

Glickenhaus is convinced 1999 could be a great year for the company, as it continues to solidify its near-monopoly position in China's satellite business. "The demand the services APT provides is going to be enormous," he maintains. "It's also a reasonably priced stock. It went public in December 1996 for $15 a share. I have no doubt the company's earnings will grow dramatically in the coming years. I'm looking for APT to make at least $2 a share in 1999."

Glickenhaus projects this stock will triple in price over the next three to five years. "It is a privately owned company, with a management team eager to make it succeed," he adds. "This is a nice investment that is going to do just fine."

Contact Information: Xie Gao Jue, Chairman
APT Satellite Holdings Limited
Room 3111-3112, 31/F.
One Pacific Place
88 Queensway, Hong Kong
011 852 2526 2281
e-mail: aptir@apstar.com
www.apstar.com

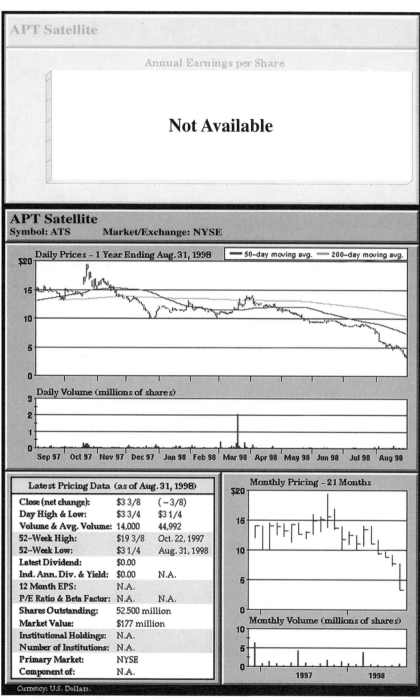

APT Satellite

Annual Earnings per Share

Not Available

APT Satellite
Symbol: ATS   **Market/Exchange: NYSE**

Daily Prices – 1 Year Ending Aug. 31, 1998   ▬ 50–day moving avg. ▬ 200–day moving avg.

Daily Volume (millions of shares)

Sep 97 Oct 97 Nov 97 Dec 97 Jan 98 Feb 98 Mar 98 Apr 98 May 98 Jun 98 Jul 98 Aug 98

Latest Pricing Data (as of Aug. 31, 1998)		
Close (net change):	$3 3/8	(–3/8)
Day High & Low:	$3 3/4	$3 1/4
Volume & Avg. Volume:	14,000	44,992
52–Week High:	$19 3/8	Oct. 22, 1997
52–Week Low:	$3 1/4	Aug. 31, 1998
Latest Dividend:	$0.00	
Ind. Ann. Div. & Yield:	$0.00	N.A.
12 Month EPS:	N.A.	
P/E Ratio & Beta Factor:	N.A.	N.A.
Shares Outstanding:	52.500 million	
Market Value:	$177 million	
Institutional Holdings:	N.A.	
Number of Institutions:	N.A.	
Primary Market:	NYSE	
Component of:	N.A.	

Monthly Pricing – 21 Months

Monthly Volume (millions of shares)

1997   1998

Currency: U.S. Dollars.

Source: IDD Information Services

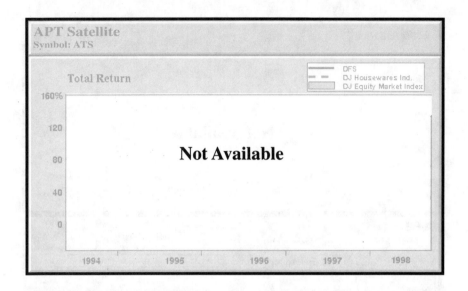

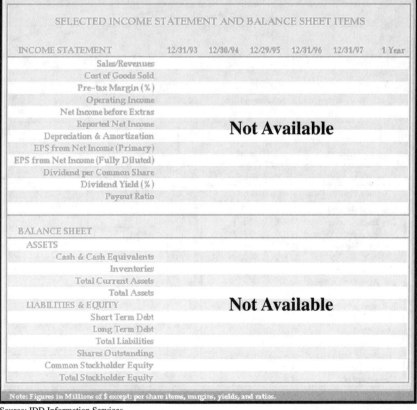

Source: IDD Information Services

B/E AEROSPACE

Ronald Muhlenkamp
Muhlenkamp & Company

Company Profile

If you've been on a commercial airplane lately, and noticed the seats were a little shabby, that could potentially be yet another business opportunity for B/E Aerospace. This Florida-based company is a leader in providing commercial aircraft seating. "It has 70 percent of the market," notes Ron Muhlenkamp, president of Muhlenkamp & Associates. B/E also manufactures individual passenger entertainment systems, food and beverage preparation and storage equipment, cooking appliances, and galley structures. The company has two primary customers: aircraft makers, like Boeing, and the individual airlines. Boeing buys seats and other equipment from B/E to put in its new jets, while the airlines look to the company to enhance and refurbish their aging fleets. "Anyone who has been on an airlane in the last few years knows that a lot of them need new seats," Muhlenkamp says. "The airlines are now making money for the first time in many years, and they can afford to replace them. They're also ordering a lot of new planes, all of which will need equipment and seating supplied by B/E."

Boeing's incredible backlog is testament to the growing airline industry. (We'll talk more about that in the next profile, which just happens to be on Boeing.) Muhlenkamp contends B/E's backlog is just like Boeing's, only better. But unlike Boeing, B/E isn't having trouble keeping up with it. "What happens is Boeing will get the order, but doesn't need seats until the plane is done," Muhlenkamp explains. "B/E can clearly see what its demand will look like. And the company has ample capacity to keep up with the orders."

B/E was formed in 1987 and has grown rapidly ever since, in large part through acquisitions. "A couple of years ago, when the airlines weren't profitable and Boeing's backlog was down, aerospace stocks were languishing," Muhlenkamp notes. "B/E used that opportunity to buy its biggest competitor. It went from having around a 20 percent market share to 70 percent. The company didn't earn much money in the process, but it was a rational strategy for growing the business. Management believed that sooner or later people would buy airplanes, and acquiring their competitor to become the dominant business in the industry made good sense."

That strategy is beginning to bear fruit. "The extraordinary airline industry recovery, the onset of which we patiently awaited while strengthening our market position and infrastructure, has now begun to be felt," says B/E chairman of the board Amin J. Khoury, who runs the company with his brother Robert. "As a result, long-deferred major aircraft refurbishment programs are now being bid and awarded; substantial increases in new aircraft, and particularly widebody, production and delivery rates are now underway; the world's major airlines are under-taking wide-scale adoption of individual-passenger entertainment systems; and our new seating, food and beverage preparation and storage equipment, and in-flight entertainment products have begun to contribute significantly to our current results and future prospects." In 1997, the company's revenue breakdown was as follows: $217 million for seating products, $101 for galley products, $52 for in-flight enter-tainment equipment, and $42 for its maintenance repair services division.

Reason for Recommendation

While Muhlenkamp expects all facets of the company's business to continue to grow, he predicts its fledgling in-flight entertainment division may really start to take off. If you've flown in first class recently, you may have already enjoyed this product. Airlines are installing small monitors on each seat, allowing passen-gers to view several channels of video entertainment during the flight. The major airlines are initially only putting these units in first-class cabins, but plans call for them to go into coach as well, especially on widebody aircraft. United Airlines, for instance, is in the midst of refitting its fleet of Boeing 777, 747-400, and 767-300 planes with B/E in-flight entertainment systems. "So here you have a company with a huge share of the market, where the backlog for new units is great and, on top of that, they have an entertainment kicker that can add on a whole new layer of business," Muhlenkamp says. "People want to be entertained in the air. If you can put something on the seat to keep them occupied on long flights, that's worth a premium." Yet Muhlenkamp points out that B/E sells at a discount to Boeing and other aerospace companies. "It's priced at a PE that's less than its sustainable return on equity, which is in the 20 percent range," he calculates. "This is a good business at a reasonable price. I expect the stock to trade in the low $40s during 1999, though I could raise that number by the time it gets there."

There is one caveat: In order for Muhlenkamp's expectations to pan out, the airline industry must remain robust. He feels it will. "Besides, I'm not paying up for the stock, so I have a cushion," he adds. "And I'm really not worried about the competition, because this isn't a business you can get into very quickly. These guys have been around a long time, they're running the company to make money, and they have many sources of revenue."

Contact Information: Amin J. Khoury, Chairman of the Board
B/E Aerospace, Inc.
1400 Corporate Center Way
Wellington, FL 33414
(561) 791-5000
www.beav.com

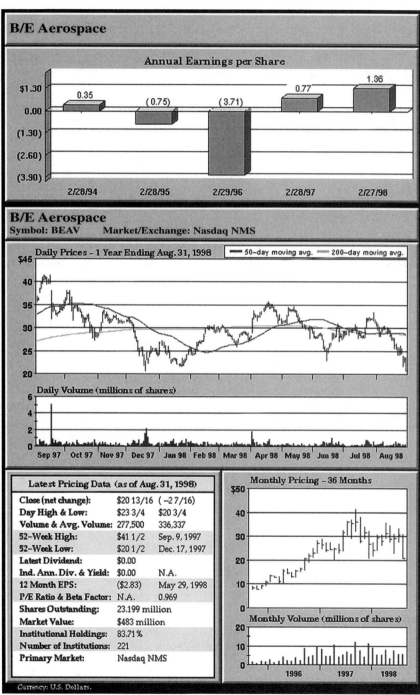

B/E Aerospace

Annual Earnings per Share

	0.35	(0.75)	(3.71)	0.77	1.36
	2/28/94	2/28/95	2/29/96	2/28/97	2/27/98

B/E Aerospace
Symbol: BEAV　　**Market/Exchange: Nasdaq NMS**

Daily Prices – 1 Year Ending Aug. 31, 1998　　50-day moving avg.　200-day moving avg.

Daily Volume (millions of shares)

Sep 97　Oct 97　Nov 97　Dec 97　Jan 98　Feb 98　Mar 98　Apr 98　May 98　Jun 98　Jul 98　Aug 98

Latest Pricing Data (as of Aug. 31, 1998)

Close (net change):	$20 13/16	(–2 7/16)
Day High & Low:	$23 3/4	$20 3/4
Volume & Avg. Volume:	277,500	336,337
52-Week High:	$41 1/2	Sep. 9, 1997
52-Week Low:	$20 1/2	Dec. 17, 1997
Latest Dividend:	$0.00	
Ind. Ann. Div. & Yield:	$0.00	N.A.
12 Month EPS:	($2.83)	May 29, 1998
P/E Ratio & Beta Factor:	N.A.	0.969
Shares Outstanding:	23.199 million	
Market Value:	$483 million	
Institutional Holdings:	83.71%	
Number of Institutions:	221	
Primary Market:	Nasdaq NMS	

Monthly Pricing – 36 Months

Monthly Volume (millions of shares)

1996　1997　1998

Currency: U.S. Dollars.

Source: IDD Information Services

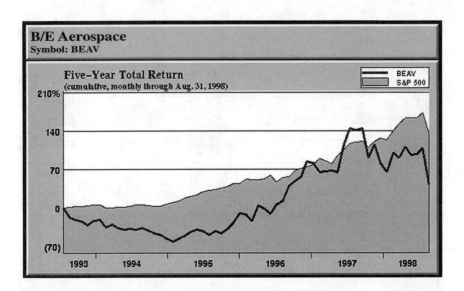

B/E Aerospace
Symbol: BEAV

Five-Year Total Return
(cumulative, monthly through Aug. 31, 1998)

Legend: BEAV, S&P 500

(Chart axis labels: 210%, 140, 70, 0, (70); years 1993, 1994, 1995, 1996, 1997, 1998)

SELECTED INCOME STATEMENT AND BALANCE SHEET ITEMS

INCOME STATEMENT	2/28/94	2/28/95	2/29/96	2/28/97	2/27/98	1 Year
Sales/Revenues	203.40	229.30	232.60	412.40	488.00	514.10
Cost of Goods Sold	123.20	148.80	151.10	257.10	296.20	310.60
Pre–tax Margin (%)	4.40	(8.20)	(25.80)	3.70	7.40	(10.10)
Operating Income	21.500	(4.000)	(41.400)	42.400	63.300	(30.700)
Net Income before Extras	5.400	(12.100)	(60.100)	13.700	30.500	(65.900)
Reported Net Income	5.400	(12.100)	(60.100)	13.700	30.500	(65.900)
Depreciation & Amortization	13.100	16.100	18.400	24.100	24.200	25.700
EPS from Net Income (Primary)	0.350	(0.750)	(3.710)	0.770	1.360	(2.830)
EPS from Net Income (Fully Diluted)	0.350	(0.750)	(3.710)	0.720	1.300	(2.870)
Dividend per Common Share	N.A.	N.A.	N.A.	N.A.	N.A.	N.A.
Dividend Yield (%)	N.A.	N.A.	N.A.	N.A.	N.A.	N.A.
Payout Ratio	N.A.	N.A.	N.A.	N.A.	N.A.	N.A.
BALANCE SHEET						
ASSETS						
Cash & Cash Equivalents	13.700	8.300	15.400	44.100	164.70	
Inventories	53.400	71.300	72.600	92.900	121.70	
Total Current Assets	136.40	142.50	149.80	213.30	382.20	
Total Assets	375.00	380.00	433.60	491.10	681.80	
LIABILITIES & EQUITY						
Short Term Debt	3.800	4.700	6.500	4.400	33.300	
Long Term Debt	159.20	172.70	273.20	225.40	349.60	
Total Liabilities	241.10	254.70	389.50	325.30	485.10	
Shares Outstanding	15.985	16.096	16.393	21.893	22.892	
Common Stockholder Equity	134.00	125.30	44.200	165.80	196.80	
Total Stockholder Equity	134.00	125.30	44.200	165.80	196.80	

Note: Figures in Millions of $ except: per share items, margins, yields, and ratios.

Source: IDD Information Services

BOEING

Joseph Battipaglia
Gruntal & Co.

Company Profile

It seemed everything was flying high for Boeing, the world's largest aerospace company, especially after its 1997 merger with arch-rival McDonnell Douglas. But then the combination of production problems and a less-than-smooth integration of the two businesses grounded Boeing's profits. "Our shareholders have every right to expect better," admits chairman and CEO Philip Condit. "So do our airline customers, who have faced (among other things) late deliveries of aircraft." Nevertheless, despite this turmoil, Boeing's balance sheet and backlog remain strong. That's why Gruntal & Co. chairman of investment policy, Joseph Battipaglia, believes the stock is attractive.

"My investment thesis is that the demand for new and replacement aircraft is on an upward slope," he reasons. "There is evidence of that just from looking at both the domestic and international order rates." Battipaglia describes the "new," postmerger Boeing as a duopoly, where each separate division shares a monopoly—Boeing with commercial aircraft and the former McDonnell Douglas with the military. "This gives Boeing a tremendous amount of power in the industry," he adds.

When you add to the mix that U.S. airlines are in the best financial health ever, and that the industry is also booming overseas, Battipaglia concludes aircraft building is a growth business. "Where Boeing has run into trouble up to this point is in executing its operating strategy," Battipaglia observes. "In effect, the company has been taking on more business than it can handle. It also hasn't been managing the production process, which means it can't make deliveries on time. The stock has been punished for that."

However, Battipaglia insists the company isn't being given credit for making such a good move strategically by acquiring McDonnell Douglas. "This action allowed Boeing to position itself in the defense industry, which is starting to rebuild," he surmises. "If it flies or goes into space, Boeing is going to be a major participant in manufacturing it, both now and in the future." As CEO Condit concurs, "Today's Boeing is a company that specializes in the design, development, production and support of almost everything that flies—from jetliners and jet fighters, through military transports, helicopters, business jets, missiles, rockets, and space-faring vehicles." On the commercial front, the company's 777 and 737 aircraft continue to be popular. In terms of the military, Boeing is involved in the development of all next-generation aircraft and missile programs for the Army, Navy, and Air Force.

But could it be that the airline industry has reached a peak in terms of needing and ordering new aircraft? No, contends Battipaglia. "The airlines have rationalized capacity," he explains. "That's why utilization rates and profits are up. This also explains why you have a hard time getting an extra seat on a flight. Capacity is in the midst of a very strong upswing. The domestic industry has been forced to replace what's out there. You also aren't finding many troubled carriers coming and going, which gives the established airlines greater pricing flexibility." Battipaglia also insists that despite the well-publicized production snafus, Boeing's product line is still as good as ever. "It isn't a question about quality," he says. "Right now investors are simply skeptical about whether management can execute its business plan."

Reason for Recommendation

Battipaglia is convinced they can. He views what's going on with Boeing right now as being similar to the transformation IBM underwent several years ago. "I'm convinced that between now and the end of 1999, Boeing will figure out how to restore its pretax margins," he predicts. "In turn, the company will stop giving the Street negative surprises. Investors can then focus on this big backlog and the company's strong position in the commercial and military markets." Battipaglia says Boeing's previous record shows it has successfully maneuvered its way through extraordinary circumstances before and can, therefore, certainly do it again.

CEO Condit further points out that the company's broader product line will give it greater stability and agility going forward. "We have the confidence of knowing that when one market is down, another is likely to be up," he says. "We have more latitude, therefore, in deploying people from one sector to another, according to business cycle changes. Moreover, with the extraordinary array of capabilities and talents that exists inside our company, we are able, and will be able, to respond quickly and decisively to opportunities, whenever and wherever they may exist—across the entire spectrum of aerospace products."

As for the stock's biggest risk, Battipaglia doesn't see one. "It's not like you're paying a premium to buy this company," he maintains. "Disappointment is already factored in. When you look at the situation closely, it reads rather ominous. Boeing has had a clunky assembly line, not to mention a price war with competitor Airbus Industries. Everybody has been pushed out of the stock because of that. But I feel this present situation can be fixed." Battipaglia is convinced the stock can easily double by the new millennium.

Contact Information: Philip M. Condit, Chairman and CEO
The Boeing Company
7755 East Marginal Way South
Seattle, WA 98108
(206) 655-2121
www.boeing.com

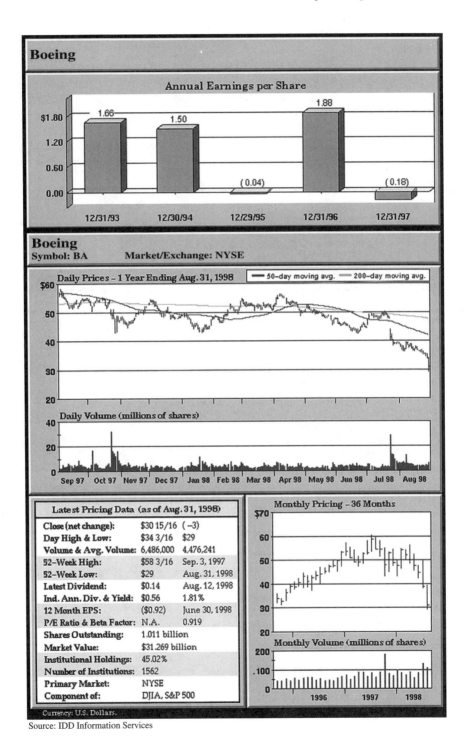

Boeing

Annual Earnings per Share

	1.66	1.50	(0.04)	1.88	(0.18)
	12/31/93	12/30/94	12/29/95	12/31/96	12/31/97

Boeing
Symbol: BA   **Market/Exchange: NYSE**

Daily Prices – 1 Year Ending Aug. 31, 1998   — 50-day moving avg.   — 200-day moving avg.

Daily Volume (millions of shares)

Sep 97 Oct 97 Nov 97 Dec 97 Jan 98 Feb 98 Mar 98 Apr 98 May 98 Jun 98 Jul 98 Aug 98

Latest Pricing Data (as of Aug. 31, 1998)		
Close (net change):	$30 15/16	(–3)
Day High & Low:	$34 3/16	$29
Volume & Avg. Volume:	6,486,000	4,476,241
52-Week High:	$58 3/16	Sep. 3, 1997
52-Week Low:	$29	Aug. 31, 1998
Latest Dividend:	$0.14	Aug. 12, 1998
Ind. Ann. Div. & Yield:	$0.56	1.81%
12 Month EPS:	($0.92)	June 30, 1998
P/E Ratio & Beta Factor:	N.A.	0.919
Shares Outstanding:	1.011 billion	
Market Value:	$31.269 billion	
Institutional Holdings:	45.02%	
Number of Institutions:	1562	
Primary Market:	NYSE	
Component of:	DJIA, S&P 500	

Monthly Pricing – 36 Months

Monthly Volume (millions of shares)

1996   1997   1998

Currency: U.S. Dollars.

Source: IDD Information Services

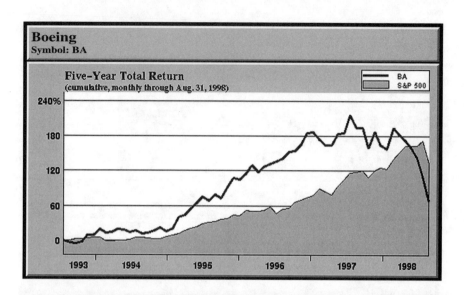

Boeing
Symbol: BA

Five-Year Total Return
(cumulative, monthly through Aug. 31, 1998)

BA
S&P 500

SELECTED INCOME STATEMENT AND BALANCE SHEET ITEMS

INCOME STATEMENT	12/31/93	12/30/94	12/29/95	12/31/96	12/31/97	1 Year
Sales/Revenues	25,438	21,924	19,515	22,681	45,800	49,428
Cost of Goods Sold	22,722	19,631	17,580	20,336	39,186	43,597
Pre–tax Margin (%)	7.20	5.20	1.80	6.00	(0.70)	(3.15)
Operating Income	1,691.0	1,151.0	902.00	1,354.0	1,045.0	15.000
Net Income before Extras	1,244.0	856.00	393.00	1,095.0	(178.00)	(886.00)
Reported Net Income	1,244.0	856.00	393.00	1,095.0	(178.00)	(886.00)
Depreciation & Amortization	1,025.0	1,142.0	1,033.0	991.00	1,458.0	1,662.0
EPS from Net Income (Primary)	1.660	1.500	(0.040)	1.880	(0.180)	(0.920)
EPS from Net Income (Fully Diluted)	1.640	1.480	(0.040)	1.850	(0.180)	(0.900)
Dividend per Common Share	0.500	0.500	0.500	0.545	0.560	0.560
Dividend Yield (%)	2.31	2.13	1.28	1.02	1.14	1.26
Payout Ratio	0.30	0.33	N.A.	0.29	N.A.	N.A.
BALANCE SHEET						
ASSETS						
Cash & Cash Equivalents	2,342.0	2,084.0	3,730.0	4,375.0	4,420.0	
Inventories	3,434.0	4,979.0	6,933.0	6,939.0	8,967.0	
Total Current Assets	9,175.0	10,414	13,178	15,080	19,263	
Total Assets	20,450	21,463	22,098	27,254	38,024	
LIABILITIES & EQUITY						
Short Term Debt	17.000	6.000	271.00	13.000	731.00	
Long Term Debt	2,613.0	2,603.0	2,344.0	3,980.0	6,123.0	
Total Liabilities	11,467	11,763	12,200	16,313	25,071	
Shares Outstanding	680.276	681.758	687.906	694.726	973.480	
Common Stockholder Equity	8,983.0	9,700.0	9,898.0	10,941	12,953	
Total Stockholder Equity	8,983.0	9,700.0	9,898.0	10,941	12,953	

Note: Figures in Millions of $ except: per share items, margins, yields, and ratios.

Source: IDD Information Services

CARNIVAL CORPORATION

Alan Bond
Bond Procope Capital Management

Company Profile

Ever since *Titanic* fever swept the nation last year, it seems the concept of cruising has never been more popular. "There's no question that movie had a positive impact on the industry," says Alan Bond of Bond Procope Capital Management. "But there's more to it than that. People are beginning to realize that cruising is a great way to go. Cruises provide for shorter and cheaper vacations, since they are all-inclusive. Besides, airfares have gone through the roof." The company best positioned to benefit from this burgeoning trend, according to Bond, is Miami-based Carnival Corporation.

Carnival is the world's largest and most profitable cruise company. It owns Carnival Cruise Lines, Holland America Line, Windstar Cruises and Cunard Line. It also owns half of Costa Cruises and the upscale Seabourn Cruise Line. In all, its combined fleet of 35 ships sails to ports around the world. "Our goal is to use our brands to reach every tier of the cruise market," says Carnival chairman and CEO Micky Arison. "Regardless of customer budget, itinerary, geography, demographics, or psychographics, our brands really do cover the waterfront. This makes us unique in the North American cruise market, if not the world." What's more, Carnival has full ownership of tour operator Holland America Westours, the largest cruise/tour operator in Alaska and the Canadian Yukon, and 28 percent interest in the British company Airtours, which specializes in travel packages to Europe.

The great thing about cruising is that you can hop aboard a ship for as little or as long as you want, unpack your bags once and travel to several different destinations. Your hotel travels with you, if you will. In addition, your cruise price includes all of your transportation, accommodations, meals plus Las Vegas-style entertainment. About the only extras are drinks and gratuities. (Are you packing your bags yet?) "One reason this concept is so popular now is that you'll notice people are taking fewer extended vacations," Bond observes. "We are so hooked on the concept of productivity and working hard that we now just go away for three or four days at a time. The cruise lines play right into this theme. They give you the experience of a full week-long vacation in only a few days. And they take you to exotic destinations like Mexico, the Caribbean and Alaska for a good price."

Carnival is quick to point out that many folks still haven't caught on to this concept yet, which means the company has a huge untapped market. Industry figures show only 8 percent of the population in North America has taken a cruise, while 80 percent of all first-timers say they'll do it again. Carnival arguably is best positioned to take advantage of this potential, because it is the most recognized name in the industry, offers the widest range of options, and is number one in every market in which it competes. "As baby boomers hit their peak earning years, and recreational spending and leisure time interest levels continue to rise, we believe more will consider cruising as an outstanding vacation choice," Arison insists.

While cruising was once viewed as a vacation only for older travelers, that's no longer the case. "I once thought of it as something only my grandparents would do," Bond concedes. "However, the cruise lines have had to change with the times. They now want to attract that younger traveler with a fairly sizable amount of disposable income and a lack of time. These ships are amazing. They allow you to see the most popular movies, exercise in state-of-the-art gyms and view first-rate live entertainment. The experience is really like staying at the finest five-star resort."

Carnival has recently entered into negotiations to develop at least six new ships. "Our earnings growth is directly impacted by our ability to increase capacity," Arison says. "The more ships we have in our fleet, the more passengers we can carry, improving economies of scale, thus lowering overhead costs on a per-berth basis. With the delivery of six new ships to the Carnival and Holland America fleets over the next three years—primarily funded by operating cash flows—we expect to increase that capacity by 40 percent. The age and size of the ships is important, too. New ships are built to run more efficiently, and large ships leverage economies of scale, benefiting margins." Bond adds that overcapacity is definitely not an issue for the company. "In fact, Carnival doesn't have enough capacity," he says. "People are canceling air vacations left and right to take cruises because the prices are more attractive. Carnival claims there aren't enough available berths to meet current demand."

Reason for Recommendation

Bond predicts the growth in this industry will continue long after people forget how many Oscars *Titanic* won. But how good is Carnival as a company? "Over the last five years, it has experienced earnings growth of 17 percent annually," Bond says. "I think it will continue to grow between 15 and 20 percent a year. In recent quarters, it has done even better." Bond estimates Carnival's earnings for 1999 will check in at around $3.10 per share, and he expects the stock to trade for at least $100 by the end of the year.

Contact Information: Micky Arison
Carnival Corporation
3655 N.W. 87th Avenue
Miami, FL 33178-2428
(305) 599-2600
www.carnivalcorp.com

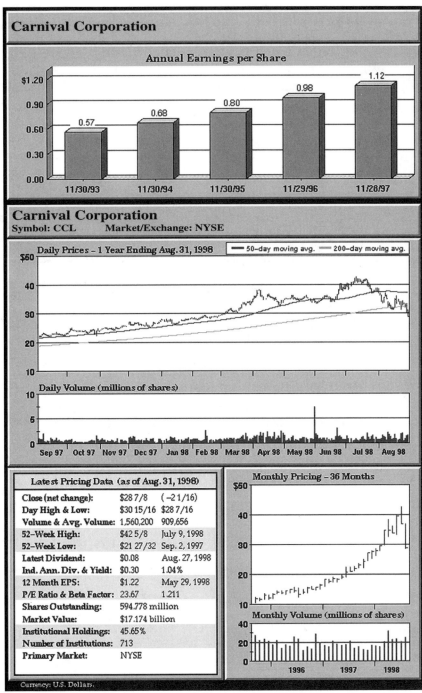

Carnival Corporation

Annual Earnings per Share

	11/30/93	11/30/94	11/30/95	11/29/96	11/28/97
EPS	0.57	0.68	0.80	0.98	1.12

Carnival Corporation

Symbol: CCL   **Market/Exchange: NYSE**

Daily Prices – 1 Year Ending Aug. 31, 1998 — 50-day moving avg. — 200-day moving avg.

Daily Volume (millions of shares)

Latest Pricing Data (as of Aug. 31, 1998)		
Close (net change):	$28 7/8	(–2 1/16)
Day High & Low:	$30 15/16	$28 7/16
Volume & Avg. Volume:	1,560,200	909,656
52–Week High:	$42 5/8	July 9, 1998
52–Week Low:	$21 27/32	Sep. 2, 1997
Latest Dividend:	$0.08	Aug. 27, 1998
Ind. Ann. Div. & Yield:	$0.30	1.04%
12 Month EPS:	$1.22	May 29, 1998
P/E Ratio & Beta Factor:	23.67	1.211
Shares Outstanding:	594.778 million	
Market Value:	$17.174 billion	
Institutional Holdings:	45.65%	
Number of Institutions:	713	
Primary Market:	NYSE	

Monthly Pricing – 36 Months

Monthly Volume (millions of shares)

Currency: U.S. Dollars.

Source: IDD Information Services

Carnival Corporation
Symbol: CCL

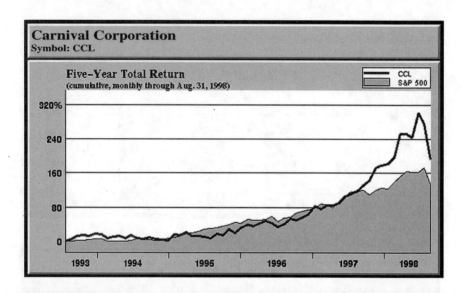

Five-Year Total Return
(cumulative, monthly through Aug. 31, 1998)

CCL
S&P 500

SELECTED INCOME STATEMENT AND BALANCE SHEET ITEMS						
INCOME STATEMENT	**11/30/93**	**11/30/94**	**11/30/95**	**11/29/96**	**11/28/97**	**1 Year**
Sales/Revenues	1,556.9	1,806.0	1,998.2	2,212.6	2,447.5	2,549.0
Cost of Goods Sold	907.90	1,028.5	1,131.1	1,241.3	1,322.7	1,358.1
Pre-tax Margin (%)	20.80	21.70	23.00	26.00	27.50	27.70
Operating Income	347.70	443.60	490.10	551.40	661.00	712.90
Net Income before Extras	318.20	381.80	451.10	566.30	666.10	723.80
Reported Net Income	318.20	381.80	451.10	566.30	666.10	723.80
Depreciation & Amortization	93.300	110.60	128.40	145.00	167.30	173.90
EPS from Net Income (Primary)	0.570	0.680	0.800	0.980	1.120	1.220
EPS from Net Income (Fully Diluted)	0.570	0.680	0.790	0.970	1.120	1.220
Dividend per Common Share	0.140	0.142	0.157	0.190	0.240	0.280
Dividend Yield (%)	1.16	1.32	1.21	1.20	0.89	0.83
Payout Ratio	0.25	0.21	0.20	0.19	0.21	0.23
BALANCE SHEET						
ASSETS						
Cash & Cash Equivalents	60.200	54.100	53.400	111.60	140.00	
Inventories	37.200	45.100	48.800	53.300	55.000	
Total Current Assets	253.80	240.40	256.40	290.90	336.00	
Total Assets	3,218.9	3,669.8	4,105.5	5,101.9	5,426.8	
LIABILITIES & EQUITY						
Short Term Debt	91.600	84.600	72.800	66.400	59.600	
Long Term Debt	1,031.2	1,161.9	1,150.0	1,316.6	1,015.3	
Total Liabilities	1,591.7	1,740.9	1,760.6	2,070.9	1,821.6	
Shares Outstanding	564.668	565.064	569.592	589.380	594.408	
Common Stockholder Equity	1,627.2	1,928.9	2,344.9	3,030.9	3,605.1	
Total Stockholder Equity	1,627.2	1,928.9	2,344.9	3,030.9	3,605.1	

Note: Figures in Millions of $ except: per share items, margins, yields, and ratios.

Source: IDD Information Services

CHUBB

Ed Walczak
Vontobel USA

Company Profile

The year was 1882. Thomas Caldecot Chubb and his son Percy collected $1,000 each from 100 prominent merchants and opened a marine underwriting business in New York's seaport district. By the turn of the century, the Chubb's had established relationships with various insurance agents and brokers, who placed their business with Chubb underwriters. That served as the foundation for what has evolved into a leading underwriter of property and casualty policies. The company was also once involved in the sale of life and health insurance, although that division was sold off to the Jefferson-Pilot Corporation in 1997. "Chubb is basically involved in three main areas," notes Vontobel USA chief investment officer Ed Walczak. "First is personal lines. If you own jewelry or a fancy house, they'll insure you. Then there is the standard lines unit, which involves underwriting worker's compensation and general liability insurance. Finally, you have the specialty commercial lines, which would provide liability insurance for directors and officers, among other things."

Of these areas, Walczak believes the personal lines business is Chubb's real gem. "The profitability on that division is just great," he says. "Chubb is well known among really affluent households and has a high market share in that demographic. The company will insure your $2 million home and your wife's $500,000 diamond necklace. It is known for providing excellent service and coming through when a hurricane blows your house away. In return for this service, it charges very high rates, so it's a profitable business." One way to figure out how profitable an insurance company is is by looking at its combined ratio. "The way it works is anything less than 100 percent is good, because it means you are making money on the actual underwriting of the business," Walczak explains. "For the personal lines area of the business, Chubb's combined ratio is around 88 percent, which means it is making good money. On top of that, once it gets the cash from your premium, it is invested in stocks and bonds, therefore, making even more from the investment income."

Walczak is also pleased that Chubb's chairman and CEO, Dean O'Hare, has been increasingly getting the company out of some underperforming areas. "He divested a real estate and underperforming life insurance business recently, which is good, since both were providing low returns," Walczak says. "With the proceeds from that, he not only retired some debt, giving the company a strong balance sheet with few liabilities, but he also repurchased shares and is going to keep doing so for the next several years. I believe that's a good use of shareholder funds." Commenting on his recent changes, O'Hare said, "Looking to the future, we have undertaken an intensive program to cut costs and allocate resources to those products, lines of business, and activities with the highest potential for profitable growth. We also are continuing our aggressive internal expansion and accelerating several initiatives to boost organic growth. In addition, we have commenced an active search for attractive acquisition candidates in the property and casualty business, both in the United States and overseas."

Reason for Recommendation

It's really not surprising to see Walczak recommend an insurance company like Chubb. After all, his investment hero is Warren Buffett, a man who has owned many insurers over the years. "Buffett spends a lot of time talking about this thing called 'float'," Walczak points out. "It means that if I'm an insurance company, and I give you insurance that you never use, I'm making money by underwriting you. That free money is the float. I never have to pay it out because you don't file any claims. It's free equity that has no cost to the insurance company. I can then invest it and make returns of 10 or 15 percent a year. Most insurers don't have great float, because they underwrite poorly and lose money that has to be made up with investment income. But Chubb has considerable float. Its combined ratio overall as a company is in the 90 percent range." Walczak further adds that Chubb has an excellent balance sheet and generates free cash flow. "This means after Chubb has paid off its employees and the rent, it actually has discretionary money left over," he says. "This can either be invested back into the business or used to pay down debt. Discretionary cash flow is another thing that's big with Buffett."

Two far-reaching trends likely to reshape the property and casualty industry going forward are continuing industry consolidation and the convergence of insurance with other financial services. Chubb admits its ability to broaden its organizational capabilities, either through internal growth or acquisition, will be a major key in addressing these challenges. CEO O'Hare has already stated he will keep a closer eye on controlling costs, accelerating the growth of high-profit businesses and making strategic acquisitions. Given Chubb's above-normal return on equity and long history of increasing earnings, Walczak insists the stock is worth at least $100. "Chubb is a very predictable company," he says. "As long as it sticks to its knitting, I think it will continue to do well."

Contact Information: Dean R. O'Hare, Chairman and CEO
The Chubb Corporation
15 Mountain View Road
Warren, NJ 07061
(908) 903-2000
www.chubb.com

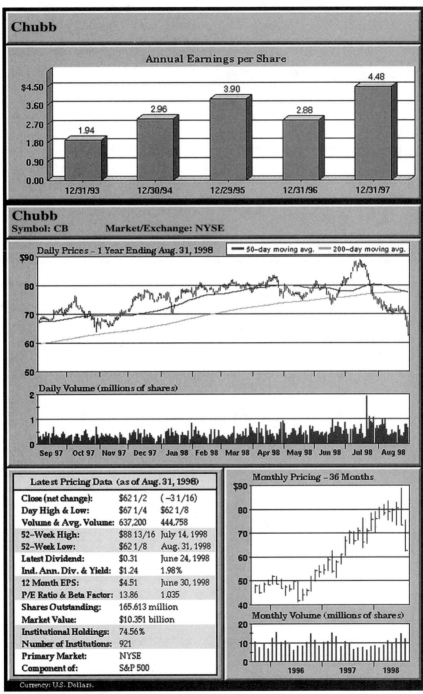

Chubb

Annual Earnings per Share

	12/31/93	12/30/94	12/29/95	12/31/96	12/31/97
EPS	1.94	2.96	3.90	2.88	4.48

Chubb
Symbol: CB   **Market/Exchange: NYSE**

Daily Prices – 1 Year Ending Aug. 31, 1998

■ 50-day moving avg. ■ 200-day moving avg.

Daily Volume (millions of shares)

Sep 97 Oct 97 Nov 97 Dec 97 Jan 98 Feb 98 Mar 98 Apr 98 May 98 Jun 98 Jul 98 Aug 98

Latest Pricing Data (as of Aug. 31, 1998)

Close (net change):	$62 1/2	(–3 1/16)
Day High & Low:	$67 1/4	$62 1/8
Volume & Avg. Volume:	637,200	444,758
52–Week High:	$88 13/16	July 14, 1998
52–Week Low:	$62 1/8	Aug. 31, 1998
Latest Dividend:	$0.31	June 24, 1998
Ind. Ann. Div. & Yield:	$1.24	1.98%
12 Month EPS:	$4.51	June 30, 1998
P/E Ratio & Beta Factor:	13.86	1.035
Shares Outstanding:	165.613 million	
Market Value:	$10.351 billion	
Institutional Holdings:	74.56%	
Number of Institutions:	921	
Primary Market:	NYSE	
Component of:	S&P 500	

Monthly Pricing – 36 Months

Monthly Volume (millions of shares)

1996   1997   1998

Currency: U.S. Dollars.

Source: IDD Information Services

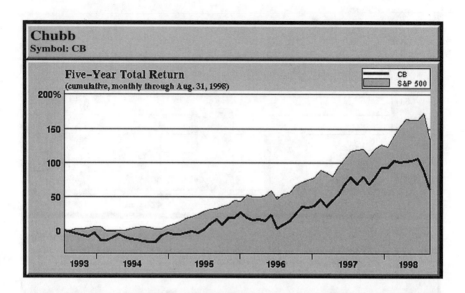

Chubb
Symbol: CB

Five-Year Total Return
(cumulative, monthly through Aug. 31, 1998)

CB
S&P 500

200%
150
100
50
0

1993   1994   1995   1996   1997   1998

SELECTED INCOME STATEMENT AND BALANCE SHEET ITEMS

INCOME STATEMENT	12/31/93	12/30/94	12/29/95	12/31/96	12/31/97	1 Year
Sales/Revenues	5,499.7	5,709.5	6,089.2	5,680.5	6,664.0	6,762.4
Cost of Goods Sold	N.A.	N.A.	N.A.	N.A.	N.A.	N.A.
Pre-tax Margin (%)	6.30	11.20	14.80	9.60	14.60	14.20
Operating Income	344.50	639.30	900.10	546.90	974.10	990.90
Net Income before Extras	344.20	528.50	696.60	486.20	769.50	764.70
Reported Net Income	344.20	528.50	696.60	512.70	769.50	764.70
Depreciation & Amortization	N.A.	N.A.	N.A.	N.A.	N.A.	N.A.
EPS from Net Income (Primary)	1.940	2.960	3.900	2.880	4.480	4.510
EPS from Net Income (Fully Diluted)	1.940	2.960	3.900	2.880	4.390	4.430
Dividend per Common Share	0.860	0.920	0.980	1.080	1.160	1.200
Dividend Yield (%)	2.21	2.38	2.03	2.01	1.53	1.49
Payout Ratio	0.44	0.31	0.25	0.38	0.26	0.27

BALANCE SHEET						
ASSETS						
Cash & Cash Equivalents	N.A.	N.A.	N.A.	N.A.	N.A.	
Inventories	N.A.	N.A.	N.A.	N.A.	N.A.	
Total Current Assets	N.A.	N.A.	N.A.	N.A.	N.A.	
Total Assets	19,437	20,723	22,996	19,939	19,616	
LIABILITIES & EQUITY						
Short Term Debt	94.800	153.30	187.60	189.50	0.000	
Long Term Debt	1,273.8	1,285.6	1,156.0	1,070.5	398.60	
Total Liabilities	15,241	16,476	17,734	14,476	13,958	
Shares Outstanding	175.418	173.642	174.602	174.861	168.718	
Common Stockholder Equity	4,196.1	4,247.0	5,262.7	5,462.9	5,657.1	
Total Stockholder Equity	4,196.1	4,247.0	5,262.7	5,462.9	5,657.1	

Note: Figures in Millions of $ except: per share items, margins, yields, and ratios.

Source: IDD Information Services

FSI INTERNATIONAL

Martin Whitman
Third Avenue Funds

Company Profile

FSI International supplies sophisticated automated processing equipment to many of the world's leading semiconductor manufacturers. "There are some 10 different processes involved in the front end of semiconductor manufacturing," explains Martin Whitman of Third Avenue Funds. "FSI is involved with three of them: microlithography, surface conditioning, and chemical management, each of which accounts for about one-third of total sales."

Here's, an explanation of what each unit does. First is the microlithography division, which supplies photoresistant processing solutions for semiconductor, flat panel display, thin film head, and multichip module manufacturing. Its POLARIS 2200 Microlithography Cluster, for example, is designed to meet the demands of today's higher-capacity wafer steppers. Next is the surface conditioning unit, which manufactures products to perform critical cleaning, etching, and stripping applications, to prepare the surfaces of silicon wafers for the production of integrated circuits. Last is the largest division, chemical management, which supplies a wide range of chemical blending, delivery, and chemical generation products for semiconductor facilities worldwide. "I like that the company is involved in three separate businesses," Whitman offers. "That way I don't have to depend on it hitting a home run in any one area."

FSI operates out of headquarters in Chaska, Minnesota, which Martin says works to its advantage. The low cost of living, compared to the Silicon Valley and Seattle, is attractive to potential workers. The company also has a large presence in Texas. FSI has a book value of around $10, but has seen its sales revenues and profits fall right along with the global recession in the semiconductor industry. Going into 1999, chairman Joel A. Elftmann has high hopes the equipment market will improve, but realizes steps must be taken to improve the company's financial position. He has implemented a number of cost-control measures, including asking all employees to take 10 unpaid days during 1998. He has also reduced plans for capital spending by more than $5 million. "FSI International has a three-part strategy designed to increase its revenues and market share," Elftmann says. "First is to develop new products and processes using internal expertise. Second is to license or acquire technology where we see a competitive advantage in our three areas of concentration. Third is to examine possible joint ventures or acquisitions of complementary technologies." Elftmann cites a study showing that by 2002, the available market for semiconductor wafer equipment should reach around $45 billion, from today's $20 billion, meaning the industry should grow by some 18 percent a year for the foreseeable future. That gives him reason to be optimistic.

Reason for Recommendation

Whitman shares Elftmann's hopes that a resurgence in the semiconductor sector will be realized, which is why he likes this stock. "I think the industry is just going to explode," he predicts. "There are two things happening here: demand is exploding and technological innovation is coming on rapidly. Semiconductor makers are reducing the size of chips, while at the same time increasing their power. All of the big players both here and overseas will have to spend billions reequipping their factories to keep up with this change. FSI looks like it's going to be a beneficiary of this."

Whitman's positive assessment of semiconductor equipment makers in general rests on three important legs, namely the extraordinary balance sheet quality of these companies, the industry's healthy long-term growth prospects, and the continuing trend of consolidation. These cash-rich, low-debt balance sheets are the result of the equipment makers' ability to attract large amounts of capital during the last strong business cycle from 1993-1995. The economic and political crises in Asia have hurt short-term prospects, but it seems apparent the overall industry growth trend remains favorable. And during times of consolidation in the industry, many companies consider acquisition as a way to expand their business at attractive prices. "At a minimum, these characteristics make the case for investment in the semiconductor equipment industry quite compelling," Whitman concludes.

Again, it's going to take time. But Whitman believes 1999 will mark a major turning point for this company. "Once conditions do improve, I think FSI has huge earnings power," he insists. "FSI's volume was under $300 million last year. However, it has completed massive capital expenditures, which will permit it to expand that to $600 million without incurring further expenses. If it has the kind of growth in it that I think it does, all of this additional revenue and incremental cost savings will go to the bottom line. We're talking about a company that could earn $3 or $4 a share some years out. When FSI comes through this difficult cycle, it could easily experience 20 percent revenue growth. Beyond that, there's obviously a lot of consolidation going on in the industry, and FSI is a merger and acquisition candidate. The company would certainly be attractive to a lot of people."

Contact Information: Joel A. Elftmann, Chairman, President and CEO
FSI International, Inc.
322 Lake Hazeltine Drive
Chaska, MN 55318
(612) 448-5440
www.fsi-intl.com

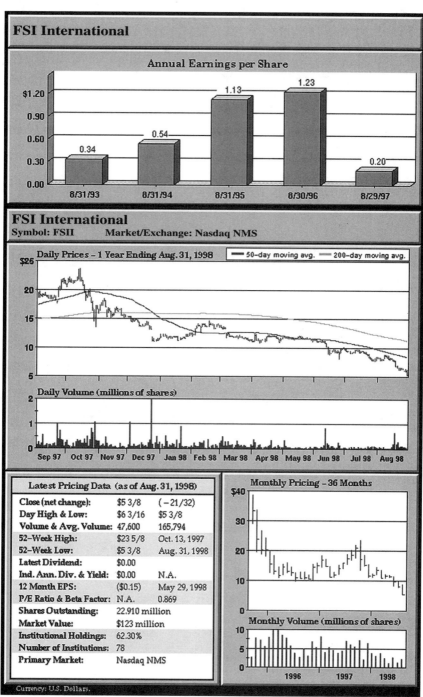

FSI International

Annual Earnings per Share

	8/31/93	8/31/94	8/31/95	8/30/96	8/29/97
EPS	0.34	0.54	1.13	1.23	0.20

FSI International
Symbol: FSII   **Market/Exchange: Nasdaq NMS**

Daily Prices – 1 Year Ending Aug. 31, 1998   ▬ 50-day moving avg.   ▬ 200-day moving avg.

Daily Volume (millions of shares)

Sep 97 Oct 97 Nov 97 Dec 97 Jan 98 Feb 98 Mar 98 Apr 98 May 98 Jun 98 Jul 98 Aug 98

Latest Pricing Data (as of Aug. 31, 1998)		
Close (net change):	$5 3/8	(–21/32)
Day High & Low:	$6 3/16	$5 3/8
Volume & Avg. Volume:	47,600	165,794
52–Week High:	$23 5/8	Oct. 13, 1997
52–Week Low:	$5 3/8	Aug. 31, 1998
Latest Dividend:	$0.00	
Ind. Ann. Div. & Yield:	$0.00	N.A.
12 Month EPS:	($0.15)	May 29, 1998
P/E Ratio & Beta Factor:	N.A.	0.869
Shares Outstanding:	22.910 million	
Market Value:	$123 million	
Institutional Holdings:	62.30%	
Number of Institutions:	78	
Primary Market:	Nasdaq NMS	

Monthly Pricing – 36 Months

Monthly Volume (millions of shares)

1996   1997   1998

Currency: U.S. Dollars.

Source: IDD Information Services

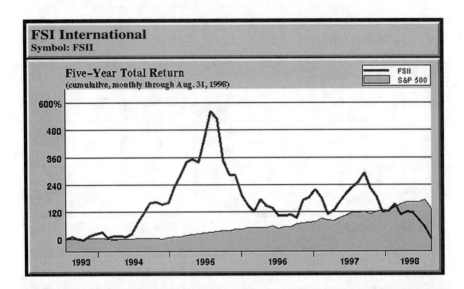

FSI International
Symbol: FSII

Five-Year Total Return
(cumulative, monthly through Aug. 31, 1998)

FSII
S&P 500

SELECTED INCOME STATEMENT AND BALANCE SHEET ITEMS

INCOME STATEMENT	8/31/93	8/31/94	8/31/95	8/30/96	8/29/97	1 Year
Sales/Revenues	77.000	94.000	190.40	304.00	252.40	254.00
Cost of Goods Sold	45.600	51.400	108.90	166.00	145.80	143.40
Pre-tax Margin (%)	4.70	8.30	13.20	12.80	1.50	(3.42)
Operating Income	3.000	6.100	19.600	30.100	(1.900)	(11.200)
Net Income before Extras	3.200	6.500	19.300	28.500	4.600	(3.300)
Reported Net Income	3.200	6.500	19.300	28.500	4.600	(3.300)
Depreciation & Amortization	2.800	2.600	3.100	8.200	12.300	15.800
EPS from Net Income (Primary)	0.340	0.540	1.130	1.230	0.200	(0.150)
EPS from Net Income (Fully Diluted)	0.340	0.540	1.130	1.230	0.200	(0.150)
Dividend per Common Share	0.000	0.000	0.000	0.000	0.000	0.000
Dividend Yield (%)	N.A.	N.A.	N.A.	N.A.	N.A.	N.A.
Payout Ratio	N.A.	N.A.	N.A.	N.A.	N.A.	N.A.
BALANCE SHEET						
ASSETS						
Cash & Cash Equivalents	2.000	10.500	97.100	48.800	79.200	
Inventories	13.100	16.100	31.900	64.100	62.000	
Total Current Assets	32.300	51.900	201.00	230.00	233.50	
Total Assets	40.400	66.000	233.80	293.30	331.20	
LIABILITIES & EQUITY						
Short Term Debt	3.300	0.100	0.000	0.200	24.500	
Long Term Debt	0.300	0.000	0.000	0.300	42.100	
Total Liabilities	19.000	23.800	55.600	75.100	106.80	
Shares Outstanding	8.420	12.162	20.260	22.362	22.583	
Common Stockholder Equity	21.300	42.100	178.20	218.10	224.30	
Total Stockholder Equity	21.300	42.100	178.20	218.10	224.30	

Note: Figures in Millions of $ except: per share items, margins, yields, and ratios.

Source: IDD Information Services

HBO & COMPANY

Fred Kobrick
Kobrick Cendant Funds

Company Profile

HBO & Company is a leading provider of information systems and technology to hospitals, integrated health delivery networks, and managed care organizations. The company implements and supports patient care, clinical, financial, and strategic management software designed to facilitate the integration of data throughout an organization. It also provides a full range of network communications technologies, electronic commerce products, and outsourcing services. The company was founded in 1974, and first became known for its minicomputer-based patient information and accounting systems. HBO grew slowly until it acquired a mainframe systems company and decision support firm in the mid-1980s. It later took on a series of acquisitions in the 1990s that expanded its product line into new markets, such as physicians' offices, reference laboratories, and the international arena. Today, HBO has approximately 9,000 customers, more than half of which are community hospitals in the U.S. The company offers a strategic mix of applications, technologies, and services to support the continued restructuring of the healthcare delivery industry.

Fund manager Fred Kobrick first invested in HBO back in the 1980s. "After visiting with management in 1985, and concluding they had no credibility whatsoever, I sold the stock," he recalls. "It was a good thing, because it managed to go down 60 percent in a bull market. Then the company brought in a new management team. At that point, I bought back in because HBO operates in such an interesting field."

Kobrick contends that without good information systems, hospitals are doomed. In his opinion, the best source of such technology is HBO. "Many hospitals have been in the dark ages, in terms of information, for a long time," he observes. "They never needed to know what was going on. Now, because of managed care, it's essential to have a good record of every pill you order and how many patient days you have. The company that hospitals are turning to for these solutions is HBO. It has products for clinical information, financial data, patient care information, and strategic management software for large medical groups."

The company offers a wide array of solutions, including the Pathways 2000 family of information systems. These client/server applications are designed to provide a common information infrastructure, enabling organizations to collect, manage, and disseminate clinically oriented information on a patient's entire medical history, regardless of where the care was provided. "One thing that really stands out is how user-friendly HBO's products are," Kobrick notes. "As these products become more powerful, they are also increasingly easy to use. They require less training, and people are making fewer mistakes with them." There are other competitors in this industry, but Kobrick contends HBO's products are much better. "They are more reliable, and customers like dealing with the company," he says. "HBO is very good at customer support."

HBO has a multiprong strategy for growth going forward. First, the company plans to leverage its existing customer base. Considering that its systems are currently installed in 52 percent of the nation's community hospitals, HBO sees the potential to sell these accounts more products and services. Second, it plans to expand into new markets, including the burgeoning area of home health care. Finally, the company hopes to continue making strategic acquisitions. HBO also believes a key component to its further growth is an ongoing focus on research and development. This will ensure its offerings continue to meet the evolving needs of existing and potential customers.

Reason for Recommendation

Kobrick points out that a round of price cutting at the end of 1996 hurt the company and the stock. That no longer seems to be an issue. He expects HBO to grow by 40 to 60 percent this year, and considers it to be a long-term, quality blue chip company. "I expect this to be at least a $50 stock this year," he predicts. The major risk is the fact that HBO deals with hospitals, which often have budgetary problems. "I'm always worried that orders could get canceled," Kobrick admits. "The reason I don't think that should stop you from investing in this company is that the more troubled a hospital is, the more it needs HBO's products." Cost cutting by HMO's is another concern, although Kobrick says that is really a positive for HBO in the long run. "The HMO's dictate how much a hospital can get paid," he reasons. "If a hospital wants to figure out how it can cut costs to meet the requirements of the HMO, it needs HBO's products. The more pressure a hospital gets from the HMO's, the more information it must gather to show where its profit margins are coming from. In other words, if a hospital doesn't have one of HBO's products to figure out whether it will make or lose money by providing a given service, it is dead. This can't be done on paper." While Wall Street estimates the company will earn $1.60 to $1.70 a share in 1999, Kobrick puts the figure at closer to $1.85.

Contact Information: Charles W. McCall, President and CEO
HBO & Company
301 Perimeter Center North
Atlanta, GA 30346
(770) 393-6000
www.hboc.com

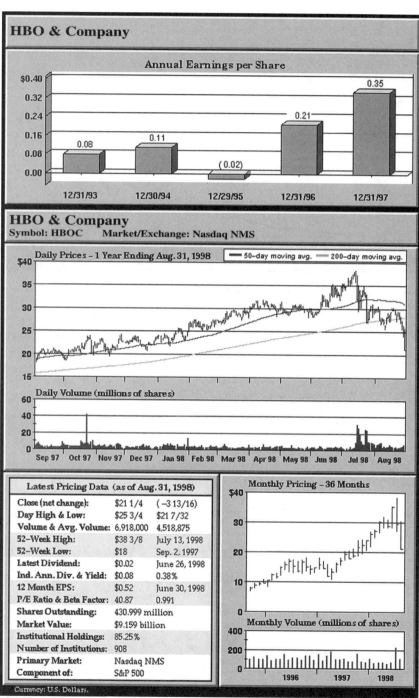

HBO & Company

Annual Earnings per Share

12/31/93	0.08	
12/30/94	0.11	
12/29/95	(0.02)	
12/31/96	0.21	
12/31/97	0.35	

HBO & Company
Symbol: HBOC   Market/Exchange: Nasdaq NMS

Daily Prices – 1 Year Ending Aug. 31, 1998   — 50–day moving avg.   — 200–day moving avg.

Daily Volume (millions of shares)

Sep 97   Oct 97   Nov 97   Dec 97   Jan 98   Feb 98   Mar 98   Apr 98   May 98   Jun 98   Jul 98   Aug 98

Latest Pricing Data (as of Aug. 31, 1998)

Close (net change):	$21 1/4	(–3 13/16)
Day High & Low:	$25 3/4	$21 7/32
Volume & Avg. Volume:	6,918,000	4,518,875
52–Week High:	$38 3/8	July 13, 1998
52–Week Low:	$18	Sep. 2, 1997
Latest Dividend:	$0.02	June 26, 1998
Ind. Ann. Div. & Yield:	$0.08	0.38%
12 Month EPS:	$0.52	June 30, 1998
P/E Ratio & Beta Factor:	40.87	0.991
Shares Outstanding:	430.999 million	
Market Value:	$9.159 billion	
Institutional Holdings:	85.25%	
Number of Institutions:	908	
Primary Market:	Nasdaq NMS	
Component of:	S&P 500	

Monthly Pricing – 36 Months

Monthly Volume (millions of shares)

1996   1997   1998

Currency: U.S. Dollars.

Source: IDD Information Services

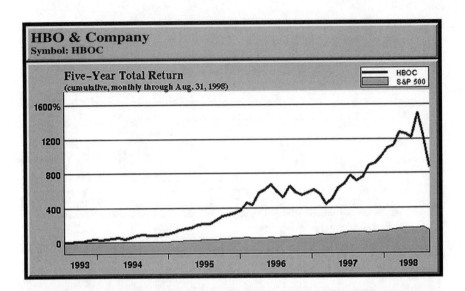

HBO & Company
Symbol: HBOC

Five-Year Total Return
(cumulative, monthly through Aug. 31, 1998)

Legend: HBOC, S&P 500

SELECTED INCOME STATEMENT AND BALANCE SHEET ITEMS

INCOME STATEMENT	12/31/93	12/30/94	12/29/95	12/31/96	12/31/97	1 Year
Sales/Revenues	237.10	327.20	495.60	796.60	1,203.2	1,406.2
Cost of Goods Sold	118.30	155.40	201.80	302.00	448.70	517.50
Pre-tax Margin (%)	12.90	14.40	(8.50)	15.40	19.90	26.90
Operating Income	31.200	48.000	95.700	179.60	318.00	409.60
Net Income before Extras	18.300	28.200	(25.200)	74.000	143.50	223.20
Reported Net Income	18.300	28.200	(25.200)	74.000	143.50	223.20
Depreciation & Amortization	9.300	17.500	30.300	49.200	62.400	70.100
EPS from Net Income (Primary)	0.080	0.110	(0.020)	0.210	0.350	0.520
EPS from Net Income (Fully Diluted)	0.080	0.110	(0.020)	0.200	0.340	0.510
Dividend per Common Share	0.019	0.018	0.020	0.020	0.030	0.050
Dividend Yield (%)	0.65	0.41	0.21	0.13	0.12	0.14
Payout Ratio	0.23	0.16	N.A.	0.10	0.09	0.10

BALANCE SHEET						
ASSETS						
Cash & Cash Equivalents	23.200	5.800	65.300	160.40	432.50	
Inventories	1.300	1.300	6.800	7.000	6.500	
Total Current Assets	73.200	122.70	252.40	519.80	923.70	
Total Assets	119.10	233.90	535.10	848.90	1,312.6	
LIABILITIES & EQUITY						
Short Term Debt	0.000	0.000	0.000	0.000	0.000	
Long Term Debt	0.000	0.000	0.600	0.200	1.000	
Total Liabilities	69.100	142.40	216.40	323.70	411.90	
Shares Outstanding	236.192	254.184	320.952	362.404	422.760	
Common Stockholder Equity	50.000	91.500	318.70	525.30	900.60	
Total Stockholder Equity	50.000	91.500	318.70	525.30	900.60	

Note: Figures in Millions of $ except: per share items, margins, yields, and ratios.

Source: IDD Information Services

HOUSEHOLD INTERNATIONAL

Cappy McGarr
McGarr Capital Management

Company Profile

Like most other companies in the financial services industry today, Household International is going through a major restructuring. "The management of the company wants to be a number of different things," notes hedge-fund manager Cappy McGarr of McGarr Capital Management. "It wants to be a low-cost provider and hold a leadership position in everything it does." Household took a major step toward becoming one of the country's most dominant consumer finance companies by merging with Beneficial Corporation in April 1998. Household chairman and CEO William Aldinger remains in charge of the combined company. At the time of the merger, Aldinger said, "This is an outstanding and unique opportunity to combine two leaders in consumer lending. Together, Household and Beneficial have the financial strength, portfolio balance, and expanded market presence that will allow us to provide superior returns for shareholders. Furthermore, our combined distribution channels, complementary product capabilities, and thirty million customer relationships should lead to higher receivables and revenue growth." Now it's up to Aldinger to deliver on these promises. If Household's past is any indication of its future, that shouldn't be a hard thing to do. Earnings per share have grown more than 20 percent for the past six years and the stock has compounded at a 37 percent clip over the last five years, far outpacing the S&P 500's 20 percent advance.

Household offers home equity, auto, and other unsecured loans, along with Visa, MasterCard, and private label credit cards throughout the United States, Canada, and the United Kingdom. Its core business, HFC, is the nation's oldest consumer finance company. Meanwhile, Beneficial's subsidiaries provide various consumer finance, credit card, banking, and insurance operations in the U.S., the United Kingdom, and Ireland.

"One thing I like is that Household has exited markets it believed it were too small to compete in," McGarr says. "For example, it sold off some unprofitable banking branches. The company is continuing to consolidate operations to become more profitable and efficient." Household is experiencing especially rapid growth in its unsecured consumer product and credit card business. Before the merger with Beneficial, it was the seventh largest issuer of Visa and MasterCards, with almost $13 billion in receivables. Household administers the popular GM-branded credit cards and the AFL-CIO's Union Privilege affinity card, among others. The breakdown of Household's total managed loan portfolio, including the Beneficial operation, is as follows: 31 percent in secured real estate, 29 percent in Visa/MasterCards, 20 percent in personal unsecured loans, 16 percent in private label credit cards (for companies like Lennox and The Good Guys), and 4 percent for other miscellaneous products. The merger transaction is expected to show up in Household's earnings beginning in 1999 and is projected to result in an annual cost savings of $450 million, although analysts were warned it would likely result in a one-time charge of $1 billion once the transaction was completed.

"The company has a computerized scoring system that I think is exceptional," McGarr adds. "It's a centralized underwriting standard. Managers know at the end of every day exactly what credit was extended. This allows them to achieve a steady stream of receivable growth. Household also has some very strong reserves, which currently stand at 4.3 percent of assets. In addition, its receivable portfolio is well-positioned. Even if we get into an economic slowdown, the company is fully reserved for this."

CEO Aldinger is currently emphasizing four themes for the company—receivables growth, customer service, credit quality, and efficiency. He believes these are key elements to ensuring future profitability. "To improve growth, we will focus on our branch network," Aldinger says. "In each of our businesses, we will supplement internal growth with acquisitions, if the economics are right. We must refine and further improve our credit risk management and get even better at collecting and underwriting. There are two pieces to our growth strategy. One is to make more loans. The other is to reduce liquidations. We will continue to focus on upselling our unsecured customers, and I include in this pool our private label customers."

Reason for Recommendation

McGarr is pleased with Aldinger's priorities. "They are extremely shareholder-friendly," he maintains. "Aldinger came over to Household from Wells Fargo Bank. He immediately froze everybody's salary, including his own, to make the company more profitable. He's done exactly what he said he was going to do. Management is required to own stock, and employees are given incentives to do well."

McGarr is convinced Household International can continue to grow at its historical rate of 20 percent annually going forward. "Interest rates do impact the company, but it manages this risk very well," he adds. "I really do think the stock is cheap, despite how well it has done in recent years. I believe you could see it trading above $65 a share in the next 12 months.

Contact Information: William Aldinger, Chairman and CEO
Household International
2700 Sanders Road
Prospect Heights, IL 60070
(847) 564-5000
www.household.com

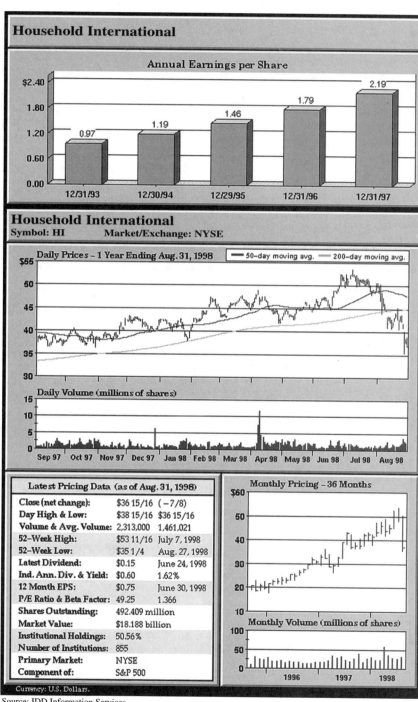

Household International

Annual Earnings per Share

Date	EPS
12/31/93	0.97
12/30/94	1.19
12/29/95	1.46
12/31/96	1.79
12/31/97	2.19

Household International
Symbol: HI   **Market/Exchange: NYSE**

Daily Prices – 1 Year Ending Aug. 31, 1998   — 50-day moving avg. — 200-day moving avg.

Daily Volume (millions of shares)

Sep 97 Oct 97 Nov 97 Dec 97 Jan 98 Feb 98 Mar 98 Apr 98 May 98 Jun 98 Jul 98 Aug 98

Latest Pricing Data (as of Aug. 31, 1998)

Close (net change):	$36 15/16	(–7/8)
Day High & Low:	$38 15/16	$36 15/16
Volume & Avg. Volume:	2,313,000	1,461,021
52–Week High:	$53 11/16	July 7, 1998
52–Week Low:	$35 1/4	Aug. 27, 1998
Latest Dividend:	$0.15	June 24, 1998
Ind. Ann. Div. & Yield:	$0.60	1.62%
12 Month EPS:	$0.75	June 30, 1998
P/E Ratio & Beta Factor:	49.25	1.366
Shares Outstanding:	492.409 million	
Market Value:	$18.188 billion	
Institutional Holdings:	50.56%	
Number of Institutions:	855	
Primary Market:	NYSE	
Component of:	S&P 500	

Currency: U.S. Dollars.

Monthly Pricing – 36 Months

Monthly Volume (millions of shares)

1996   1997   1998

Source: IDD Information Services

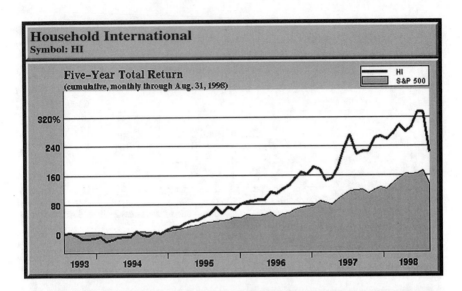

Household International
Symbol: HI

Five-Year Total Return
(cumulative, monthly through Aug. 31, 1998)

	HI
	S&P 500

SELECTED INCOME STATEMENT AND BALANCE SHEET ITEMS

INCOME STATEMENT	12/31/93	12/30/94	12/29/95	12/31/96	12/31/97	1 Year
Sales/Revenues	4,454.5	4,603.3	5,144.4	5,058.8	5,503.1	6,373.2
Cost of Goods Sold	N.A.	N.A.	N.A.	N.A.	N.A.	N.A.
Pre-tax Margin (%)	10.10	11.50	14.70	16.30	18.70	7.65
Operating Income	1,600.2	1,771.0	2,310.8	2,342.9	2,532.6	2,010.6
Net Income before Extras	298.70	367.60	453.20	538.60	686.60	73.500
Reported Net Income	298.70	367.60	453.20	538.60	686.60	73.500
Depreciation & Amortization	N.A.	N.A.	N.A.	N.A.	N.A.	N.A.
EPS from Net Income (Primary)	0.970	1.190	1.460	1.790	2.190	0.750
EPS from Net Income (Fully Diluted)	0.950	1.170	1.430	1.770	2.160	0.720
Dividend per Common Share	0.393	0.410	0.437	0.487	0.540	0.580
Dividend Yield (%)	3.62	3.31	2.20	1.58	1.27	1.17
Payout Ratio	0.41	0.34	0.30	0.27	0.25	0.77
BALANCE SHEET						
ASSETS						
Cash & Cash Equivalents	N.A.	N.A.	N.A.	N.A.	N.A.	
Inventories	N.A.	N.A.	N.A.	N.A.	N.A.	
Total Current Assets	N.A.	N.A.	N.A.	N.A.	N.A.	
Total Assets	32,962	34,338	29,219	29,594	30,303	
LIABILITIES & EQUITY						
Short Term Debt	0.000	0.000	0.000	0.000	0.000	
Long Term Debt	14,756	14,646	17,887	21,230	20,930	
Total Liabilities	30,544	31,815	26,248	26,273	25,461	
Shares Outstanding	284.685	290.099	291.778	291.486	321.796	
Common Stockholder Equity	2,078.3	2,200.4	2,690.9	2,941.2	4,516.2	
Total Stockholder Equity	2,417.6	2,523.0	2,970.9	3,321.2	4,841.2	

Note: Figures in Millions of $ except: per share items, margins, yields, and ratios.

Source: IDD Information Services

INACOM

Philip Carret
Carret & Company

Company Profile

When Fortune 500 companies want to create state-of-the-art computer systems for their specific needs, they often call on a relatively unknown firm called Inacom. "Basically these guys are integrators and facilitators, though the world thinks of them as marketers of desktop computers," the late Philip Carret told me just prior to his passing in May, 1998. Carret first learned of this company from his grand-daughter Renee Carret, a portfolio manager at his firm. "For years, Inacom has been the biggest distributor of IBM boxes in the country. But it's never been a particularly profitable business. What the company has done, in my opinion, is use desktop computers as loss leaders, while implementing servers and network solutions for companies around the world."

Inacom was formed in 1982 as a provider of computers and software solutions to farmers and ranchers. It went public in 1987 and has since grown into a $3.5 billion global technology management company. While it is IBM's single largest customer, Inacom also does significant business with Compaq, Hewlett-Packard, and Intel. In essence, Inacom buys computers from these companies, tears them apart and rebuilds them to the specifications of its corporate customers. It then adds on any other components needed to make the systems complete. "This is the only firm in the country, to my knowledge, that can buy individual components from IBM and assemble their own boxes to meet the requirements of their clients," Carret said. "It used to be that IBM and other computer makers would only sell completed boxes. So Inacom would have to call and custom order the machine built to its specifications. By building the boxes themselves, this cuts the time it takes to get a computer working for the client by six weeks or more."

Inacom sells its PCs across the U.S. through a channel of about 1,000 independent resellers and through 51 company-owned business centers. While some 90 percent of all revenues come from selling boxes, Inacom makes more than half of its profits from designing, installing, and maintaining the systems. "The company has a huge share of the market," Carret added. "Inacom is national, while most of its competitors are regional and lack the capital needed to survive. That means many of them will either fall by the wayside or be acquired. For that matter, Inacom appears to be an attractive acquisition target itself."

Inacom has been on an acquiring binge of its own, gobbling up competitors like Inacomp, Computer Biz and AM Computer Services over the past year. "A focused acquisition strategy has paid dividends in our ability to penetrate key markets, expand our service capabilities and maximize profitability," says Inacom president and CEO Bill Fairfield. "We believe Inacom is the leading company in our industry, offering the fully integrated life cycle approach to clients. Our investments in improved and expanded resources and systems are paying considerable dividends. Our services-based strategy has been shown to be the wave of the future. Our global marketing presence gives Inacom powerful leverage with multinational corporations. We've established the industry benchmark for build-to-order. And our sound acquisitions have helped support solid growth."

Reason for Recommendation

"This is the perfect kind of situation for the type of investing that I do," Carret maintained. "This is a company I have looked at for years. It's undervalued, undiscovered, and everybody seems to think it's a technology company. Really, it's not. This company sells for around 11 times earnings. It is gaining market share, and once Inacom gets an account, unless it really screws up, it has a client for life. Corporations don't want to change computer facilitators. They like to keep in place the guys who design the systems and make sure they run properly. Therefore, Inacom has an ongoing stream of revenue and additional business. New clients keep coming on board, and the existing ones are continually upgrading and expanding."

Analysts estimate that the technology services market, in which Inacom operates, will grow at around 15 percent annually through the year 2000, while overall PC growth should expand from 15 to 20 percent during this same period. Inacom has an impressive financial history. It grew sales by some 70 percent and operating profits by 200 percent from 1994-1996, and Goldman Sachs predicts the company will earn $3.05 a share in 1999. "There has never been a moment in Inacom's history when so many critical factors were in place at the same time to allow us to realize our most optimistic goals," CEO Fairfield insists. "And in the coming years, our journey toward market leadership will continue to be a demonstration of how well we can leverage our considerable advantages." While Carret had high hopes for Inacom this year, he didn't have a specific price target in mind for the stock when he recommended it to me. "I think it's absolutely nuts to set targets," he retorted. "As long as management stays on the ball and lives up to its promises, I'd stay with the company."

Contact Information: Bill Fairfield, President and CEO
Inacom Corp.
10810 Farnam Drive
Omaha, NE 61854
(402) 392-3900
www.inacom.com

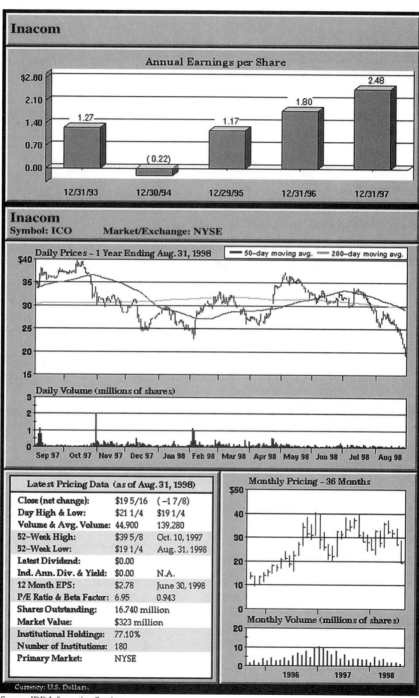

Inacom

Annual Earnings per Share

Date	EPS
12/31/93	1.27
12/30/94	(0.22)
12/29/95	1.17
12/31/96	1.80
12/31/97	2.48

Inacom
Symbol: ICO   **Market/Exchange: NYSE**

Daily Prices – 1 Year Ending Aug. 31, 1998   — 50-day moving avg.   — 200-day moving avg.

Daily Volume (millions of shares)

Sep 97 Oct 97 Nov 97 Dec 97 Jan 98 Feb 98 Mar 98 Apr 98 May 98 Jun 98 Jul 98 Aug 98

Latest Pricing Data (as of Aug. 31, 1998)

Close (net change):	$19 5/16	(−1 7/8)
Day High & Low:	$21 1/4	$19 1/4
Volume & Avg. Volume:	44,900	139,280
52–Week High:	$39 5/8	Oct. 10, 1997
52–Week Low:	$19 1/4	Aug. 31, 1998
Latest Dividend:	$0.00	
Ind. Ann. Div. & Yield:	$0.00	N.A.
12 Month EPS:	$2.78	June 30, 1998
P/E Ratio & Beta Factor:	6.95	0.943
Shares Outstanding:	16.740 million	
Market Value:	$323 million	
Institutional Holdings:	77.10%	
Number of Institutions:	180	
Primary Market:	NYSE	

Monthly Pricing – 36 Months

Monthly Volume (millions of shares)

1996   1997   1998

Currency: U.S. Dollars.

Source: IDD Information Services

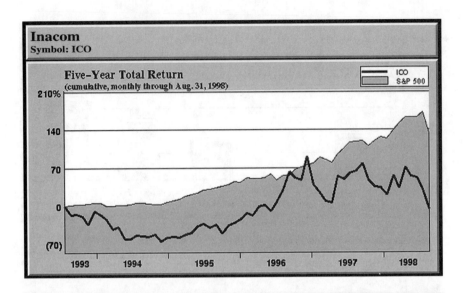

Inacom
Symbol: ICO

Five-Year Total Return
(cumulative, monthly through Aug. 31, 1998)

ICO
S&P 500

SELECTED INCOME STATEMENT AND BALANCE SHEET ITEMS

INCOME STATEMENT	12/31/93	12/30/94	12/29/95	12/31/96	12/31/97	1 Year
Sales/Revenues	1,545.2	1,800.5	2,200.3	3,102.1	3,896.3	4,222.2
Cost of Goods Sold	1,362.5	1,612.0	1,977.4	2,796.9	3,463.9	3,790.2
Pre-tax Margin (%)	1.30	(0.20)	0.90	1.00	1.30	1.53
Operating Income	28.300	8.300	34.500	52.200	78.900	97.000
Net Income before Extras	11.700	(2.300)	11.700	18.700	29.500	38.400
Reported Net Income	11.700	(2.300)	11.700	18.700	29.500	38.400
Depreciation & Amortization	13.300	19.800	19.100	21.800	31.300	37.800
EPS from Net Income (Primary)	1.270	(0.220)	1.170	1.800	2.480	2.780
EPS from Net Income (Fully Diluted)	1.250	(0.220)	1.160	1.660	2.170	2.400
Dividend per Common Share	N.A.	N.A.	N.A.	N.A.	N.A.	N.A.
Dividend Yield (%)	N.A.	N.A.	N.A.	N.A.	N.A.	N.A.
Payout Ratio	N.A.	N.A.	N.A.	N.A.	N.A.	N.A.
BALANCE SHEET						
ASSETS						
Cash & Cash Equivalents	9.700	10.500	20.700	31.400	52.600	
Inventories	186.90	228.70	352.90	386.60	429.40	
Total Current Assets	364.10	430.20	539.90	712.30	747.80	
Total Assets	456.90	519.90	624.20	847.60	960.50	
LIABILITIES & EQUITY						
Short Term Debt	171.40	96.700	83.500	140.80	0.000	
Long Term Debt	23.100	30.300	23.700	55.300	141.50	
Total Liabilities	320.40	384.20	475.50	670.90	635.30	
Shares Outstanding	9.808	9.864	10.020	10.850	14.825	
Common Stockholder Equity	136.50	135.60	148.80	176.80	325.20	
Total Stockholder Equity	136.50	135.60	148.80	176.80	325.20	

Note: Figures in Millions of $ except: per share items, margins, yields, and ratios.

Source: IDD Information Services

INTEL

Vita Nelson
The Moneypaper

Company Profile

If you own a personal computer, chances are Intel makes the brains that help to run it. By far the most recognized brand name in the technology field, thanks in large part to its successful "Intel Inside" advertising program, the company's microprocessors control the central processing of data in computers. "This is the world's leading manufacturer of integrated circuits," notes Vita Nelson, publisher of *The Moneypaper*. "In addition to microprocessors, Intel's main products include related peripherals, microcontrollers, and other memory components."

The world's first microprocessor, the Intel 4004, was developed in 1971. It provided astonishing performance for its time. The chip contained 2,300 transistors and was capable of handling 60,000 instructions per second. But that's snail speed compared to what's available today for a small fraction of the price. Intel's Pentium Pro, for example, contains 5.5 million transistors and is able to accept 300 million instructions per second. "The company is now working on its next generation of chips, called 'Merced,'" Nelson points out. "Merced is scheduled to be released in 1999. This much faster new chip has already been endorsed and licensed for use by all the major computer systems software and hardware producers, thus ensuring its compatibility and market success. I expect it to become the new industry standard."

This wouldn't be surprising, since Intel is known for being a company that sets the standards others follow. Intel's revolutionary Pentium and Pentium II processors with MMX technology boost multimedia performance in PCs by 60 percent, compared to equivalent-speed processors without them. The company's networking and communications products enhance the capabilities of PC systems and networks, making them easier to use and manage. Its flash memory products provide easily reprogrammable memory for computers, mobile phones, and many other devices. And Intel's embedded control chips are used to perform specific functions in such things as automobile engine and braking systems, laser printers, hard disk drives, cellular phones, and home appliances. While Intel's major customers are computer manufacturers, individual PC users can also buy the company's enhancement products directly.

Intel's sales, profits and stock price have surged throughout most of the company's history. A $100 investment at the time of Intel's IPO 26 years ago would be worth more than $100,000 today. But the past couple of years have been challenging for the company. To begin with, computer systems retailing for below $1,000 are the hottest selling items in the industry right now, and many of these units contain less expensive chips supplied by Intel's competitors. Intel has responded by

55

announcing plans to fabricate a more cost effective alternative of its own. This, combined with problems in Asia, has slowed the company's growth and caused Wall Street to become concerned about its future. It's not that they fear Intel will go out of business. Instead, investors worry the company won't give them the kind of explosive growth going forward that it has experienced in the past, especially since foreign sales account for more than half of Intel's revenues. These fears were further amplified when Intel reported that earnings and income fell in the fourth quarter of 1997 compared to the same period in the previous year.

What's more, shortly after being named *Time* magazine's man of the year in 1997, former Intel president and CEO Andrew Grove announced he was stepping down, to be replaced by second-in-command Craig Barrett. Investors actually seemed to be little concerned about this handover. Some even suggested it could be good for the company.

Reason for Recommendation

Nelson isn't worried about any of the changes taking place in the company. In fact, she says this current uncertainty has given investors an excellent opportunity to buy the company at giveaway levels. "This is a high-tech juggernaut whose earnings have been growing faster than its current PE," she says. "Enough is enough. I don't see how the price can go any lower." Nelson forecasts the company will grow at a rate of 30 percent in 1999, with earnings well above the $30 billion mark.

In addition to the release of Merced, Nelson points out that Intel has a number of new products and alliances in the pipeline that should bode well for its fortunes going forward. "Three Asian companies will manufacture PC cameras using its 971 PC camera kit," she says. "Plus, insiders own 7 percent of the outstanding shares, which is a good sign." Nelson adds that Intel has a terrific dividend reinvestment plan, which allows existing shareholders to reinvest dividends and buy additional stock from the company each month without paying a commission. (Incidentally, this is the third time in the past four years that a *Wall Street's Picks* panelist has selected Intel as their favorite company for the year ahead. In each previous case, the stock went on to become a standout performer.)

Contact Information: Craig R. Barrett, President and CEO
Intel Corporation
2200 Mission College Boulevard
Santa Clara, CA 95052
(800) 628-8686
www.intel.com

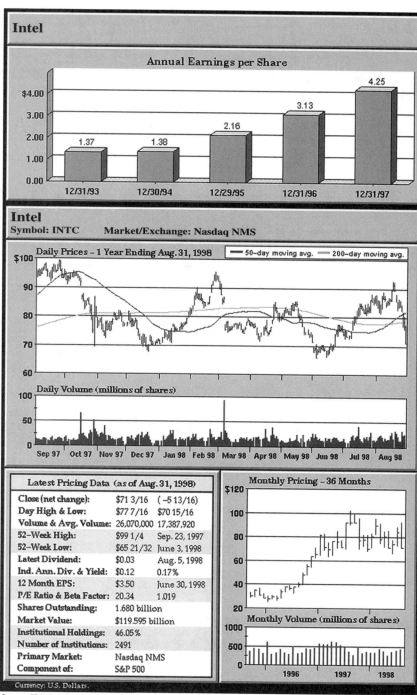

Intel

Annual Earnings per Share

1.37	1.38	2.16	3.13	4.25
12/31/93	12/30/94	12/29/95	12/31/96	12/31/97

Intel

Symbol: INTC　　　**Market/Exchange: Nasdaq NMS**

Daily Prices – 1 Year Ending Aug. 31, 1998　　50-day moving avg.　200-day moving avg.

Daily Volume (millions of shares)

Sep 97　Oct 97　Nov 97　Dec 97　Jan 98　Feb 98　Mar 98　Apr 98　May 98　Jun 98　Jul 98　Aug 98

Latest Pricing Data (as of Aug. 31, 1998)

Close (net change):	$71 3/16	(–5 13/16)
Day High & Low:	$77 7/16	$70 15/16
Volume & Avg. Volume:	26,070,000	17,387,920
52–Week High:	$99 1/4	Sep. 23, 1997
52–Week Low:	$65 21/32	June 3, 1998
Latest Dividend:	$0.03	Aug. 5, 1998
Ind. Ann. Div. & Yield:	$0.12	0.17%
12 Month EPS:	$3.50	June 30, 1998
P/E Ratio & Beta Factor:	20.34	1.019
Shares Outstanding:	1.680 billion	
Market Value:	$119.595 billion	
Institutional Holdings:	46.05%	
Number of Institutions:	2491	
Primary Market:	Nasdaq NMS	
Component of:	S&P 500	

Currency: U.S. Dollars.

Monthly Pricing – 36 Months

Monthly Volume (millions of shares)

1996　1997　1998

Source: IDD Information Services

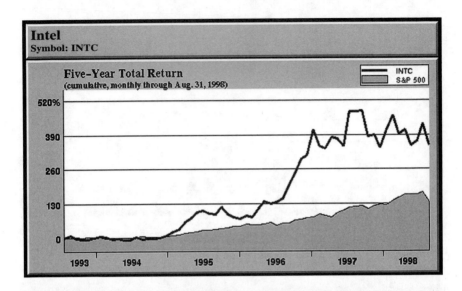

Intel
Symbol: INTC

Five-Year Total Return
(cumulative, monthly through Aug. 31, 1998)

INTC
S&P 500

SELECTED INCOME STATEMENT AND BALANCE SHEET ITEMS

INCOME STATEMENT	12/31/93	12/30/94	12/29/95	12/31/96	12/31/97	1 Year
Sales/Revenues	8,782.0	11,521	16,202	20,847	25,070	24,590
Cost of Goods Sold	2,535.0	4,529.0	6,432.0	7,276.0	7,753.0	8,625.0
Pre-tax Margin (%)	40.20	31.30	34.80	38.10	42.50	35.50
Operating Income	3,392.0	3,387.0	5,252.0	7,553.0	9,887.0	8,069.0
Net Income before Extras	2,295.0	2,288.0	3,566.0	5,157.0	6,945.0	5,762.0
Reported Net Income	2,295.0	2,288.0	3,566.0	5,157.0	6,945.0	5,762.0
Depreciation & Amortization	717.00	1,047.0	1,379.0	1,888.0	2,192.0	2,446.0
EPS from Net Income (Primary)	1.370	1.380	2.160	3.130	4.250	3.500
EPS from Net Income (Fully Diluted)	1.300	1.310	2.020	2.900	3.870	3.230
Dividend per Common Share	0.050	0.056	0.070	0.090	0.110	0.120
Dividend Yield (%)	0.32	0.35	0.25	0.14	0.16	0.16
Payout Ratio	0.04	0.04	0.03	0.03	0.03	0.03
BALANCE SHEET						
ASSETS						
Cash & Cash Equivalents	1,475.0	1,180.0	1,463.0	4,165.0	4,102.0	
Inventories	838.00	1,169.0	2,004.0	1,293.0	1,697.0	
Total Current Assets	5,802.0	6,167.0	8,097.0	13,684	15,867	
Total Assets	11,344	13,816	17,504	23,735	28,880	
LIABILITIES & EQUITY						
Short Term Debt	497.00	517.00	346.00	389.00	322.00	
Long Term Debt	426.00	392.00	400.00	728.00	448.00	
Total Liabilities	3,844.0	4,549.0	5,364.0	6,863.0	9,585.0	
Shares Outstanding	1,672.000	1,652.000	1,642.000	1,642.000	1,628.000	
Common Stockholder Equity	7,500.0	9,267.0	12,140	16,872	19,295	
Total Stockholder Equity	7,500.0	9,267.0	12,140	16,872	19,295	

Note: Figures in Millions of $ except: per share items, margins, yields, and ratios.

Source: IDD Information Services

INTERNATIONAL PAPER

James O'Shaughnessy
O'Shaughnessy Capital Management

Company Profile

How is it that International Paper wound up in this book as Jim O'Shaughnessy's favorite stock for the second year in a row? Simple. By sheer coincidence, it once again was the company that met the strict requirements he adheres to when selecting his preferred pick. At least that was the case as this book went to press.

Here's what I mean: O'Shaughnessy chose International Paper because it fits his strategy of buying the second-lowest priced of the top ten highest yielding stocks in the Dow Jones Industrial Average. It's one derivation of the increasingly popular "Dogs of the Dow" investment technique. "I tested this strategy back to 1928 and found that while it is considerably more volatile than the traditional Dogs of the Dow approach (which calls for buying all 10 of the highest yielding stocks), the returns it generates are outstanding," he says. "It has averaged about 26 percent annually going back over 60 years."

The premise behind this strategy is simple. The high yield is a sign the stock is out of favor. "Essentially, you're buying a well-known blue chip company when it is under some degree of distress and/or is unloved or misunderstood on Wall Street," he explains. "The fact is, if you were to do additional fundamental research on these companies, you would probably find a reason not to invest in them. This strategy works because it forces you to buy Union Carbide after it has blown up India, or Exxon when the oil is still glistening on the bay or Philip Morris as 18 other states sue it for reimbursement. If you do additional outside research, you will be absolutely certain this is the one stock you don't want to buy." In the case of International Paper, you would find that the company reported a loss of 50 cents a share in 1997, after special items. This was caused by a series of negative factors, including a substantial decline in pulp profits, most of which were attributed to the ongoing economic crisis in Asia. "For this year, we will take whatever steps are necessary to improve the financial performance of the company," International Paper chairman and CEO John T. Dillon says. "These include extending our internal performance improvements, further strengthening relationships with customers, focusing all businesses to achieve their return on investment objectives, keeping inventories at the lowest possible levels, and not adding any significant new capacity."

That's really what an investor following this strategy is banking on. The idea is that you are buying a company on the verge of turning around a negative situation. You know the stock is having trouble because of its relatively high yield. Once conditions improve, the share price should go up, thus lowering the yield. "These are not brand new babies," O'Shaughnessy points out. "They're wise old guys. They've been around the block a million times and can weather virtually any downturn. If the movie 'Independence Day' comes true, these companies will still be around."

In all fairness, International Paper is a solid company, now in its 100th year of business. It is one of the world's preeminent manufacturers of printing papers, packaging materials, forest products, and specialty items. It operates more than 6 million acres of forestland and manages production plants in some 30 different countries. Its white and colored papers are marketed under the Hammermill, Strathmore, Beckett, and Springhill brand names. Its coated papers are used by a variety of magazine publishers, including *Forbes* and *Parents*. Its forestry products are turned into everything from kitchen cabinets to entire homes. Clearly, we use items made by International Paper on a daily basis.

Reason for Recommendation

As you know by now, O'Shaughnessy doesn't care about any of this He doesn't even know the company's CEO and has no plans to visit its headquarters in Purchase, New York for a personal inspection. He only likes the stock because it fit into his investment strategy at the time this book was being written. In fact, by the time you read this, there's a good chance the company matching this profile will have changed. Therefore, assuming you want to take O'Shaughnessy's advice, you should jot down a list of the ten highest yielding Dow stocks at the moment, which are listed in *The Wall Street Journal* each month, and see which one has the second lowest price. If it's still International Paper, that's the stock to buy. If it's another company, put your money there instead.

It's important to point out that you should use this technique only for selecting a stock to add to your overall portfolio. You should never put your entire portfolio into any one name, even when following a strategy like this one. O'Shaughnessy himself recommends you own at least 10 and preferably 25 different companies for proper diversification. By the way, this isn't the first time the same stock has met O'Shaughnessy's test for this particular strategy. "It's not that common but it does happen occasionally," he says. "Talk about the ultimate strategy. If you followed my advice last year, this time around you don't have to do a thing."

Contact Information: John T. Dillon, Chairman and CEO
International Paper Company
Two Manhattanville Road
Purchase, NY 10577
(914) 397-1500
www.ipaper.com

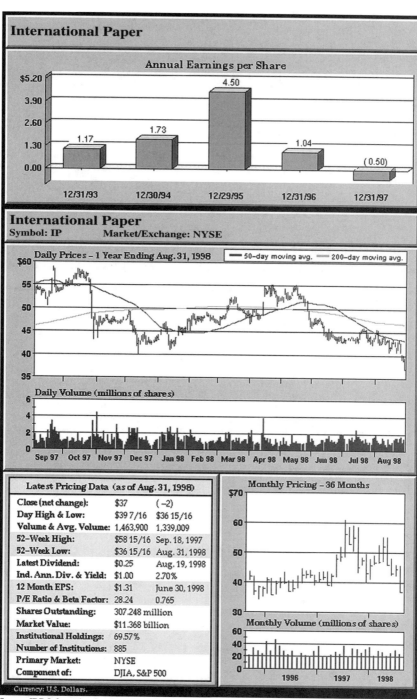

International Paper

Annual Earnings per Share

$5.20	
3.90	
2.60	
1.30	
0.00	

1.17   1.73   4.50   1.04   (0.50)

12/31/93   12/30/94   12/29/95   12/31/96   12/31/97

International Paper
Symbol: IP   **Market/Exchange: NYSE**

Daily Prices – 1 Year Ending Aug. 31, 1998   — 50-day moving avg.   — 200-day moving avg.

Daily Volume (millions of shares)

Sep 97   Oct 97   Nov 97   Dec 97   Jan 98   Feb 98   Mar 98   Apr 98   May 98   Jun 98   Jul 98   Aug 98

Latest Pricing Data (as of Aug. 31, 1998)

Close (net change):	$37	(−2)
Day High & Low:	$39 7/16	$36 15/16
Volume & Avg. Volume:	1,463,900	1,339,009
52–Week High:	$58 15/16	Sep. 18, 1997
52–Week Low:	$36 15/16	Aug. 31, 1998
Latest Dividend:	$0.25	Aug. 19, 1998
Ind. Ann. Div. & Yield:	$1.00	2.70%
12 Month EPS:	$1.31	June 30, 1998
P/E Ratio & Beta Factor:	28.24	0.765
Shares Outstanding:	307.248 million	
Market Value:	$11.368 billion	
Institutional Holdings:	69.57%	
Number of Institutions:	885	
Primary Market:	NYSE	
Component of:	DJIA, S&P 500	

Monthly Pricing – 36 Months

Monthly Volume (millions of shares)

1996   1997   1998

Currency: U.S. Dollars.

Source: IDD Information Services

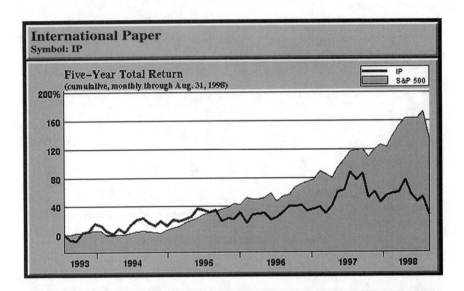

International Paper
Symbol: IP

Five-Year Total Return
(cumulative, monthly through Aug. 31, 1998)

IP
S&P 500

SELECTED INCOME STATEMENT AND BALANCE SHEET ITEMS

INCOME STATEMENT	12/31/93	12/30/94	12/29/95	12/31/96	12/31/97	1 Year
Sales/Revenues	13,685	14,966	19,797	20,143	20,096	19,775
Cost of Goods Sold	10,191	11,143	13,896	14,901	14,973	14,729
Pre-tax Margin (%)	3.70	4.40	9.50	3.10	(0.60)	3.22
Operating Income	810.00	1,013.0	2,521.0	1,420.0	1,146.0	1,197.0
Net Income before Extras	289.00	432.00	1,153.0	303.00	(151.00)	395.00
Reported Net Income	289.00	432.00	1,153.0	303.00	(151.00)	395.00
Depreciation & Amortization	898.00	885.00	1,031.0	1,194.0	1,258.0	1,209.0
EPS from Net Income (Primary)	1.170	1.730	4.500	1.040	(0.500)	1.310
EPS from Net Income (Fully Diluted)	1.170	1.730	4.500	1.040	(0.500)	1.310
Dividend per Common Share	0.840	0.840	0.920	1.000	1.000	1.000
Dividend Yield (%)	2.48	2.23	2.43	2.47	2.32	2.33
Payout Ratio	0.72	0.49	0.20	0.96	N.A.	0.76

BALANCE SHEET						
ASSETS						
Cash & Cash Equivalents	242.00	270.00	312.00	352.00	398.00	
Inventories	2,024.0	2,075.0	2,784.0	2,840.0	2,760.0	
Total Current Assets	4,401.0	4,830.0	5,873.0	5,998.0	5,945.0	
Total Assets	16,631	17,836	23,977	28,252	26,754	
LIABILITIES & EQUITY						
Short Term Debt	2,089.0	2,083.0	2,283.0	3,296.0	2,212.0	
Long Term Debt	3,601.0	4,464.0	5,946.0	6,691.0	7,154.0	
Total Liabilities	10,406	11,322	15,730	18,458	17,594	
Shares Outstanding	247.800	251.800	261.000	300.200	302.200	
Common Stockholder Equity	6,225.0	6,514.0	7,797.0	9,344.0	8,710.0	
Total Stockholder Equity	6,225.0	6,514.0	8,247.0	9,794.0	9,160.0	

Note: Figures in Millions of $ except: per share items, margins, yields, and ratios.

Source: IDD Information Services

NEWMONT MINING

Anthony Gallea

Smith Barney

Company Profile

It should come as no surprise that Tony Gallea has selected a gold stock as his favorite investment idea for 1999. After all, almost every investor on Wall Street has written gold off, to the point of laughing at the mere mention it may still have some value. These pundits have good reason to be skeptical. Gold is just now climbing back above $300 an ounce, after falling to an 18-year low of $278 in January 1998. It has been an abysmal investment during this entire time. Newmont Mining's stock alone lost 34 percent of its value in 1997, in a year when the S&P 500 *rose* more than 33 percent. So why has Gallea risked putting his name on a company like Newmont this year? Because he's a devoted contrarian who is always out buying what everyone else is shunning.

"What I'm really doing is making a play on gold," he explains. "Newmont is the proxy I have selected to do this." Newmont is the largest gold company in the world, outside of South Africa, and the lowest cost producer among the major mining houses. The company ended 1997 with 52.7 million ounces of proven and probable gold reserves. It produces gold from operations in Nevada and California, along with Peru, Indonesia, and the Central Asian Republic of Uzhekistan. In mid-1997, Newmont merged with Santa Fe Pacific Gold, thus increasing its industry dominance.

Gallea's reasons for choosing Newmont are many. "I start with the long-term view that gold has been around ever since man has been bipedal," he says. "One of the things I look for in an investment is I want it to be down at least 50 percent from its high at the time of purchase. Gold is down more than that from its high of over $800 an ounce some two decades ago. Then when you look out at what analysts are projecting, you'll hear them talk about a modest increase or decrease in gold prices, but there aren't any extreme opinions in either direction. However, all of the recent selling by the central bank that has put the market on its heels has been subsiding a bit, and it appears the new European Central Bank will have 20 to 25 percent of its reserves in gold."

So, as Gallea's thesis goes, there is continuing demand for gold with an ongoing decrease in overall mine production. Then there's the issue of price. "Some 40 percent of the world's gold production has a cash cost above $290 an ounce," he observes. "At these current prices, the mines can't make any money. A quarter of the total production has a cost of more than $320 an ounce. South Africa is a particularly high production area with very deep mines, many of which have been shuttered. Russian gold production is also down. The Asians have not been buying, and many producers have stopped selling forward because prices are so low."

By now you probably have the picture that things couldn't possibly get any worse for gold and gold producers. And that's exactly Gallea's point. "It seems to me that when you have gold trading at an 18-year low, and sentiment is so bearish on gold mining, it may be time to start buying some gold mining stocks," he asserts. "The stock you want to own is Newmont. It's a class act in the industry. The company owns 90 percent of Newmont Gold Corporation. This is a big company with 1997 sales of $1.4 billion. Newmont also has some oil and gas production, though it's a relatively small piece of the pie."

Reason for Recommendation

Gallea is definitely in the minority. Many educated investors are now arguing that gold is no longer relevant, especially because it doesn't even seem to move upward in times when the stock market goes into temporary turmoil. "As a contrarian, I like to hear that," Gallea insists. "The pundits are right on that point, and it has discouraged people from owning gold stocks. I don't know of many folks out there pounding the table for gold. And the statistics don't look good. Newmont got up to $80 in 1987. That means you could have owned this stock for the past 12 years and lost a lot of money on it. However, when you have 1,000 metric tons a year of deficit, unless the central banks keep selling to close that gap, the only thing that should happen is for the price to go up."

Another popular complaint is that gold is no longer relevant as a store of value. "This is a commodity that's been around for thousands of years," Gallea counters. "Of the currencies around 1,000 years ago, only gold has survived. The reason this stock is cheap now is because everyone is calling for the death of gold. If you wait until people realize that's not going to happen, these shares could more than double. And if I'm wrong, I don't think you have much risk from here."

Newmont chairman, president and CEO, Ronald Cambre, points out that the company is taking steps to ensure it remains profitable in the current environment. "We are significantly reducing cash outlays this year through a deferral of capital projects, revised mining plans, reduced exploration and administrative spending, and (by reducing) the quarterly dividend to 3 cents per share from 12 cents." The last major move in Newmont's stock was back in 1996, when it got up to $60 a share. That's also Gallea's 1999 target.

Contact Information: Ronald Cambre, Chairman, President and CEO
Newmont Mining
1700 Lincoln Street
Denver, CO 80203
(303) 863-7414
www.newmont.com

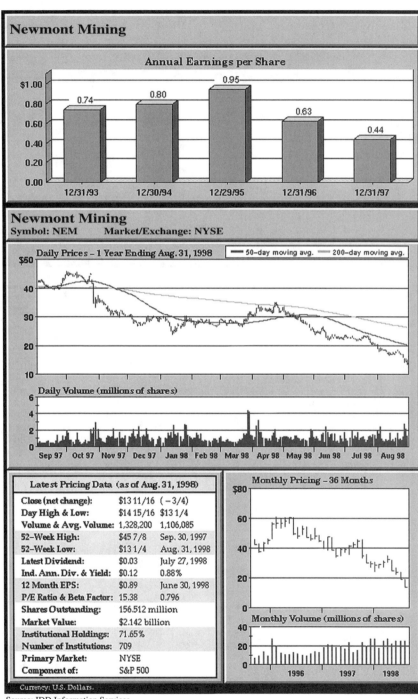

Newmont Mining

Annual Earnings per Share

	12/31/93	12/30/94	12/29/95	12/31/96	12/31/97
	0.74	0.80	0.95	0.63	0.44

Newmont Mining
Symbol: NEM   Market/Exchange: NYSE

Daily Prices – 1 Year Ending Aug. 31, 1998   ▬ 50–day moving avg. ▬ 200–day moving avg.

Daily Volume (millions of shares)

Sep 97 Oct 97 Nov 97 Dec 97 Jan 98 Feb 98 Mar 98 Apr 98 May 98 Jun 98 Jul 98 Aug 98

Latest Pricing Data (as of Aug. 31, 1998)		
Close (net change):	$13 11/16	(–3/4)
Day High & Low:	$14 15/16	$13 1/4
Volume & Avg. Volume:	1,328,200	1,106,085
52–Week High:	$45 7/8	Sep. 30, 1997
52–Week Low:	$13 1/4	Aug. 31, 1998
Latest Dividend:	$0.03	July 27, 1998
Ind. Ann. Div. & Yield:	$0.12	0.88%
12 Month EPS:	$0.89	June 30, 1998
P/E Ratio & Beta Factor:	15.38	0.796
Shares Outstanding:	156.512 million	
Market Value:	$2.142 billion	
Institutional Holdings:	71.65%	
Number of Institutions:	709	
Primary Market:	NYSE	
Component of:	S&P 500	

Currency: U.S. Dollars.

Monthly Pricing – 36 Months

Monthly Volume (millions of shares)

1996   1997   1998

Source: IDD Information Services

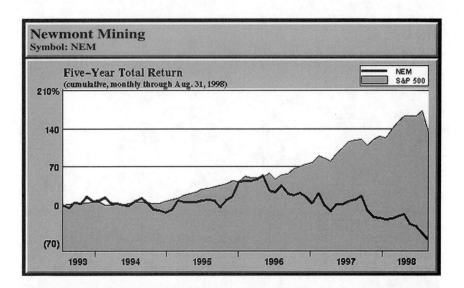

Newmont Mining
Symbol: NEM

Five-Year Total Return
(cumulative, monthly through Aug. 31, 1998)

NEM
S&P 500

SELECTED INCOME STATEMENT AND BALANCE SHEET ITEMS

INCOME STATEMENT	12/31/93	12/30/94	12/29/95	12/31/96	12/31/97	1 Year
Sales/Revenues	634.30	597.40	636.20	768.50	1,572.8	1,548.1
Cost of Goods Sold	339.20	326.40	370.60	476.10	744.80	737.90
Pre-tax Margin (%)	17.90	7.80	20.40	8.50	3.80	10.45
Operating Income	82.100	26.200	(5.900)	46.900	342.20	298.10
Net Income before Extras	94.700	76.100	112.60	85.100	68.400	138.30
Reported Net Income	94.700	76.100	112.60	85.100	68.400	138.30
Depreciation & Amortization	110.00	91.100	106.80	124.80	321.00	370.50
EPS from Net Income (Primary)	0.740	0.800	0.950	0.630	0.440	0.890
EPS from Net Income (Fully Diluted)	0.740	0.800	0.950	0.630	0.440	0.890
Dividend per Common Share	0.481	0.480	0.480	0.480	0.390	0.210
Dividend Yield (%)	1.04	1.33	1.06	1.07	1.33	0.89
Payout Ratio	0.65	0.60	0.51	0.76	0.89	0.24
BALANCE SHEET						
ASSETS						
Cash & Cash Equivalents	69.800	160.60	59.100	185.70	146.20	
Inventories	122.20	130.90	174.00	188.30	339.50	
Total Current Assets	229.00	370.10	289.50	455.90	641.40	
Total Assets	1,186.4	1,656.7	1,773.8	2,081.1	3,614.0	
LIABILITIES & EQUITY						
Short Term Debt	15.700	15.700	33.600	65.200	69.100	
Long Term Debt	192.00	593.60	604.30	585.00	1,179.4	
Total Liabilities	556.60	983.20	1,030.9	1,056.2	2,023.0	
Shares Outstanding	85.796	86.080	94.802	99.522	156.500	
Common Stockholder Equity	615.50	659.10	742.90	1,024.9	1,591.1	
Total Stockholder Equity	629.90	673.50	742.90	1,024.9	1,591.1	

Note: Figures in Millions of $ except: per share items, margins, yields, and ratios.

Source: IDD Information Services

NIKE

Robert Sanborn
The Oakmark Fund

Company Profile

Nike is unquestionably one of the most recognized brands on the planet. Whether it's on Tiger Woods' cap, or on your child's T-shirt, the company's famous "swoosh" logo can be seen just about everywhere. And we all know that Nike's message to the world is "Just Do It." But while 1997 was the best year in the company's history, a glance at Nike's third quarter 1998 financial highlights shows how good fortunes can change in a matter of months. Revenues were down 8 percent, global footwear and apparel sales fell in double digits, and the company was forced to take a restructuring charge of up to $175 million. "In spirit, Nike remains a company that is about change," said chairman and CEO Philip H. Knight after announcing the disappointing results. "Going forward into this challenging period, we must look at new initiatives, ambitious thinking and new metrics for measuring our success to supplement our core value of creating the best products for athletes. Our goal is to continually invest in the future of Nike, so that we are better poised to leverage those investments when our business is back on the path of growth."

What caused Nike's reversal of fortune? "The same things that have caused it to underperform two other times in its history," surmises Robert Sanborn, portfolio manager of The Oakmark Fund. "The basic structure of Nike's business is one that involves very fast-moving end markets, combined with a fairly slow-moving product development process. Earnings slowdowns, while intermittent, will occur from time to time in the context of a good long-term trend rate. I think that's where we're at right now. It happened in the late 1980s and in 1993. What happens is there's a fashion change of some sort. People are less likely to be wearing sneakers around these days. The second thing that occurred was the whole Asian situation. Asia is a very big foreign market for Nike, and the company has tremendous inventories built up there and here in the U.S. as well. The last factor, I believe, is that the whole basketball category has tanked industry-wide. The NBA had a lot of bad publicity in 1997, and the effects of that are lingering on."

Nike clearly won't be filing for bankruptcy any time soon. Its athletic footwear products remain popular, and the company is known for its emphasis on high quality construction and innovative design. What's more, Nike sells active sports apparel, performance equipment, and various other products in 100 countries around the world, most of which feature the company's trademark logo. "Shoes are clearly the core business," Sanborn points out. "The shoes make the apparel and equipment business possible for them. Nike has clearly leveraged its brand name well, without being piggy about it."

Reason for Recommendation

So far, you're probably thinking that Nike should be one of "Wall Street's *Pans* for 1999," instead of a featured pick. But that's precisely the point. According to Sanborn, investors are treating this company like times are going to be tough forever. But he's convinced this is just a temporary setback that has created an excellent opportunity to snap up shares at cheap prices. And, as a value investor, that's exactly the kind of stock that makes him drool. "I owned Nike several years ago and sold it after it went sky high in a matter of months," Sanborn says. "I've been waiting for the right time to buy it back ever since. Now is the time."

However, Sanborn admits the turnaround won't happen overnight. "It's going to take a long time," he says. "The company has to work off inventories. It has already taken some major steps, such as cutting jobs, which it has traditionally been reluctant to do." (Nike's workforce jumped from 9,500 to 22,000 during 1994-1997 alone.) Chairman Knight concurs. "Looking ahead into fiscal 1999, we foresee continued pressure on our earnings resulting from our difficulties in the Asia Pacific market," he states. However, Knight remains convinced that "the Asia Pacific region holds the greatest long-term opportunities for growth."

In addition, Sanborn says the stock is so reasonable, he's willing to wait for the picture to improve. "Given the quality of the brand name and Nike's potential for growth, this company is trading at a phenomenally attractive valuation," he insists. "Nike has invested heavily in the brand name, while improving on foreign distribution and awareness. And it has done all this without issuing one new share of stock or raising a dollar in debt. It's one heck of a free cash-flow business. Nike spends more on marketing than its next four competitors combined. I feel this is a very good opportunity for the long run."

Sanborn also admires Knight and has full faith in his ability to make the company shine again. "He doesn't run the business for Wall Street, he runs it for the long term," Sanborn says. "More importantly, he's creating a culture at Nike that's very special and unique." Sanborn estimates the company will earn $2.40 a share in 1999, and has a near-term target for the stock of $70.

Contact Information: Philip H. Knight, Chairman and CEO
Nike, Inc.
One Bowerman Drive
Beaverton, OR 97005
(503) 671-6453
www.info.nike.com

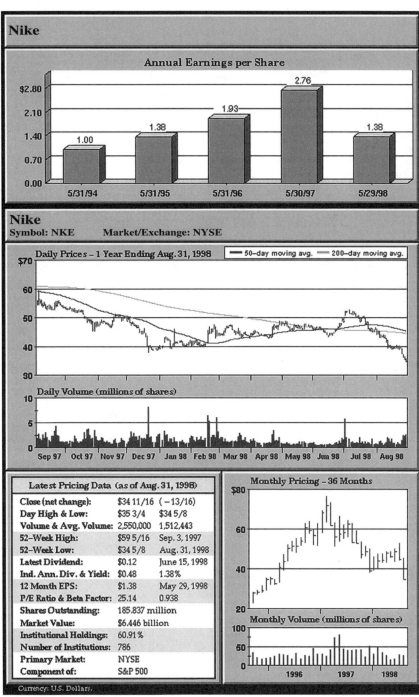

Nike

Annual Earnings per Share

1.00	1.38	1.93	2.76	1.38
5/31/94	5/31/95	5/31/96	5/30/97	5/29/98

Nike
Symbol: NKE   Market/Exchange: NYSE

Daily Prices – 1 Year Ending Aug. 31, 1998   ▬ 50-day moving avg.   ▬ 200-day moving avg.

Daily Volume (millions of shares)

Sep 97   Oct 97   Nov 97   Dec 97   Jan 98   Feb 98   Mar 98   Apr 98   May 98   Jun 98   Jul 98   Aug 98

Latest Pricing Data (as of Aug. 31, 1998)

Close (net change):	$34 11/16	(−13/16)
Day High & Low:	$35 3/4	$34 5/8
Volume & Avg. Volume:	2,550,000	1,512,443
52–Week High:	$59 5/16	Sep. 3, 1997
52–Week Low:	$34 5/8	Aug. 31, 1998
Latest Dividend:	$0.12	June 15, 1998
Ind. Ann. Div. & Yield:	$0.48	1.38%
12 Month EPS:	$1.38	May 29, 1998
P/E Ratio & Beta Factor:	25.14	0.938
Shares Outstanding:	185.837 million	
Market Value:	$6.446 billion	
Institutional Holdings:	60.91%	
Number of Institutions:	786	
Primary Market:	NYSE	
Component of:	S&P 500	

Currency: U.S. Dollars.

Monthly Pricing – 36 Months

Monthly Volume (millions of shares)

1996   1997   1998

Source: IDD Information Services

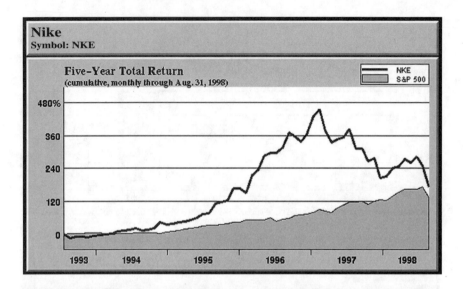

Nike
Symbol: NKE

Five-Year Total Return
(cumulative, monthly through Aug. 31, 1998)

— NKE
▬ S&P 500

SELECTED INCOME STATEMENT AND BALANCE SHEET ITEMS

INCOME STATEMENT	5/31/94	5/31/95	5/31/96	5/30/97	5/29/98	1 Year
Sales/Revenues	3,789.7	4,760.8	6,470.6	9,186.5	9,553.1	9,553.1
Cost of Goods Sold	2,236.9	2,775.1	3,774.3	5,334.7	5,832.0	5,832.0
Pre–tax Margin (%)	12.90	13.70	13.90	14.10	6.80	6.45
Operating Income	514.20	685.70	975.30	1,379.8	863.80	863.80
Net Income before Extras	298.80	399.70	553.20	795.80	399.60	399.50
Reported Net Income	298.80	399.70	553.20	795.80	399.60	399.50
Depreciation & Amortization	64.500	90.200	132.40	168.30	233.50	233.50
EPS from Net Income (Primary)	1.000	1.380	1.930	2.760	1.380	1.380
EPS from Net Income (Fully Diluted)	0.990	1.360	1.880	2.680	1.350	1.350
Dividend per Common Share	0.200	0.225	0.275	0.350	0.440	0.440
Dividend Yield (%)	1.36	1.14	0.55	0.61	0.96	0.96
Payout Ratio	0.20	0.16	0.14	0.13	0.32	0.32
BALANCE SHEET						
ASSETS						
Cash & Cash Equivalents	518.80	216.10	262.10	445.40	108.60	
Inventories	470.00	629.70	931.20	1,338.6	1,396.6	
Total Current Assets	1,770.4	2,045.9	2,726.9	3,830.9	3,532.6	
Total Assets	2,373.8	3,142.7	3,951.6	5,361.2	5,397.4	
LIABILITIES & EQUITY						
Short Term Debt	131.20	429.00	452.40	555.40	481.80	
Long Term Debt	12.400	10.600	9.600	296.00	379.40	
Total Liabilities	632.60	1,177.8	1,520.0	2,205.0	2,135.5	
Shares Outstanding	292.800	285.780	287.258	289.270	287.000	
Common Stockholder Equity	1,740.9	1,964.7	2,431.1	3,155.8	3,261.6	
Total Stockholder Equity	1,741.2	1,965.0	2,431.4	3,156.1	3,261.9	

Note: Figures in Millions of $ except: per share items, margins, yields, and ratios.

Source: IDD Information Services

ORCKIT COMMUNICATIONS

Robert Kern

Kern Capital Management

Company Profile

When Bob Kern looks at the big picture of what's going on in the area of technology, he finds that people are trying to communicate with each other by computer as quickly as possible. That's why he believes companies offering the best solutions for broadband communications and high speed Internet access will prosper as we enter the new millennium. "We have already increased the speed of modems by a factor of 2, from 28.8K to 56K," he notes. "And even though the 56K modem just came out, it's already obsolete." It's not just Kern who has taken notice of this trend. At the beginning of 1998, a group of companies including Microsoft, Intel, Compaq, and the regional Bell operators met to discuss this very issue. "You have guys like Bill Gates and Andy Grove realizing that for their businesses to be successful, they have got to overcome this bottleneck with bandwidth," Kern says. "It's vitally important to them that this technology is adopted and utilized on a widespread basis. We're not only talking the United States, but this is a worldwide challenge. So companies with technology that will bring increased bandwidth to the home and small business are going to do very well. And I feel the best positioned company to take advantage of this opportunity is Orckit Communications."

Orckit is an Israeli-based business that designs, develops, manufactures, and markets high-speed data systems which enable telephone companies and Internet service providers to optimize the bandwidth utilization of the "last mile" of copper wire in the local loop, or that segment from the central office to the customer's premises. The company is one of only a handful in the digital subscriber line (DSL) industry with not only core technology—a self-developed silicon chip and proprietary software—but also a full range of DSL products and systems. The one thing Kern is most impressed with is the company's asymmetric digital subscriber line (ADSL) technology. ADSL is expected increase the current speed of Internet access by a factor of 30 to 50 times what is currently available. "It will allow you to achieve this high bandwidth over ordinary telephone lines," he notes. "This is important because you can't go out there and rebuild the entire infrastructure using fiber optics. Therefore, you need technologies that will allow you to communicate quickly over what exists today, namely copper wire."

This ADSL technology will reside in both the telephone company's central office and in your computer. "Orckit provides the technology and is partnered with semiconductor manufacturers and equipment suppliers to bring ADSL technology to consumers and small businesses," Kern says. So at some point, Compaq, for example, could put an ADSL board in its computer, allowing you to take it home, plug it in, and enjoy this higher bandwidth." Orckit got a huge endorsement for the technology last April when GTE announced it would begin offering network-based ADSL service in 16 U.S. states, creating the nation's largest deployment of ADSL to date. GTE tapped Fujitsu Network Communications of Texas to supply the ADSL equipment, using Orckit as its digital subscriber line partner. During the initial phases, GTE expects the technology to allow for World Wide Web access at speeds of up to 1.5 megabits per second. "This was really a blockbuster announcement for the company," Kern contends. "I think it will cause other telephone companies here and around the world to focus more on the Orckit solution for this issue of speed. Orckit has already had a lot of success outside the United States, especially in Europe and China. Investors haven't focused on that much. I think they will now."

Reason for Recommendation

Which brings us to the reason Kern likes Orckit's prospects for 1999 so much. "It's going to take awhile, but the aggressive rollout GTE plans is going to be the beginning of some great advances for Orckit," Kern predicts. "You might say this technology was in field trials before. It is now ready to be used by the masses." Orckit is not the only company offering ADSL. In fact, Kern admits this is likely to be a very competitive area, because the global potential for the technology is so huge. "Nevertheless, in terms of investment opportunities in smaller companies, which are my area of expertise, there are very few that compare to Orckit," he reasons. "The selection by GTE was a major endorsement. The company is also attractive from a valuation standpoint. Orckit has about 15 million shares outstanding, with a current market capitalization of around $300 million. The GTE contract alone should be worth $80 million or more over the next several years. The impact of this will likely start to kick in during 1999. The company is also redesigning its semiconductor silicon chip to be a lower cost product. That reduction effort will reduce expenses as volumes increase." Kern adds there are few analysts covering Orckit today. The company came public at $16 in September of 1996, ran up to $20, then down to $10. It's been in a trading range ever since. "No one has noticed how well the company has progressed fundamentally," Kern says. "And I don't think investors appreciate how quickly Orckit's broad range of technologies are catching favor with GTE and other leading international phone companies."

Contact Information: Eric Paneth, Chairman of the Board and CEO
Orckit Communications
38 Nahalat Yitzhak St.
Tel Aviv 67448, Israel
U.S. Contact: (212) 983-1702
www.orckit.com

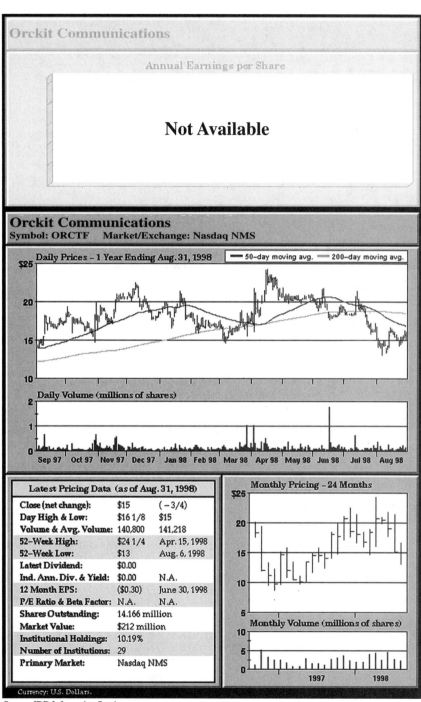

Source: IDD Information Services

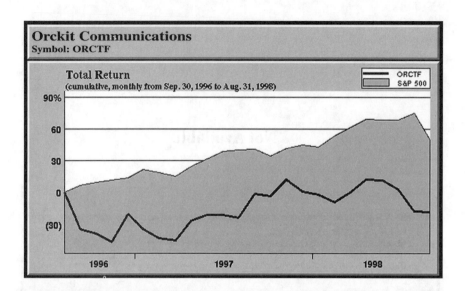

Orckit Communications
Symbol: ORCTF

Total Return
(cumulative, monthly from Sep. 30, 1996 to Aug. 31, 1998)

ORCTF
S&P 500

90%
60
30
0
(30)

1996   1997   1998

SELECTED INCOME STATEMENT AND BALANCE SHEET ITEMS

INCOME STATEMENT	1/01/00	1/01/00	1/01/00	1/01/00	1/01/00	1 Year
Sales/Revenues	N.A.	N.A.	N.A.	N.A.	N.A.	32.000
Cost of Goods Sold	N.A.	N.A.	N.A.	N.A.	N.A.	N.A.
Pre–tax Margin (%)	N.A.	N.A.	N.A.	N.A.	N.A.	N.A.
Operating Income	N.A.	N.A.	N.A.	N.A.	N.A.	N.A.
Net Income before Extras	N.A.	N.A.	N.A.	N.A.	N.A.	(4.700)
Reported Net Income	N.A.	N.A.	N.A.	N.A.	N.A.	(4.700)
Depreciation & Amortization	N.A.	N.A.	N.A.	N.A.	N.A.	N.A.
EPS from Net Income (Primary)	N.A.	N.A.	N.A.	N.A.	N.A.	(0.300)
EPS from Net Income (Fully Diluted)	N.A.	N.A.	N.A.	N.A.	N.A.	(0.300)
Dividend per Common Share	N.A.	N.A.	N.A.	N.A.	N.A.	N.A.
Dividend Yield (%)	N.A.	N.A.	N.A.	N.A.	N.A.	N.A.
Payout Ratio	N.A.	N.A.	N.A.	N.A.	N.A.	N.A.
BALANCE SHEET						
ASSETS						
Cash & Cash Equivalents	N.A.	N.A.	N.A.	N.A.	N.A.	
Inventories	N.A.	N.A.	N.A.	N.A.	N.A.	
Total Current Assets	N.A.	N.A.	N.A.	N.A.	N.A.	
Total Assets	N.A.	N.A.	N.A.	N.A.	N.A.	
LIABILITIES & EQUITY						
Short Term Debt	N.A.	N.A.	N.A.	N.A.	N.A.	
Long Term Debt	N.A.	N.A.	N.A.	N.A.	N.A.	
Total Liabilities	N.A.	N.A.	N.A.	N.A.	N.A.	
Shares Outstanding	N.A.	N.A.	N.A.	N.A.	N.A.	
Common Stockholder Equity	N.A.	N.A.	N.A.	N.A.	N.A.	
Total Stockholder Equity	N.A.	N.A.	N.A.	N.A.	N.A.	

Note: Figures in Millions of $ except: per share items, margins, yields, and ratios.

Source: IDD Information Services

PAGENET

Elizabeth Dater
Warburg Pincus Asset Management

Company Profile

PageNet is in a stage of evolution. As the cover of its 1997 report states, "We are expanding from a paging or wireless messaging company to something significantly broader in potential and scope: a wireless information provider." In other words, while basic word and numeric messaging will continue to be the cornerstone of this 17-year-old company's business, it is also expanding into other areas that can capitalize on its ability to transmit instant information, such as golf scores and stock quotes. Company executives also hope this change will return PageNet to profitability, after several years of losses.

PageNet provides paging services throughout the United States, Puerto Rico, the Virgin Islands, and Canada. "It's in all of the nation's 100 largest markets and has in excess of 10.5 million subscribers," notes Beth Dater of Warburg Pincus Asset Management. "This means the company has around 23 percent of the total available paging business." Dater admits the company is not in the best shape financially. "It got itself overextended with a lot of debt," she says. "It overexpanded and didn't pay attention to profitability or pricing." At one time, PageNet had a "win-at-all-costs" mentality, in which it tried to gain market share in the wireless industry by underpricing the competition. But that hurt the bottom line. Now new chairman and CEO John Frazee vows to grow the company by providing value to customers, not by lowering rates. "We will continue to raise prices as we improve our customer service and other aspects of our core offerings," Frazee states. "Specifically, we are working to create a world-class organization that will achieve long-term profitable growth through the creation and delivery of branded, customized wireless information services."

While Dater has followed PageNet off and on for many years, she is especially impressed by the major changes taking place in the company right now. Most notably, PageNet has a completely revamped management team spearheaded by Frazee, who previously worked for both Sprint and Centel. "He was on the board before and took over as CEO in August 1997," Dater observes. "He has focused on restructuring the company and restoring profitability, primarily by slowing down subscriber growth and lowering capital expenditures."

Looking ahead, Frazee sees PageNet's services falling into two basic categories. First is messaging, which encompasses traditional word and numeric paging, along with newer products like two-way and voice messaging. Second is information services, which include broadcast or customized feeds from such content providers as CNN and The Golf Channel. "While the messaging side of our business is strong and getting stronger, I'd like to focus on our opportunities in information services because they are truly staggering," Frazee adds. "This is the Information Age, and consumer demand for information is more voracious than it has ever been. PageNet is in a unique position to supply this kind of targeted information, both to its current paging customers and to individuals who may have never considered carrying a pager before. We intend to offer information services that span the worlds of business and finance, government and education, sports and entertainment, and information oriented to consumers and to individual corporations."

Another area the company has experimented with and failed, thus far, is two-way messaging. "This product just didn't work out," Dater says. "The good news is the infrastructure for it is now in place. Most of the spending is behind the company, so it can focus on new product development, new software and technology, and building marketing expertise to leverage that infrastructure by bringing out additional products and services which can add greatly to profitability down the road."

Reason for Recommendation

PageNet has always been a leader in the paging business. That hasn't translated into profitability, though, for many of the reasons I've already discussed. But if this restructuring program is successful, as Dater expects it to be, the company's fortunes could soon take a turn for the better. "Unit growth in this business has always been good, and it continues to grow at about 15 percent annually," she says. "You will continue to see a period of flat or negative subscriber growth as the company moves out of its less profitable business areas. However, the effect of that will be far more profitable subscriber growth on the overall base. This is clearly a growth business. In fact, alpha numeric and voice and data communications is probably the most attractive technology there is."

Dater further notes that PageNet has only one major competitor now, although its future success depends heavily on the company's ability to put its restructuring plan in place. "I'm not looking for any earnings for awhile. This is more of a cash flow story," she says. "Based on the increasing margins I see, I expect PageNet to be free cash flow positive by the end of 1999. If that happens, I think this stock will have a value in excess of $30 a share going into the new millennium."

Contact Information: John Frazee, Jr., Chairman, President, and CEO
Paging Network (PageNet)
4965 Preston Park Blvd., Suite 800
Plano, TX 75093
(972) 985-4100
www.pagenet.com

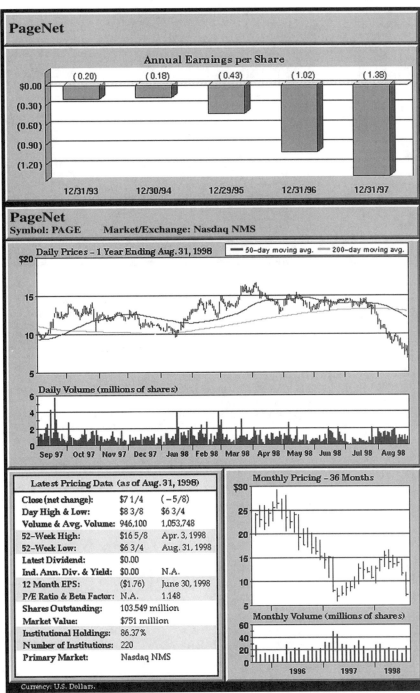

PageNet

Annual Earnings per Share

(0.20)   (0.18)   (0.43)   (1.02)   (1.38)

$0.00
(0.30)
(0.60)
(0.90)
(1.20)

12/31/93   12/30/94   12/29/95   12/31/96   12/31/97

PageNet
Symbol: PAGE   **Market/Exchange: Nasdaq NMS**

Daily Prices – 1 Year Ending Aug. 31, 1998   ▬ 50-day moving avg.   ▬ 200-day moving avg.

$20
15
10
5

Daily Volume (millions of shares)

6
4
2
0

Sep 97 Oct 97 Nov 97 Dec 97 Jan 98 Feb 98 Mar 98 Apr 98 May 98 Jun 98 Jul 98 Aug 98

Latest Pricing Data (as of Aug. 31, 1998)		
Close (net change):	$7 1/4	(−5/8)
Day High & Low:	$8 3/8	$6 3/4
Volume & Avg. Volume:	946,100	1,053,748
52–Week High:	$16 5/8	Apr. 3, 1998
52–Week Low:	$6 3/4	Aug. 31, 1998
Latest Dividend:	$0.00	
Ind. Ann. Div. & Yield:	$0.00	N.A.
12 Month EPS:	($1.76)	June 30, 1998
P/E Ratio & Beta Factor:	N.A.	1.148
Shares Outstanding:	103.549 million	
Market Value:	$751 million	
Institutional Holdings:	86.37%	
Number of Institutions:	220	
Primary Market:	Nasdaq NMS	

Monthly Pricing – 36 Months

$30
25
20
15
10
5

Monthly Volume (millions of shares)

60
40
20
0

1996   1997   1998

Currency: U.S. Dollars.

Source: IDD Information Services

PageNet
Symbol: PAGE

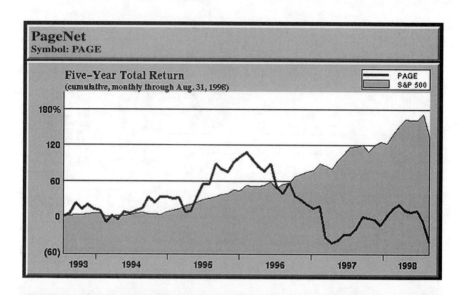

Five-Year Total Return
(cumulative, monthly through Aug. 31, 1998)

SELECTED INCOME STATEMENT AND BALANCE SHEET ITEMS						
INCOME STATEMENT	12/31/93	12/30/94	12/29/95	12/31/96	12/31/97	1 Year
Sales/Revenues	373.90	489.70	646.00	822.50	961.00	1,022.8
Cost of Goods Sold	62.500	78.100	89.100	111.40	113.00	216.20
Pre–tax Margin (%)	(5.30)	(3.70)	(6.80)	(9.90)	(14.70)	(17.65)
Operating Income	12.800	32.700	52.100	43.400	20.200	51.500
Net Income before Extras	(20.000)	(18.000)	(44.200)	(81.800)	(141.40)	(180.10)
Reported Net Income	(20.000)	(18.000)	(44.200)	(81.800)	(141.40)	(180.10)
Depreciation & Amortization	87.400	107.40	153.30	218.70	297.90	300.90
EPS from Net Income (Primary)	(0.200)	(0.180)	(0.430)	(1.020)	(1.380)	(1.760)
EPS from Net Income (Fully Diluted)	(0.200)	(0.180)	(0.430)	(1.020)	(1.380)	(1.760)
Dividend per Common Share	0.000	0.000	0.000	0.000	0.000	0.000
Dividend Yield (%)	N.A.	N.A.	N.A.	N.A.	N.A.	N.A.
Payout Ratio	N.A.	N.A.	N.A.	N.A.	N.A.	N.A.
BALANCE SHEET						
ASSETS						
Cash & Cash Equivalents	2.500	2.500	198.20	3.800	2.900	
Inventories	7.400	9.900	14.100	57.700	24.100	
Total Current Assets	29.000	39.400	262.40	130.40	105.20	
Total Assets	371.60	706.00	1,228.3	1,462.1	1,597.2	
LIABILITIES & EQUITY						
Short Term Debt	0.000	0.000	0.000	0.000	0.000	
Long Term Debt	342.50	504.00	1,150.0	1,459.2	1,779.5	
Total Liabilities	394.90	745.90	1,309.1	1,621.8	1,935.1	
Shares Outstanding	101.086	101.406	102.246	102.621	102.660	
Common Stockholder Equity	(23.400)	(39.900)	(80.800)	(159.70)	(337.90)	
Total Stockholder Equity	(23.400)	(39.900)	(80.800)	(159.70)	(337.90)	

Note: Figures in Millions of $ except: per share items, margins, yields, and ratios.

Source: IDD Information Services

PIERCE LEAHY

Michael DiCarlo
DFS Advisors

Company Profile

If you've ever wondered what happened to all of those applications you've filled out and signed over the years for everything from insurance to credit cards, chance are they're sitting in one of Pierce Leahy's storage facilities somewhere around the country. "This company has a very simple business," says Michael DiCarlo, partner and portfolio manager at DFS Advisors. "It is the largest archive management company in North America. In other words, it's in the storage business."

Any sort of record that needs to be saved for some amount of time is fair game for finding a home at one of Pierce Leahy's facilities. "Big insurance companies need to archive their policies, while mutual fund firms file away their applications. Keep in mind that an original signature is still required for any legal or financial document, and companies have to keep these things on file," DiCarlo explains. "But Pierce Leahy's buildings aren't just full of paper. They also house video tapes, X-rays, microfilm, optical discs, computer tapes—you name it." It is the paper storage business that typically accounts for 95 percent of all revenues, though as we become a more computer-based society, that model may start to change.

The concept is really simple. Pierce Leahy buys or leases vacant buildings around the country and rents out space to its clients. "When company executives go out and search for a site, they're not looking at square footage," DiCarlo points out. "They're keeping an eye on cubic footage. In other words, they want the ceilings to be high so they can keep stacking to the sky." Company president and CEO J. Peter Pierce agrees that's the most important consideration. "Cubic footage of client records is the key driver of our business," he says. "That's what produces the strong recurring revenue stream that drives our business and our industry."

And recurring revenue is almost a given in this business, according to DiCarlo. "If you look at the sustainability and visibility of earnings and cash flow, this is an unbelievable business model, because the company keeps getting paid over and over again," he says. "Once your documents are at one of Pierce Leahy's storage facilities, it's very unlikely that you'll decide to switch to another provider. And most of these documents need to be kept for a long time."

Pierce Leahy is by far the largest archive records management company in the country, with almost 60 million cubic feet of records currently under its control. It operates 150 records centers across the United States, including vital business locations like San Francisco, Los Angeles, New York, Philadelphia, Chicago, Houston, Boston, and Washington, D.C. The company also has another 13 locations in 5 of Canada's 6 largest markets. Pierce Leahy's client list includes more than 22,000 businesses in such industries as financial services, manufacturing, transportation, healthcare, and law. Although the company has been around for some time as a family-owned operation, it has only been publicly traded since July 1997, when it debuted as an IPO priced at $18 a share.

Why would companies want to pay Pierce Leahy to store these documents, instead of just keeping them stacked in an on-site facility? "That's easy," DiCarlo offers. "Using Pierce Leahy's remote site is much less expensive than the high-cost space at a corporation's headquarters. Plus, it's what they do for a business. There's no reason for a company to take on the hassle of keeping track of this stuff when it can hire Pierce Leahy to do it for them."

Reason for Recommendation

DiCarlo insists the company doesn't need to do anything fancy to have another banner year in 1999. "If it simply keeps running the business the same way it has in the past, this will be a very solid 25 percent grower this year and into the future," he says. "There's very low debt on the balance sheet and that translates into tons of free cash flow. And the company doesn't need to add a lot of new capacity to double current revenues." Revenues jumped 41 percent from 1996 to 1997, while earnings rose 43.6 percent during that same period.

Pierce Leahy agrees that the nationwide trend toward outsourcing should continue to benefit it going forward. It also estimates that it has only tapped 25 percent of the potential market for its services. The company plans to continue its growth strategy this year by targeting new customers, increasing its business with existing clients, and continuing an aggressive program of acquisitions. In 1997 alone, the company bought out 13 competitors. "These acquisitions have been complemented by a significant investment in building a larger sales force as another way to grow our business," CEO Pierce says.

Because of these acquisitions, earnings haven't been that impressive of late. DiCarlo estimates the company will earn 75 cents a share in 1999. But he maintains the stock is cheap based on the cash it throws off. "This company also has terrific management," he adds. "I think they do a great job running a simple business. I'm convinced the stock could trade for $40 by the end of 1999."

Contact Information: J. Peter Pierce, President and CEO
Pierce Leahy Corp.
631 Park Avenue
King of Prussia, PA 19406
(610) 992-8200
www.pierceleahy.com

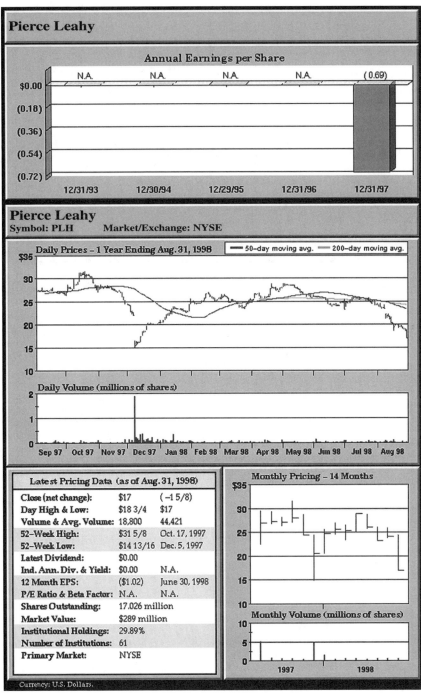

Pierce Leahy

Annual Earnings per Share

	N.A.	N.A.	N.A.	N.A.	(0.69)
$0.00					
(0.18)					
(0.36)					
(0.54)					
(0.72)					
	12/31/93	12/30/94	12/29/95	12/31/96	12/31/97

Pierce Leahy
Symbol: PLH   Market/Exchange: NYSE

Daily Prices – 1 Year Ending Aug. 31, 1998   ▬ 50-day moving avg.   ▬ 200-day moving avg.

Daily Volume (millions of shares)

Sep 97 Oct 97 Nov 97 Dec 97 Jan 98 Feb 98 Mar 98 Apr 98 May 98 Jun 98 Jul 98 Aug 98

Latest Pricing Data (as of Aug. 31, 1998)

Close (net change):	$17	(–1 5/8)
Day High & Low:	$18 3/4	$17
Volume & Avg. Volume:	18,800	44,421
52-Week High:	$31 5/8	Oct. 17, 1997
52-Week Low:	$14 13/16	Dec. 5, 1997
Latest Dividend:	$0.00	
Ind. Ann. Div. & Yield:	$0.00	N.A.
12 Month EPS:	($1.02)	June 30, 1998
P/E Ratio & Beta Factor:	N.A.	N.A.
Shares Outstanding:	17.026 million	
Market Value:	$289 million	
Institutional Holdings:	29.89%	
Number of Institutions:	61	
Primary Market:	NYSE	

Monthly Pricing – 14 Months

Monthly Volume (millions of shares)

1997   1998

Currency: U.S. Dollars.

Source: IDD Information Services

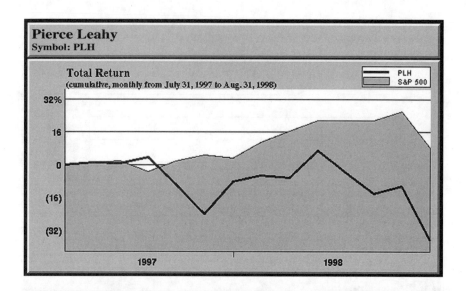

Pierce Leahy
Symbol: PLH

Total Return
(cumulative, monthly from July 31, 1997 to Aug. 31, 1998)

SELECTED INCOME STATEMENT AND BALANCE SHEET ITEMS

INCOME STATEMENT	12/31/93	12/30/94	12/29/95	12/31/96	12/31/97	1 Year
Sales/Revenues	N.A.	N.A.	N.A.	N.A.	183.50	217.40
Cost of Goods Sold	N.A.	N.A.	N.A.	N.A.	100.80	121.70
Pre-tax Margin (%)	N.A.	N.A.	N.A.	N.A.	(1.00)	(2.72)
Operating Income	N.A.	N.A.	N.A.	N.A.	30.000	29.200
Net Income before Extras	N.A.	N.A.	N.A.	N.A.	(9.200)	(14.700)
Reported Net Income	N.A.	N.A.	N.A.	N.A.	(9.200)	(14.700)
Depreciation & Amortization	N.A.	N.A.	N.A.	N.A.	22.600	29.200
EPS from Net Income (Primary)	N.A.	N.A.	N.A.	N.A.	(0.690)	(1.020)
EPS from Net Income (Fully Diluted)	N.A.	N.A.	N.A.	N.A.	(0.690)	(1.020)
Dividend per Common Share	N.A.	N.A.	N.A.	N.A.	N.A.	N.A.
Dividend Yield (%)	N.A.	N.A.	N.A.	N.A.	N.A.	N.A.
Payout Ratio	N.A.	N.A.	N.A.	N.A.	N.A.	N.A.
BALANCE SHEET						
ASSETS						
Cash & Cash Equivalents	N.A.	N.A.	N.A.	N.A.	1.800	
Inventories	N.A.	N.A.	N.A.	N.A.	0.800	
Total Current Assets	N.A.	N.A.	N.A.	N.A.	32.200	
Total Assets	N.A.	N.A.	N.A.	N.A.	394.70	
LIABILITIES & EQUITY						
Short Term Debt	N.A.	N.A.	N.A.	N.A.	1.100	
Long Term Debt	N.A.	N.A.	N.A.	N.A.	277.80	
Total Liabilities	N.A.	N.A.	N.A.	N.A.	335.30	
Shares Outstanding	N.A.	N.A.	N.A.	N.A.	16.478	
Common Stockholder Equity	N.A.	N.A.	N.A.	N.A.	59.300	
Total Stockholder Equity	N.A.	N.A.	N.A.	N.A.	59.300	

Note: Figures in Millions of $ except: per share items, margins, yields, and ratios.

Source: IDD Information Services

POWERWAVE TECHNOLOGIES

Margarita Perez
Fortaleza Asset Management

Company Profile

With the increasing number of technologies using wireless communications, it seems logical there will be a continued demand for products made by Powerwave Technologies. The company designs, manufactures, and markets what are known as ultra-linear radio frequency power amplifiers. These devices are key components in most wireless communications networks. They increase the signal strength of transmissions, while reducing the level of interference. This enables wireless service providers to offer clearer call connections and fewer interrupted calls. Powerwave makes both single and multicarrier amplifiers, although its primary emphasis is on the latter.

"The company's potential markets include cellular phones, mobile radios, paging, and even the phones you find on airplanes," notes Margarita Perez, president of Fortaleza Asset Management. "These amplifiers are typically the most expensive component in a cellular base station. This little company has been profitable every year since its founding in 1985."

In its early days, Powerwave developed a line of amplifiers for use with VHF/UHF and AM/FM transceivers. It then branched out into products for the land mobile radio industry. The company's first radio frequency amplifiers for digital cellular networks came on line in 1996 in South Korea. That same year, the company went public. "Initially, this stock was really hot," Perez says. "The risk was always that about 70 percent of its business came from Korea, which had the fastest growing market for the digital wireless network using the CDMA protocol. Powerwave was at the forefront of this technology. The company had an engineer who had connections in Korea and managed to make Powerwave the dominant player in that market. Wireless communications in Korea began growing by leaps and bounds, and so did the company." This was fueled primarily by orders from three major customers: Hyundai, LGIC, and Samsung.

Then came the Asian financial meltdown in October 1997. Investors, realizing that Powerwave got most of its business from the troubled area, drove the company's stock down from $49 to $9. Some even figured Powerwave might go out of business, because its largest customer base effectively disappeared overnight, at least in the short run. But that wasn't to be. "I'm really impressed with the way management has handled this," Perez says. "You would think that having so much business in Korea would cause them to go cash-flow negative and start losing money. Instead the company is making money. It still has around $57 million in cash with no debt."

In a recent quarter, Powerwave reported that business in Korea dropped 65 percent. But Perez points out it has been able to make up for some of these losses by attracting new customers in the U.S. and Latin America. "For planning purposes, the company has warned investors to assume this loss in business to Korea will drop by another 50 percent for the foreseeable future," she says. "Some analysts have actually taken the Korean business out of the numbers completely. Even at that, they are still projecting earnings of about $1 a share next year."

Reason for Recommendation

Perez maintains that Powerwave's opportunities in the U.S. and Latin America are enormous. If that's the case, why hasn't the company pursued these areas more aggressively before? "I keep asking myself that question," Perez admits. "Perhaps it had too much opportunity in Korea and couldn't handle anything else. All along, the company has been successfully trying to garner market share in the U.S. and has been pretty successful. The company recently signed deals with LM Ericsson, Motorola, Lucent Technologies, Nokia, and Northern Telecom." But Powerwave competes head-on in the U.S. with several other firms, including Avantek (a division of Hewlett-Packard), AML Communications, Microwave Power Devices, and Spectrian. In South Korea, it virtually had the entire field to itself. "It's important to point out that about 75 percent of the market here is still captive," Perez insists. "A lot of potential customers build this technology in-house right now. But, from what I can gather, Powerwave makes the best multichannel amplifier available. As we move more into becoming a digital society, and demand increases for these amplifiers, I expect more of these providers to outsource their business to Powerwave. I'm also impressed with how the company has dealt with the huge loss of its Asian business in such a short period of time, while managing to keep making money."

In addition, Perez is quick to add that Powerwave's business in South Korea hasn't disappeared. It has simply been postponed until the area can get back on solid financial footing again. "I feel very confident these customers will come back," she predicts. "Even if they don't, remember that the Korean business is no longer being counted in the numbers. Therefore, there will be a huge financial impact once Korea addresses its problems and gets itself back together. I think it's only a matter of time." Perez looks for shares of Powerwave to trade for at least $30 by the end of the 1999. If the fundamentals improve faster than expected, she adds it could go even higher.

Contact Information: Bruce Edwards, President and CEO
Powerwave Technologies, Inc.
2026 McGaw Avenue
Irvine, CA 92614
(888) 797-9283
www.powerwave.com

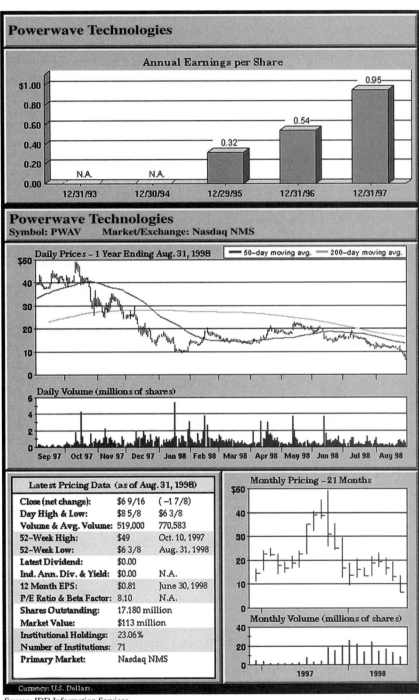

Powerwave Technologies

Annual Earnings per Share

	12/31/93	12/30/94	12/29/95	12/31/96	12/31/97
	N.A.	N.A.	0.32	0.54	0.95

Powerwave Technologies
Symbol: PWAV   Market/Exchange: Nasdaq NMS

Daily Prices - 1 Year Ending Aug. 31, 1998   ▬ 50-day moving avg. ▬ 200-day moving avg.

Daily Volume (millions of shares)

Sep 97 Oct 97 Nov 97 Dec 97 Jan 98 Feb 98 Mar 98 Apr 98 May 98 Jun 98 Jul 98 Aug 98

Latest Pricing Data (as of Aug. 31, 1998)

Close (net change):	$6 9/16	(−1 7/8)
Day High & Low:	$8 5/8	$6 3/8
Volume & Avg. Volume:	519,000	770,583
52–Week High:	$49	Oct. 10, 1997
52–Week Low:	$6 3/8	Aug. 31, 1998
Latest Dividend:	$0.00	
Ind. Ann. Div. & Yield:	$0.00	N.A.
12 Month EPS:	$0.81	June 30, 1998
P/E Ratio & Beta Factor:	8.10	N.A.
Shares Outstanding:	17.180 million	
Market Value:	$113 million	
Institutional Holdings:	23.06%	
Number of Institutions:	71	
Primary Market:	Nasdaq NMS	

Monthly Pricing – 21 Months

Monthly Volume (millions of shares)

1997   1998

Currency: U.S. Dollars.

Source: IDD Information Services

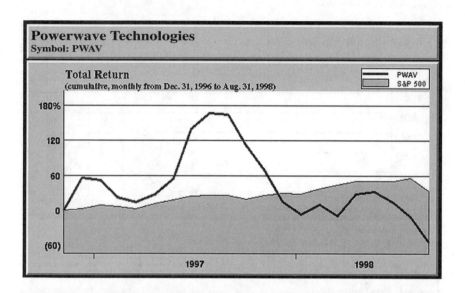

Powerwave Technologies
Symbol: PWAV

Total Return
(cumulative, monthly from Dec. 31, 1996 to Aug. 31, 1998)

Legend: PWAV, S&P 500

Y-axis: 180%, 120, 60, 0, (60)
X-axis: 1997, 1998

SELECTED INCOME STATEMENT AND BALANCE SHEET ITEMS

INCOME STATEMENT	12/31/93	12/30/94	12/29/95	12/31/96	12/31/97	1 Year
Sales/Revenues	N.A.	N.A.	36.000	60.300	119.70	115.80
Cost of Goods Sold	N.A.	N.A.	22.300	34.100	69.300	66.800
Pre–tax Margin (%)	N.A.	N.A.	21.10	21.40	21.60	18.45
Operating Income	N.A.	N.A.	7.500	12.400	23.300	19.200
Net Income before Extras	N.A.	N.A.	4.500	7.600	16.200	14.100
Reported Net Income	N.A.	N.A.	4.500	7.600	16.200	14.100
Depreciation & Amortization	N.A.	N.A.	0.400	0.700	1.700	2.200
EPS from Net Income (Primary)	N.A.	N.A.	0.320	0.540	0.950	0.810
EPS from Net Income (Fully Diluted)	N.A.	N.A.	0.310	0.520	0.920	0.790
Dividend per Common Share	N.A.	N.A.	N.A.	N.A.	N.A.	N.A.
Dividend Yield (%)	N.A.	N.A.	N.A.	N.A.	N.A.	N.A.
Payout Ratio	N.A.	N.A.	N.A.	N.A.	N.A.	N.A.
BALANCE SHEET						
ASSETS						
Cash & Cash Equivalents	N.A.	N.A.	5.900	32.400	67.400	
Inventories	N.A.	N.A.	4.700	4.700	8.800	
Total Current Assets	N.A.	N.A.	15.300	42.600	92.500	
Total Assets	N.A.	N.A.	16.500	46.900	101.70	
LIABILITIES & EQUITY						
Short Term Debt	N.A.	N.A.	0.100	0.300	0.500	
Long Term Debt	N.A.	N.A.	0.100	0.500	0.700	
Total Liabilities	N.A.	N.A.	5.900	10.100	26.200	
Shares Outstanding	N.A.	N.A.	14.762	15.863	17.264	
Common Stockholder Equity	N.A.	N.A.	(3.900)	36.800	75.500	
Total Stockholder Equity	N.A.	N.A.	10.600	36.800	75.500	

Note: Figures in Millions of $ except: per share items, margins, yields, and ratios.

Source: IDD Information Services

SPECIALTY EQUIPMENT COMPANIES

John Rogers
Ariel Capital Management

Company Profile

This is the first year since I began writing *Wall Street's Picks* in 1996 that McDonald's has failed to make the list of recommended stocks for the year ahead. But John Rogers of Ariel Capital Management has found a small company that truly is a play on the global growth of the giant restaurant chain. "Specialty Equipment is involved in two exciting areas right now," Rogers says. "It is most well-known for manufacturing the Taylor soft-serve ice cream machines used in every McDonald's around the world. But these machines are also found in frozen yogurt stores, and restaurants that sell frozen margaritas. Taylor is the preeminent brand when it comes to these soft-serve machines."

Now the company has taken that relationship with McDonald's one step further. For one thing, McDonald's now offers a new dessert called McFlurry, a soft-serve concoction similar to Dairy Queen's Blizzard. "Taylor's ice cream machine will be used to make the McFlurry, and Taylor will also be providing the disposable cups and spoons," Rogers says. "In addition, Taylor manufactures what it calls a 'clam shape' grill. These two-sided grills cook hamburgers on both sides at the same time. McDonald's has been using them for several years and it has really increased the cooking speed."

Specialty Equipment manufactures a diversified line of food service equipment used by restaurant chains, convenience stores, soft drink bottlers, and brewers. In addition to Taylor, the company has four other global brands—Gamko, Wells, World Dryer, and Beverage-Air. Gamko produces commercial refrigeration, beer dispensing, and merchandising equipment. Wells manufacturers food warming and cooking equipment, coffee/tea brewers and dispensers, and expresso/cappuccino equipment. World Dryer makes those warm air hand dryers found in public restrooms. And Beverage-Air develops commercial refrigeration equipment. "If you go into a convenience store, you'll often see these little coolers full of ice cream, soft drinks or juices," Rogers notes. "These are made by Beverage-Air. They're like large refrigerators with a clear window. It's a relatively mundane business, but it's doing really well. Specialty has been able to dominate this niche, with only one major competitor."

Although the company has been around for close to 80 years, it remains relatively underfollowed on Wall Street. One reason may be that it has been privately held for much of that time. Specialty Equipment first went public about a decade ago, before returning to private ownership. After running into some severe financial difficulties, and being forced into Chapter 11 in 1991, management reorganized, got its act together and decided to go public again in 1993. "I think that once analysts start to pick up on what a wonderful story Specialty Equipment has, the coverage will increase," Rogers predicts. That, in turn, should bring more buyers into the stock and, therefore, a higher share price.

Reason for Recommendation

"This is my favorite stock by far," Rogers says. "For one thing, it's cheap, based on my earnings estimate for 1999 of $1.63 per share. What's more, I love the products this company makes." As I previously mentioned, he also views this as a great way to piggyback on McDonald's incredible growth overseas. "McDonald's is going to open something like 1,500 restaurants in the Far East alone over the next few years," he observes. "You know that Taylor will be right there alongside them. That's the real story here. Specialty Equipment is also paying down its debt quite rapidly. This will give it a higher debt rating and enhance earnings. The company is also retiring some of its high-interest debt, which should increase earnings by 13 or 14 percent a share in 1999."

Another possibility, in Roger's mind, is that Specialty Equipment could be an attractive acquisition target. "The restaurant industry is ripe for consolidation, and it wouldn't be a shock to see a company like this gobbled up," he says. "With a $450 million market capitalization, it would be a bite-sized acquisition for a larger corporation."

Although the company sells its products to many other businesses besides McDonald's, the restaurant chain accounts for roughly 25 percent of Specialty Equipment's overall revenues. Therefore, if McDonald's decided to end its relationship for one reason or another, that would be a big blow to the bottom line. "I've spent a lot of time talking with McDonald's management about that issue," Rogers shares. "McDonald's is typically very loyal to its suppliers. Taylor has such an entrenched brand there, I think it would be difficult for anyone else to come in and compete. It would be easier for them to buy the company than try to duplicate this complicated technology. I'm more concerned about the fact that Beverage-Air's business is booming in the U.S., and you wonder how long that will continue. But the other big positive is that in many foreign countries where McDonald's is opening up, especially in the emerging markets, local residents are being exposed to this new treat of soft-serve ice cream for the first time. As other restaurateurs find out about it, they want to own Taylor machines too. There is huge potential for them to continue to grow overseas."

Contact Information: Jeff Rhodenbaugh, President & CEO
Specialty Equipment Companies
1245 Corporate Blvd., Suite 401
Aurora, IL 60504
(630) 585-5111
www.specialty-equipment.com

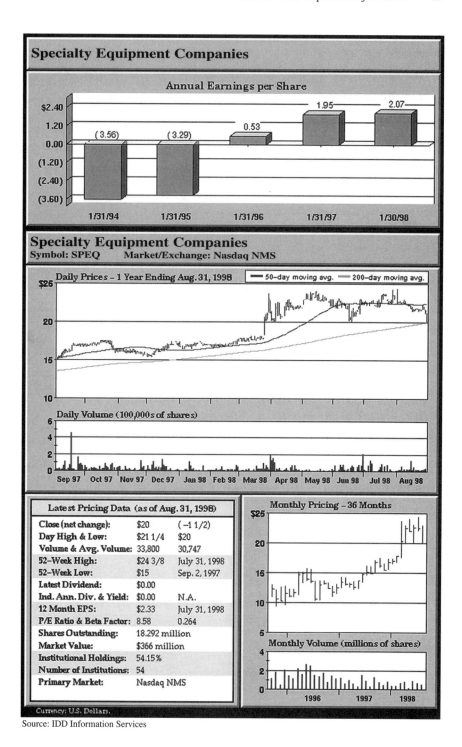

Specialty Equipment Companies

Annual Earnings per Share

	1/31/94	1/31/95	1/31/96	1/31/97	1/30/98
EPS	(3.56)	(3.29)	0.53	1.95	2.07

Specialty Equipment Companies
Symbol: SPEQ   Market/Exchange: Nasdaq NMS

Daily Prices – 1 Year Ending Aug. 31, 1998
— 50-day moving avg.   — 200-day moving avg.

Daily Volume (100,000s of shares)

Sep 97 Oct 97 Nov 97 Dec 97 Jan 98 Feb 98 Mar 98 Apr 98 May 98 Jun 98 Jul 98 Aug 98

Latest Pricing Data (as of Aug. 31, 1998)

Close (net change):	$20	(–1 1/2)
Day High & Low:	$21 1/4	$20
Volume & Avg. Volume:	33,800	30,747
52–Week High:	$24 3/8	July 31, 1998
52–Week Low:	$15	Sep. 2, 1997
Latest Dividend:	$0.00	
Ind. Ann. Div. & Yield:	$0.00	N.A.
12 Month EPS:	$2.33	July 31, 1998
P/E Ratio & Beta Factor:	8.58	0.264
Shares Outstanding:	18.292 million	
Market Value:	$366 million	
Institutional Holdings:	54.15%	
Number of Institutions:	54	
Primary Market:	Nasdaq NMS	

Monthly Pricing – 36 Months

Monthly Volume (millions of shares)

1996   1997   1998

Currency: U.S. Dollars.

Source: IDD Information Services

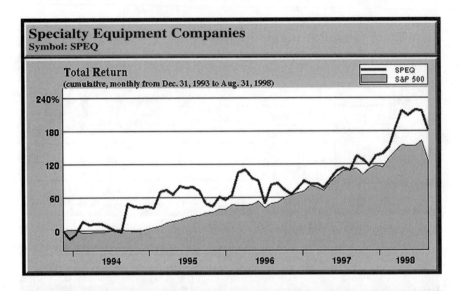

Specialty Equipment Companies
Symbol: SPEQ

Total Return
(cumulative, monthly from Dec. 31, 1993 to Aug. 31, 1998)

SPEQ
S&P 500

SELECTED INCOME STATEMENT AND BALANCE SHEET ITEMS						
INCOME STATEMENT	**1/31/94**	**1/31/95**	**1/31/96**	**1/31/97**	**1/30/98**	**1 Year**
Sales/Revenues	320.90	371.70	392.50	401.20	433.10	478.50
Cost of Goods Sold	217.40	248.50	264.40	273.90	294.40	N.A.
Pre-tax Margin (%)	(16.00)	(11.10)	4.70	10.50	10.90	N.A.
Operating Income	(34.000)	(18.600)	39.300	60.300	63.000	N.A.
Net Income before Extras	(58.400)	(54.000)	8.900	34.100	37.500	42.400
Reported Net Income	(58.400)	(54.000)	8.900	34.100	37.500	42.400
Depreciation & Amortization	79.800	79.000	26.700	6.900	5.800	N.A.
EPS from Net Income (Primary)	(3.560)	(3.290)	0.530	1.950	2.070	2.330
EPS from Net Income (Fully Diluted)	(3.560)	(3.290)	0.450	1.700	1.860	2.100
Dividend per Common Share	N.A.	N.A.	N.A.	N.A.	N.A.	N.A.
Dividend Yield (%)	N.A.	N.A.	N.A.	N.A.	N.A.	N.A.
Payout Ratio	N.A.	N.A.	N.A.	N.A.	N.A.	N.A.
BALANCE SHEET						
ASSETS						
Cash & Cash Equivalents	2.800	3.200	28.400	7.800	39.900	
Inventories	49.400	53.800	51.500	55.300	54.000	
Total Current Assets	99.400	105.00	135.70	132.40	175.50	
Total Assets	231.60	168.60	180.20	176.90	241.50	
LIABILITIES & EQUITY						
Short Term Debt	2.400	0.300	0.200	0.100	18.400	
Long Term Debt	217.00	198.90	193.00	155.40	159.60	
Total Liabilities	298.90	289.40	287.80	248.10	280.30	
Shares Outstanding	16.426	16.446	17.315	17.986	18.083	
Common Stockholder Equity	(67.200)	(120.80)	(107.60)	(71.200)	(38.800)	
Total Stockholder Equity	(67.200)	(120.80)	(107.60)	(71.200)	(38.800)	

Note: Figures in Millions of $ except: per share items, margins, yields, and ratios.

Source: IDD Information Services

STAAR SURGICAL

Marcus Robins
The Red Chip Review

Company Profile

If you have any kind of vision problem, you will most likely be interested in this next company, even if you ultimately decide not to invest in it. That's because STAAR Surgical has a number of new technologies for vision correction, whether you suffer from cataracts, glaucoma, nearsightedness, or farsightedness. The company's original development, which now boasts an almost 30 percent market penetration, is an intraocular lens implanted through a small incision in cataract patients. "The surgeon goes in with some kind of device that fractures and pulverizes the old, hardened human lens," explains *Red Chip Review* editor Marcus Robins. "Then they inject one of STAAR's lenses through this small opening, which may be only 1 millimeter in size. The patient walks in with cloudy vision and leaves 15 to 30 minutes later with fully restored site. In the old days, the doctor would just pop your God-given lens out and give you Coke bottle-like glasses that you had to wear for the rest of your life." STAAR's intraocular lens business has gone from $20 million to $60 million in just a few short years.

But the reason Robins singles STAAR out as his favorite idea for the year ahead is because of several exciting new products in the pipeline. "First, the company has something called a glaucoma wick," he says. Glaucoma is a disease that affects some 67 million people worldwide and is a leading cause of blindness. It causes fluid buildup, which puts pressure on the optic nerve and can lead to blindness. "The wick is a rice grain-sized matrix of material you implant into the eye. It allows excess fluid to seep out, preventing pressure from building up, and therefore, preserving sight. This should be a nice $5 or $10 million product in the next several years," Robins adds.

An even bigger potential blockbuster, however, is STAAR's new implantable contact lens. "I have pretty thick glasses and am getting quite vain in my old age," Robins admits. "I haven't had much in the way of changes to my correction in the last decade, and I'm not any good at messing around with contacts. One solution for nearsighted people like me is to have either radial keratonomy (RK) or photorefractive keratectomy (PRK) surgery. But there have been horror stories about complications with those procedures. I would never take a chance like that. Now STAAR has come out with a procedure employing virtually the same technique as that used on millions of cataract patients. The doctor goes in, makes a small sutureless incision and actually lays an implantable contact lens on top of the lens on your eye, giving you corrected vision. Quite literally you go in, have the procedure and within 30 minutes you leave with 20-20 sight. It sounds too good to be true, but it really does seem to work." This technology is currently in phase-two clinical trials. Robins expects STAAR to receive final approval for it from the Food and Drug Administration by the end of 1999.

A major advantage to this technique over the other two more commonly used surgical procedures is that it is less painful and reversible. "If your eyesight changes, or there is some kind of problem, you can remove the lens," Robins notes. "It also sounds like this procedure will be advanced enough to take into consideration other variables like astigmatism, which is generally hard to correct with regular contacts." Those who have had this procedure done in current trials report an excellent rate of success. Unlike the other two surgical options available today, the STAAR lens can be implanted in those with farsighted vision as well.

Reason for Recommendation

It is this implantable lens technology that has Robins most enthusiastic about STAAR. "This is going to be a very sensible alternative, and it is a far less expensive procedure to perform," Robins insists. "Instead of shelling out $200,000 for a piece of equipment to perform the laser surgery, doctors only need a syringe to implant the lens."

STAAR is not without competition in its two existing businesses. There are others with similar cataract correction technologies. STAAR's glaucoma wick procedure, which was developed in Russia, is also being replicated by fellow contenders with less success. However, Robins points out that there is really no other company close to perfecting the implantable contact lens technology. "I think you will start to see doctors perform this surgery aggressively in 1999," he says. "What you have is a market that currently only offers some very cumbersome and unpleasant alternatives for vision correction. I have every reason to believe this will be a multibillion dollar business. Even if the company's revenues went from $100 to $500 million, the stock would go crazy." Robins' target price for shares of STAAR is $24 by the end of the year, although this is a company he says he'll hold on to as long as the new technology is as successful as he expects it to be.

Contact Information: John Wolf, Chairman and CEO
STAAR Surgical
1811 Walker Avenue
Monrovia, CA 91016
(818) 303-7902
www.staar.com

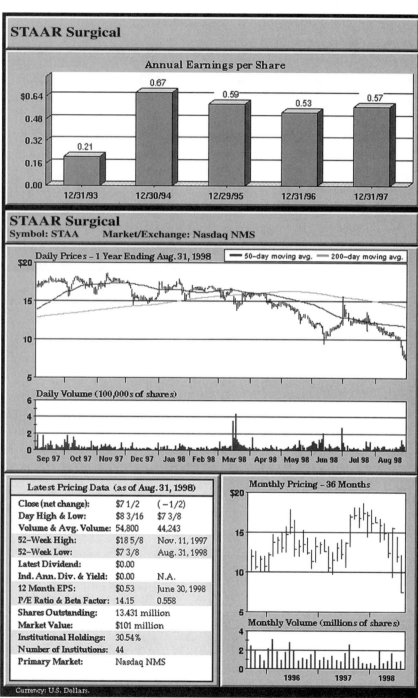

STAAR Surgical

Annual Earnings per Share

12/31/93	12/30/94	12/29/95	12/31/96	12/31/97
0.21	0.67	0.59	0.53	0.57

STAAR Surgical
Symbol: STAA   Market/Exchange: Nasdaq NMS

Daily Prices – 1 Year Ending Aug. 31, 1998   ▬ 50–day moving avg.   ▬ 200–day moving avg.

Daily Volume (100,000s of shares)

Sep 97 Oct 97 Nov 97 Dec 97 Jan 98 Feb 98 Mar 98 Apr 98 May 98 Jun 98 Jul 98 Aug 98

Latest Pricing Data (as of Aug. 31, 1998)		
Close (net change):	$7 1/2	(–1/2)
Day High & Low:	$8 3/16	$7 3/8
Volume & Avg. Volume:	54,800	44,243
52–Week High:	$18 5/8	Nov. 11, 1997
52–Week Low:	$7 3/8	Aug. 31, 1998
Latest Dividend:	$0.00	
Ind. Ann. Div. & Yield:	$0.00	N.A.
12 Month EPS:	$0.53	June 30, 1998
P/E Ratio & Beta Factor:	14.15	0.558
Shares Outstanding:	13.431 million	
Market Value:	$101 million	
Institutional Holdings:	30.54%	
Number of Institutions:	44	
Primary Market:	Nasdaq NMS	

Monthly Pricing – 36 Months

Monthly Volume (millions of shares)

1996   1997   1998

Currency: U.S. Dollars.

Source: IDD Information Services

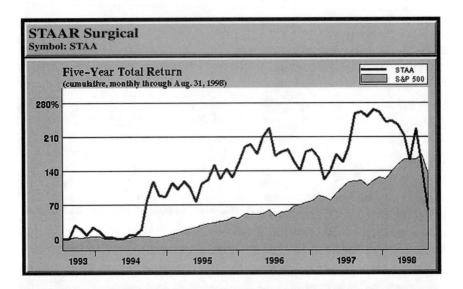

STAAR Surgical
Symbol: STAA

Five-Year Total Return
(cumulative, monthly through Aug. 31, 1998)

STAA
S&P 500

SELECTED INCOME STATEMENT AND BALANCE SHEET ITEMS

INCOME STATEMENT	12/31/93	12/30/94	12/29/95	12/31/96	12/31/97	1 Year
Sales/Revenues	20.100	27.400	34.700	42.200	42.500	48.400
Cost of Goods Sold	3.100	4.800	6.900	7.900	6.800	N.A.
Pre–tax Margin (%)	12.90	22.30	21.30	24.20	27.50	N.A.
Operating Income	1.900	5.500	7.100	10.100	9.300	N.A.
Net Income before Extras	2.500	8.300	7.500	6.900	7.400	6.900
Reported Net Income	2.500	8.300	7.500	6.900	7.400	6.900
Depreciation & Amortization	0.900	1.300	1.500	2.300	3.500	N.A.
EPS from Net Income (Primary)	0.210	0.670	0.590	0.530	0.570	0.530
EPS from Net Income (Fully Diluted)	0.200	0.630	0.550	0.500	0.530	0.490
Dividend per Common Share	N.A.	N.A.	N.A.	N.A.	N.A.	N.A.
Dividend Yield (%)	N.A.	N.A.	N.A.	N.A.	N.A.	N.A.
Payout Ratio	N.A.	N.A.	N.A.	N.A.	N.A.	N.A.
BALANCE SHEET						
ASSETS						
Cash & Cash Equivalents	1.400	3.200	3.800	6.500	6.300	
Inventories	8.000	8.600	9.600	12.400	14.700	
Total Current Assets	13.600	20.100	25.100	28.700	35.400	
Total Assets	18.800	28.900	38.800	51.100	62.400	
LIABILITIES & EQUITY						
Short Term Debt	1.600	1.800	4.000	8.200	1.600	
Long Term Debt	0.000	0.600	1.200	0.800	5.800	
Total Liabilities	6.700	6.800	10.000	14.500	17.700	
Shares Outstanding	12.466	12.704	12.784	13.071	13.246	
Common Stockholder Equity	12.000	22.000	28.700	36.600	44.800	
Total Stockholder Equity	12.000	22.000	28.700	36.600	44.800	

Note: Figures in Millions of $ except: per share items, margins, yields, and ratios.

Source: IDD Information Services

STATE STREET

L. Roy Papp
L. Roy Papp & Associates

Company Profile

Although State Street was originally founded as a traditional bank in Boston back in 1792, today it's a much different company. Instead of making most of its money from loans or other traditional banking activities, State Street provides a wide range of products and services for large portfolios of investment assets. "It offers safekeeping and custodian services for a lot of mutual fund companies, corporations, pension funds, nonprofit organizations, and high net-worth individuals," observes L. Roy Papp of L. Roy Papp & Associates. "State Street has more than $4 trillion in assets under its care."

The company began providing mutual fund services in 1924, shortly after these regulated investment pools were created. The company takes charge of the assets held by some 40 percent of the nation's mutual fund portfolios. Unlike the competition, State Street also offers accounting, daily pricing, and other administrative services to its various fund clients.

While State Street already has a big chunk of the available fund business in the U.S., Papp believes the potential to capture more market share overseas is tremendous. "This is truly a global company," he says. "The growth rate of its non-U.S. custodianship business for the past five years has been about 35 percent annually, which means it doubles every two years." The current asset breakdown is 70 percent domestic and 30 percent overseas. State Street has offices in such countries as Austria, Australia, Canada, France, Germany, Japan, the People's Republic of China, and the United Kingdom. It also operates its own investment management division, with $390 billion in assets, including the SSgA family of mutual funds.

With more than 14,000 employees, the company prides itself on having the latest technology. "State Street spends tons of money updating its computer systems," Papp says. "It has largely licked the Year 2000 problem, which is something many banks haven't even started to tackle. That's another reason I don't invest directly abroad. Many foreign corporations don't even begin to understand the problems they're going to face in 2000. They've got a ticking time bomb on their hands." (The Year 2000 problem refers to the inability of some computer software programs to adjust their dates to 2000 next year, instead rolling back to 1900.) Papp's also impressed with State Street's progressive management team. He singles out their aggressiveness to steal business away from competitors, even if it means underpricing them and settling for lower profits in the short run.

During the most recent fiscal year, 64 percent of State Street's operating profit came from services for institutional investors, 21 percent from commercial lending and 15 percent from investment management. Revenues increased 24 percent from the previous year, while earnings per share rose 30 percent. Still, the stock has lagged the S&P financial index since 1992. Papp surmises that's largely because Wall Street has failed to realize how unique State Street is compared to other financial companies.

"Our commitment is clear," says State Street chairman and chief executive officer Marshall N. Carter. "We continue to build our business for future growth by developing a broader product array for our customers." Among these products is Global Link, an integrated, electronic market information, trade execution and reporting platform, which includes unique currency markets research and other foreign exchange management tools. "In investment management, we are focused on continuing the expansion of both our global reach and diversified product lines," Carter adds. "Anticipating industry changes and investing to develop the resources to handle them before they occur is an important element of State Street's industry leadership. The market for services to institutional investors is large and growing. Analysts estimate the $6 trillion global mutual fund industry will grow 15 percent annually over the next five years, the $8 trillion pension fund industry 10 percent, the $9 trillion insurance industry 9 percent, and the $15 trillion asset management industry 10 percent."

Reason for Recommendation

Those impressive numbers, and that incredible potential, are major reasons Papp believes State Street will be a stellar performer in 1999. "Another thing is Wall Street is finally pricing this company more like a growth stock, instead of like a bank," he notes. "You're now looking at a stock that trades at roughly a market multiple. However, it's important to remember that if the banks get hit for some reason, this company will go down as well."

There are two things that could derail State Street's impressive growth streak. One is the incredible amount of competition in the industry, which comes from such sources as other investment management firms, insurance companies, law firms, and even leasing companies. Secondly, if the mutual fund industry goes into the tank, State Street will follow it down. "I'm betting that the international markets will grow, not slow down," Papp predicts. "This is clearly the best play on the global mutual fund industry and financial globalization that I know of."

Contact Information: Marshall N. Carter, Chairman and CEO
State Street Corporation
225 Franklin Street
Boston, MA 02171
(617) 786-3000
www.statestreet.com

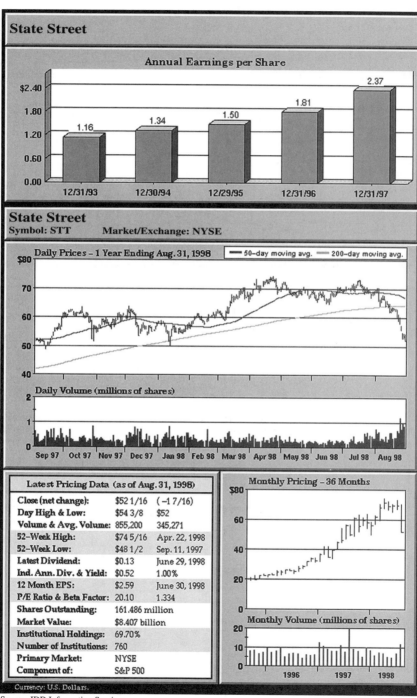

State Street

Annual Earnings per Share

Date	EPS
12/31/93	1.16
12/30/94	1.34
12/29/95	1.50
12/31/96	1.81
12/31/97	2.37

State Street
Symbol: STT   Market/Exchange: NYSE

Daily Prices – 1 Year Ending Aug. 31, 1998

— 50–day moving avg. — 200–day moving avg.

Daily Volume (millions of shares)

Sep 97 Oct 97 Nov 97 Dec 97 Jan 98 Feb 98 Mar 98 Apr 98 May 98 Jun 98 Jul 98 Aug 98

Latest Pricing Data (as of Aug. 31, 1998)		
Close (net change):	$52 1/16	(–1 7/16)
Day High & Low:	$54 3/8	$52
Volume & Avg. Volume:	855,200	345,271
52–Week High:	$74 5/16	Apr. 22, 1998
52–Week Low:	$48 1/2	Sep. 11, 1997
Latest Dividend:	$0.13	June 29, 1998
Ind. Ann. Div. & Yield:	$0.52	1.00%
12 Month EPS:	$2.59	June 30, 1998
P/E Ratio & Beta Factor:	20.10	1.334
Shares Outstanding:	161.486 million	
Market Value:	$8.407 billion	
Institutional Holdings:	69.70%	
Number of Institutions:	760	
Primary Market:	NYSE	
Component of:	S&P 500	

Currency: U.S. Dollars.

Monthly Pricing – 36 Months

Monthly Volume (millions of shares)

1996   1997   1998

Source: IDD Information Services

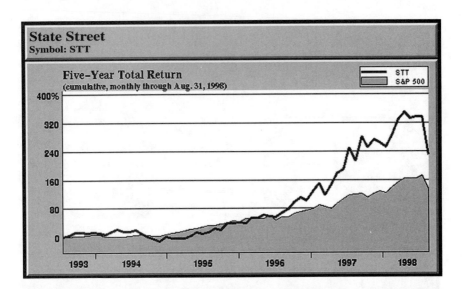

State Street
Symbol: STT

Five-Year Total Return
(cumulative, monthly through Aug. 31, 1998)

STT
S&P 500

400%

320

240

160

80

0

1993   1994   1995   1996   1997   1998

SELECTED INCOME STATEMENT AND BALANCE SHEET ITEMS

INCOME STATEMENT	12/31/93	12/30/94	12/29/95	12/31/96	12/31/97	1 Year
Sales/Revenues	1,532.3	1,885.7	2,455.7	2,745.0	3,428.0	3,830.0
Cost of Goods Sold	N.A.	N.A.	N.A.	N.A.	N.A.	N.A.
Pre-tax Margin (%)	18.10	17.00	14.90	16.30	16.50	16.25
Operating Income	658.70	857.70	1,273.7	1,339.0	1,678.0	1,905.0
Net Income before Extras	179.80	207.40	247.10	293.00	380.00	416.00
Reported Net Income	179.80	207.40	247.10	293.00	380.00	416.00
Depreciation & Amortization	N.A.	N.A.	N.A.	N.A.	N.A.	N.A.
EPS from Net Income (Primary)	1.160	1.340	1.500	1.810	2.370	2.590
EPS from Net Income (Fully Diluted)	1.140	1.320	1.470	1.780	2.320	2.530
Dividend per Common Share	0.260	0.300	0.340	0.380	0.440	0.480
Dividend Yield (%)	1.39	2.10	1.51	1.18	0.76	0.69
Payout Ratio	0.22	0.22	0.23	0.21	0.19	0.19
BALANCE SHEET						
ASSETS						
Cash & Cash Equivalents	N.A.	N.A.	N.A.	N.A.	N.A.	
Inventories	N.A.	N.A.	N.A.	N.A.	N.A.	
Total Current Assets	N.A.	N.A.	N.A.	N.A.	N.A.	
Total Assets	18,720	21,730	25,785	31,524	37,975	
LIABILITIES & EQUITY						
Short Term Debt	469.30	649.10	5,564.2	649.00	609.00	
Long Term Debt	278.90	127.50	301.80	562.00	818.00	
Total Liabilities	17,615	20,498	24,198	29,749	35,980	
Shares Outstanding	151.748	153.758	164.776	162.308	160.836	
Common Stockholder Equity	1,105.0	1,231.3	1,587.5	1,775.0	1,995.0	
Total Stockholder Equity	1,105.0	1,231.3	1,587.5	1,775.0	1,995.0	

Note: Figures in Millions of $ except: per share items, margins, yields, and ratios.

Source: IDD Information Services

STERLING SOFTWARE

Susan Byrne
Westwood Management

Company Profile

Even though Sterling Software has been around since 1981, in many respects it's a brand new company. "It has undergone more than one evolution," notes Susan Byrne of Westwood Management. "This Texas-based company originally made defense electronics software. Then it got a patent for what became a whole industry called electronic data interchange, or EDI. EDI software allows computers to talk to each other. For instance, the ATM at your bank is hooked in to the same information as the ATM at other banks around the world thanks to EDI technology." Creating EDI software was Sterling's primary business, and the one it was best known for. But when the EDI unit was spun off as a stand-alone company called Sterling Commerce in 1996, Sterling Software was left with little more than a stash of cash.

"It no longer had a fast-growing business," Byrne observes. "What happened is $165 million of that cash was used to purchase the applications division of Texas Instruments in mid-1997. That money, which was earning less than 6 percent in the bank, was turned into an operating division that's growing by 25 to 30 percent a year." Now, instead of being a slow-growing defense electronics business, Sterling is a cutting-edge software applications company. "Applications software is what programmers need to make other programs," Byrne explains. "Sterling makes all kinds of software for various users."

The acquisition allowed Sterling to combine the Composer™ technology, developed by Texas Instruments Software, with its own KEY™ software suite to create the first and most complete development environment for planning, modeling, designing, and building applications and components. "This has been the most exhilarating time in the history of Sterling Software," says company president and CEO Sterling Williams. "The acquisition of Texas Instruments Software makes Sterling Software the unquestioned leader in applications development."

Following the acquisition, the company was reshaped into three major business groups—applications management, systems management, and federal systems. The applications management unit creates software that allows for business modeling through code generation. Its COOL product family offers solutions for mission critical application development, data design and analysis, plus business and workflow modeling. "In the applications management market, there is a growing trend toward assembling software from prefabricated, reusable components," says CEO Williams. "We are the leader in this market, which industry analysts predict will be the primary method for developing software applications in the future." The systems management division specializes in automation, network management, service desk and storage management products. It provides software under the SAMS family name. These solutions manage, monitor, and automate data storage in both distributed and centralized environments. "The trend is toward systems management tools that enable IT (information technology) organizations to manage, automate, and respond to systems problems based on their impact on the mission-critical services that keep business operations up and running," Williams adds. "We are at the forefront of this opportunity with a strong background in systems and network automation and with new systems management automation products." The federal systems division provides information technology services to the federal government under numerous multiyear contracts. The division's engineers designed and now operate the NASA Science Internet. They also developed the prototypes of new knowledge-based air traffic management software, which was successfully field-tested by the FAA at airports in Denver and Dallas/Fort Worth.

Sterling kept more than 900 of the 1,300 Texas Instruments employees effected by the merger. Byrne says they are all reenergized and, therefore, more productive. "Before they were just a small part of a huge company," she says. "Now these bright people have been able to take an equity stake and create products for essentially a brand new company." Recent contracts, with such technology heavyweights as IBM and Hewlett-Packard, affirm in Byrne's mind that Sterling is on the right track. The company now has 3,100 employees in 85 offices around the globe. Its customers include some 400 of the 500 largest industrial and service corporations in the U.S.

Reason for Recommendation

Despite the money it took to buy the Texas Instruments division, Sterling has no debt and an impressive amount of cash still left on the balance sheet. "What's amazing is the company made money in its first quarter following the acquisition," Byrne observes. "I think Sterling will grow by 30 percent a year. A reasonable price-earnings multiple would be 25. Based on my estimated earnings for fiscal 1999 of at least $1.50 per share, that would put the stock at close to $38 by the end of the year." In addition, Byrne says few people on Wall Street even cover the stock right now, and those who do don't realize all of the positive changes taking place in the company.

Contact Information: Sterling Williams, President and CEO
Sterling Software
300 Crescent Court, Suite 1200
Dallas, TX 75201
(214) 981-1000
www.sterling.com

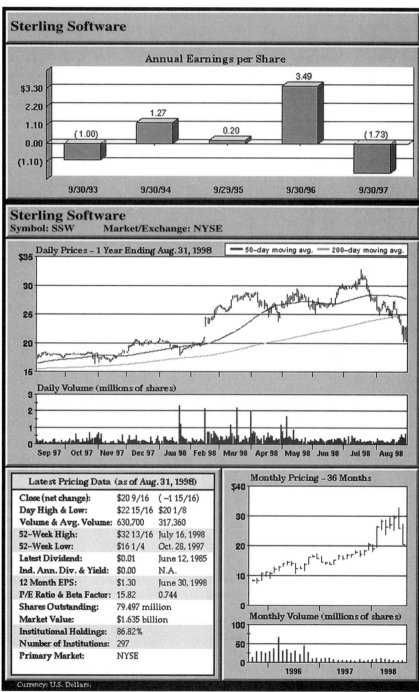

Sterling Software

Annual Earnings per Share

			3.49	
(1.00)	1.27	0.20		(1.73)
9/30/93	9/30/94	9/29/95	9/30/96	9/30/97

$3.30
2.20
1.10
0.00
(1.10)

Sterling Software
Symbol: SSW   Market/Exchange: NYSE

Daily Prices – 1 Year Ending Aug. 31, 1998   — 50-day moving avg.   — 200-day moving avg.

Daily Volume (millions of shares)

Sep 97   Oct 97   Nov 97   Dec 97   Jan 98   Feb 98   Mar 98   Apr 98   May 98   Jun 98   Jul 98   Aug 98

Latest Pricing Data (as of Aug. 31, 1998)

Close (net change):	$20 9/16	(–1 15/16)
Day High & Low:	$22 15/16	$20 1/8
Volume & Avg. Volume:	630,700	317,360
52–Week High:	$32 13/16	July 16, 1998
52–Week Low:	$16 1/4	Oct. 28, 1997
Latest Dividend:	$0.01	June 12, 1985
Ind. Ann. Div. & Yield:	$0.00	N.A.
12 Month EPS:	$1.30	June 30, 1998
P/E Ratio & Beta Factor:	15.82	0.744
Shares Outstanding:	79.497 million	
Market Value:	$1.635 billion	
Institutional Holdings:	86.82%	
Number of Institutions:	297	
Primary Market:	NYSE	

Monthly Pricing – 36 Months

Monthly Volume (millions of shares)

1996   1997   1998

Currency: U.S. Dollars.

Source: IDD Information Services

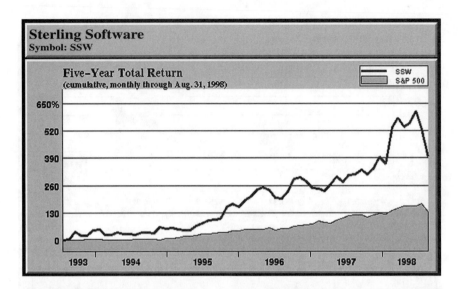

Sterling Software
Symbol: SSW

Five-Year Total Return
(cumulative, monthly through Aug. 31, 1998)

SSW
S&P 500

SELECTED INCOME STATEMENT AND BALANCE SHEET ITEMS						
INCOME STATEMENT	**9/30/93**	**9/30/94**	**9/29/95**	**9/30/96**	**9/30/97**	**1 Year**
Sales/Revenues	411.80	473.40	588.20	439.20	489.00	640.60
Cost of Goods Sold	139.70	137.40	145.10	150.60	165.30	207.80
Pre–tax Margin (%)	(11.80)	19.50	9.00	19.30	(27.90)	23.65
Operating Income	(45.500)	95.600	70.400	60.900	(175.10)	13.700
Net Income before Extras	(33.400)	58.300	9.300	60.600	(133.00)	100.10
Reported Net Income	(33.400)	58.300	9.300	237.90	(133.00)	100.10
Depreciation & Amortization	31.500	34.300	45.400	31.600	34.500	39.900
EPS from Net Income (Primary)	(1.000)	1.270	0.200	3.490	(1.730)	1.300
EPS from Net Income (Fully Diluted)	(1.000)	1.160	0.200	3.330	(1.730)	1.250
Dividend per Common Share	0.000	0.000	0.000	0.000	0.000	0.000
Dividend Yield (%)	N.A.	N.A.	N.A.	N.A.	N.A.	N.A.
Payout Ratio	N.A.	N.A.	N.A.	N.A.	N.A.	N.A.
BALANCE SHEET						
ASSETS						
Cash & Cash Equivalents	29.800	101.90	179.30	524.20	435.70	
Inventories	0.000	0.000	0.000	0.000	0.000	
Total Current Assets	214.80	297.20	444.10	914.60	826.90	
Total Assets	397.70	488.80	714.20	1,097.6	1,065.7	
LIABILITIES & EQUITY						
Short Term Debt	4.000	7.300	5.900	0.400	0.000	
Long Term Debt	116.80	115.90	116.70	0.000	0.000	
Total Liabilities	300.40	312.90	365.90	218.10	317.40	
Shares Outstanding	35.546	41.170	52.946	76.870	77.104	
Common Stockholder Equity	97.200	175.80	348.30	879.50	748.30	
Total Stockholder Equity	97.200	175.80	348.30	879.50	748.30	

Note: Figures in Millions of $ except: per share items, margins, yields, and ratios.

Source: IDD Information Services

VITESSE

Kevin Landis
Firsthand Funds

Company Profile

Talk about a technology company with blue chip clients! The list of Vitesse Semiconductor Corporation's satisfied customers includes Cisco Systems, IBM, Newbridge Networks, Seagate, Lucent Technologies, Alcatel Alsthom (one of *Wall Street's Picks for 1999*), Ericsson, and many more. Most of the major players in the industry do business with Vitesse. And according to technology fund manager Kevin Landis, if you believe in the future of these companies, you can't help but be interested in Vitesse.

"Vitesse is a chip company, although it doesn't make the standard silicon chips that many people are familiar with," Landis says. "It manufactures gallium arsenide chips." What's the difference? Chips made with gallium arsenide do two things really well: they can run at high speeds, and they operate using very low power. "As such, these chips are great for high-performance applications," Landis explains. "When you're sending information through a transponder line, for example, you need an extremely high performance chip, and you're willing to pay up for it. That's what Vitesse provides."

You don't have to know much about technology to realize that we're living in a society that places a heavy emphasis on speed. The faster, the better. Therefore, the need for the chips Vitesse makes is increasing. "You won't find gallium arsenide chips in your personal computer, because they are far too fast and expensive for that," Landis notes. "But if you send somebody e-mail, it will probably pass through a Vitesse chip. And if you make a long distance call, chances are it too will travel through a circuit using a Vitesse chip. Imagine you and I are talking over a fiber optic cable. Fiber travels at the speed of light. What happens when you go from the world of light to the world of electronics? You have information coming so fast that you need a really fast chip to slow it down and interpret it. Vitesse makes that chip." In fact, telecommunications products account for 52 percent of the company's total revenues.

Gallium arsenide will never replace silicon, but Landis maintains the two technologies are complementary. "The thing about gallium arsenide is that it's really hard to manufacture," he points out. "There's a big barrier to entry. Even though it's a profitable business, and many people would like to be in it, there's a lot of learning and history that goes into successfully manufacturing these chips because they're really hard to work with. Vitesse is probably the best out there. There are a few other companies on the horizon trying to emulate Vitesse, although they are far behind. Besides, by the time someone was able to knock off today's products, Vitesse would no doubt be on to something even faster and more leading edge."

Reason for Recommendation

With computer prices falling, and more people gaining access to the Internet, Landis predicts that the need for Vitesse chips will explode in the coming years. "This company has demonstrated it has a key technology that's needed by the Lucents, Nortels, and Cisco Systems of the world," he says. "It has the exact right end customers. These are the companies you would select if you had your pick of any in the world. Every argument you can make that Cisco's going to sell more networking equipment and move more e-mail is an argument for Vitesse. Vitesse sells that key silver bullet Cisco needs right at the critical spot in the network." (Incidentally, Landis selected Cisco as his favorite idea for the year in *Wall Street's Picks for 1998*. Because of price appreciation, he now rates that stock a hold.)

"Top-line growth at Vitesse has been expanding anywhere from 11 to 14 percent a quarter," Landis observes. "The company's biggest obstacle is that it has been constrained by capacity. That problem appears to have been solved now that it's getting production out of a new facility in Colorado Springs. This should take the company into a new realm. It will no longer be capacity constrained. Management has said the company's natural growth rate should be in the mid-teens. That's sequential, quarter to quarter. So if we just take a conservative mid-teens number, the company could grow anywhere from 50 to 75 percent in 1999 over 1998."

Revenues topped $100 million for the first time ever in 1997, reaching $104.8 million. Operating income increased 113 percent, earnings per share jumped 105 percent and the company's backlog vaulted from $36 million to $62 million. Unfortunately, the stock is no bargain at current levels. Landis admits, compared to the overall market, it's expensive. But he contends this is a solid company with such a competitive position that it should be able to trade at a premium to its growth rate. "I think the market could easily value this company at 50 times earnings, which is pretty amazing," he predicts. "This company has the strongest competitive position of any I have seen. I believe Vitesse can earn $2 a share in 1999. If I place a more conservative valuation of 40 times earnings on the stock, it could trade for $80 by the end of the year."

Contact Information: Louis R. Tomasetta, President and CEO
Vitesse Semiconductor Corporation
741 Calle Plano
Camarillo, CA 93012
(805) 388-3700
www.vitesse.com

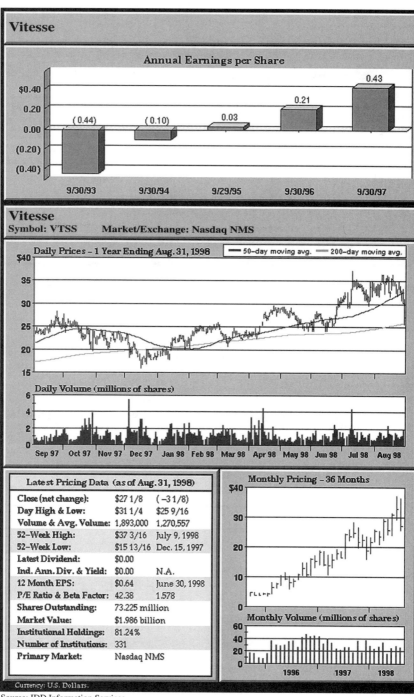

Vitesse

Annual Earnings per Share

Date	EPS
9/30/93	(0.44)
9/30/94	(0.10)
9/29/95	0.03
9/30/96	0.21
9/30/97	0.43

Vitesse
Symbol: VTSS   Market/Exchange: Nasdaq NMS

Daily Prices - 1 Year Ending Aug. 31, 1998   — 50-day moving avg.   — 200-day moving avg.

Daily Volume (millions of shares)

Sep 97 Oct 97 Nov 97 Dec 97 Jan 98 Feb 98 Mar 98 Apr 98 May 98 Jun 98 Jul 98 Aug 98

Latest Pricing Data (as of Aug. 31, 1998)

Close (net change):	$27 1/8	(−3 1/8)
Day High & Low:	$31 1/4	$25 9/16
Volume & Avg. Volume:	1,893,000	1,270,557
52–Week High:	$37 3/16	July 9, 1998
52–Week Low:	$15 13/16	Dec. 15, 1997
Latest Dividend:	$0.00	
Ind. Ann. Div. & Yield:	$0.00	N.A.
12 Month EPS:	$0.64	June 30, 1998
P/E Ratio & Beta Factor:	42.38	1.578
Shares Outstanding:	73.225 million	
Market Value:	$1.986 billion	
Institutional Holdings:	81.24%	
Number of Institutions:	331	
Primary Market:	Nasdaq NMS	

Monthly Pricing – 36 Months

Monthly Volume (millions of shares)

1996   1997   1998

Currency: U.S. Dollars.

Source: IDD Information Services

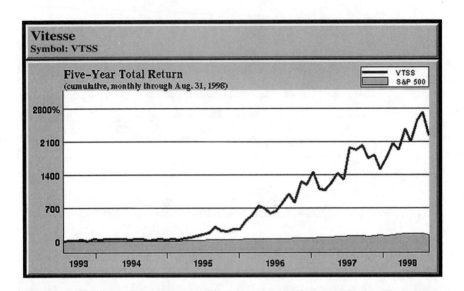

Vitesse
Symbol: VTSS

Five-Year Total Return
(cumulative, monthly through Aug. 31, 1998)

— VTSS
☐ S&P 500

SELECTED INCOME STATEMENT AND BALANCE SHEET ITEMS

INCOME STATEMENT	9/30/93	9/30/94	9/29/95	9/30/96	9/30/97	1 Year
Sales/Revenues	26.400	35.600	42.900	66.000	104.90	151.90
Cost of Goods Sold	21.500	16.600	17.200	26.800	38.600	49.600
Pre-tax Margin (%)	(72.30)	(11.50)	3.70	21.20	34.90	37.42
Operating Income	(18.100)	(3.200)	2.800	13.400	28.800	47.400
Net Income before Extras	(19.100)	(4.100)	1.500	12.600	32.900	46.600
Reported Net Income	(19.100)	(4.100)	1.500	12.600	32.900	46.600
Depreciation & Amortization	5.600	5.600	5.300	5.000	6.900	11.800
EPS from Net Income (Primary)	(0.440)	(0.100)	0.030	0.210	0.430	0.640
EPS from Net Income (Fully Diluted)	(0.440)	(0.100)	0.030	0.210	0.430	0.610
Dividend per Common Share	0.000	0.000	0.000	0.000	0.000	0.000
Dividend Yield (%)	N.A.	N.A.	N.A.	N.A.	N.A.	N.A.
Payout Ratio	N.A.	N.A.	N.A.	N.A.	N.A.	N.A.

BALANCE SHEET						
ASSETS						
Cash & Cash Equivalents	9.300	4.200	6.300	52.400	97.400	
Inventories	8.800	9.000	9.900	10.000	11.800	
Total Current Assets	27.000	26.600	29.500	81.900	204.60	
Total Assets	44.000	39.500	42.100	100.40	292.30	
LIABILITIES & EQUITY						
Short Term Debt	4.900	6.600	6.200	0.900	0.300	
Long Term Debt	8.800	5.900	5.500	0.400	0.100	
Total Liabilities	19.300	18.000	17.200	12.000	27.200	
Shares Outstanding	43.862	44.918	46.506	58.192	71.828	
Common Stockholder Equity	24.600	21.500	25.000	88.400	265.10	
Total Stockholder Equity	24.600	21.500	25.000	88.400	265.10	

Note: Figures in Millions of $ except: per share items, margins, yields, and ratios.

Source: IDD Information Services

WESTERN DIGITAL

Al Frank
The Prudent Speculator

Company Profile

This isn't the best of times to be in the disk drive business, but you wouldn't know it from reading Western Digital's latest annual report. Chairman and CEO Chuck Haggerty has nothing but wonderful things to say about his company, and predicts that revenues will more than double to $10 billion within the next five years. However, the numbers from Western Digital's second fiscal quarter report tell a different story. Including special charges resulting from an oversupply of goods and competitive pricing pressures, the company reported a net loss of $145.2 million, or $1.66 per share. This compares to a profit of 68 cents a share in the same period the previous year.

What's going on? According to Al Frank, editor of *The Prudent Speculator*, a chain of negative events can be blamed for dragging down disk drive makers like Western Digital right along with many others in the high-tech industry. "First there was an oversupply of chips on the market, which caused Wall Street to punish the chip makers," he explains. "Then came the Asian contagion, which hurt just about everyone. After that, big manufacturers like Compaq and Gateway postponed purchases because they had an oversupply of certain kinds of computers. Since Western Digital relies on these computer companies for the bulk of its business, when they hurt, it hurts too."

Traders are also pretty fickle when it comes to buying stocks like this. They either love or hate the disk drive makers. And when they're out of favor, look out below. "One year disk drive makers are called a commodity business, and everyone sells them off," Frank says. "Then when the supply tightens up the following year, they become a growth industry again and the shares go through the roof." Right now, at least as this book goes to press, Western Digital is viewed as an unloved commodity business and a company only a value investor like Frank could love.

Founded in 1970, Western Digital designs and manufacturers computer hard drives. Some of its drives are installed directly into the box by the manufacturer, and others can be purchased at resellers after the initial sale. Its product line includes the 3.5-inch hard drives used in desktop PCs and enterprise systems, and the 3.0-inch hard drives found in mobile PCs. The company's "Caviar" family of drives offers storage capacities ranging from 1.2 to 5.1 gigabytes. In 1997, Western Digital began shipping its latest drives, dubbed WD Enterprise, with storage capacities of 2.1, 4.3 and 9 gigabytes.

"This has been such a good company," Frank says. "I first bought it in 1993 for around $10 a share and everybody told me the company was a generation behind everyone else and probably wouldn't survive. They were wrong. Western Digital has thrived in a very competitive environment. Unfortunately it has come across another glitch in the PC world." Frank believes the current problems are only short term in nature and insists the outlook for the computer industry remains strong. "The consensus is that PC sales will grow between 15 and 20 percent annually over the next five years," he notes. "The real negative folks put the number at 13 percent, while the bulls are forecasting more than 20 percent. Either way, this is definitely the kind of business you want to be invested in. There are millions of people in the United States and around the world who still don't have a computer. Western Digital is a good company that will get its fair share of this market. Even if you go with the low-end numbers, PC sales are going to at least double in the next five years." If that's true, maybe Western Digital does have a shot at reaching CEO Haggerty's goal of hitting $10 billion in revenues.

Reason for Recommendation

The company is taking drastic steps to improve its financial picture. It has entirely eliminated all long-term debt and secured $250 million in new financing. It has also terminated some of its less profitable businesses. "The recent actions we have taken will allow Western Digital to focus fully on executing its plan to maintain leadership in the desktop hard drive business and to continue growing its successful high-end enterprise business," Haggerty says. "As the hard drive industry works its way through the current cycle, we want to be in a position to take full advantage of the growth opportunities in the data storage industry in the next several years." Frank has no doubt they will. "I look at the big picture and conclude that this company is going to come out of the current slump just fine," Frank maintains. "My goal price for this stock over the next three to five years is around $47 a share. It could go higher if earnings pick up."

The biggest risk, in Frank's mind, is that some computer maker invents a server that allows you to hook directly to the Internet using your TV set without requiring any storage space. In such a case, you wouldn't need a disk drive to hold any information. "But if something like this is coming, it won't be for several years down the line," Frank predicts. "In the meantime, the demand for storage will continue to increase because people want more and more memory. Even if they don't use it, they still want their computers to have it."

Contact Information: Charles A. Haggerty, Chairman, President and CEO
Western Digital Corporation
8105 Irvine Center Drive
Irvine, CA 92618
(714) 932-5000
www.wdc.com

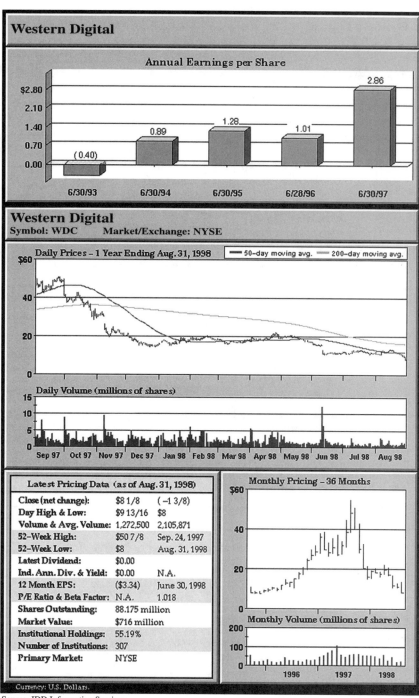

Western Digital

Annual Earnings per Share

	6/30/93	6/30/94	6/30/95	6/28/96	6/30/97
	(0.40)	0.89	1.28	1.01	2.86

Western Digital
Symbol: WDC   Market/Exchange: NYSE

Daily Prices – 1 Year Ending Aug. 31, 1998 ▬ 50-day moving avg. ▬ 200-day moving avg.

Daily Volume (millions of shares)

Sep 97 Oct 97 Nov 97 Dec 97 Jan 98 Feb 98 Mar 98 Apr 98 May 98 Jun 98 Jul 98 Aug 98

Latest Pricing Data (as of Aug. 31, 1998)

Close (net change):	$8 1/8	(–1 3/8)
Day High & Low:	$9 13/16	$8
Volume & Avg. Volume:	1,272,500	2,105,871
52-Week High:	$50 7/8	Sep. 24, 1997
52-Week Low:	$8	Aug. 31, 1998
Latest Dividend:	$0.00	
Ind. Ann. Div. & Yield:	$0.00	N.A.
12 Month EPS:	($3.34)	June 30, 1998
P/E Ratio & Beta Factor:	N.A.	1.018
Shares Outstanding:	88.175 million	
Market Value:	$716 million	
Institutional Holdings:	55.19%	
Number of Institutions:	307	
Primary Market:	NYSE	

Currency: U.S. Dollars.

Monthly Pricing – 36 Months

Monthly Volume (millions of shares)

1996 1997 1998

Source: IDD Information Services

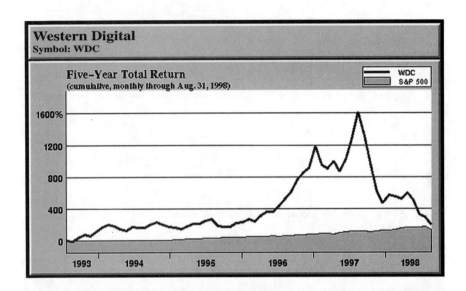

Western Digital
Symbol: WDC

Five-Year Total Return
(cumulative, monthly through Aug. 31, 1998)

Legend: WDC, S&P 500

SELECTED INCOME STATEMENT AND BALANCE SHEET ITEMS

INCOME STATEMENT	6/30/93	6/30/94	6/30/95	6/28/96	6/30/97	1 Year
Sales/Revenues	1,225.2	1,539.7	2,130.9	2,865.2	4,177.9	3,541.6
Cost of Goods Sold	989.40	1,175.6	1,693.2	2,431.6	3,464.1	N.A.
Pre-tax Margin (%)	(2.00)	5.60	6.80	3.80	7.50	N.A.
Operating Income	(10.000)	91.800	133.00	77.400	301.60	N.A.
Net Income before Extras	(25.100)	73.100	123.30	96.900	267.60	(290.20)
Reported Net Income	(25.100)	73.100	123.30	96.900	267.60	(290.20)
Depreciation & Amortization	53.700	46.200	43.600	51.600	63.500	N.A.
EPS from Net Income (Primary)	(0.400)	0.890	1.280	1.010	2.860	(3.340)
EPS from Net Income (Fully Diluted)	(0.400)	0.850	1.240	1.010	2.850	(3.340)
Dividend per Common Share	0.000	0.000	0.000	0.000	0.000	0.000
Dividend Yield (%)	N.A.	N.A.	N.A.	N.A.	N.A.	N.A.
Payout Ratio	N.A.	N.A.	N.A.	N.A.	N.A.	N.A.

BALANCE SHEET						
ASSETS						
Cash & Cash Equivalents	33.800	243.50	217.50	182.60	208.30	
Inventories	112.50	79.600	98.900	142.60	224.50	
Total Current Assets	318.50	537.50	730.10	794.30	1,017.9	
Total Assets	531.20	640.50	858.80	984.10	1,307.1	
LIABILITIES & EQUITY						
Short Term Debt	23.500	0.000	0.000	0.000	0.000	
Long Term Debt	182.60	58.600	0.000	0.000	0.000	
Total Liabilities	400.30	352.20	385.40	530.30	687.10	
Shares Outstanding	70.676	89.790	99.354	87.142	85.896	
Common Stockholder Equity	131.00	288.20	473.40	453.90	620.00	
Total Stockholder Equity	131.00	288.20	473.40	453.90	620.00	

Note: Figures in Millions of $ except: per share items, margins, yields, and ratios.

Source: IDD Information Services

part

2

THE TOP
MUTUAL
FUNDS
FOR 1999

A FEW WORDS ABOUT MUTUAL FUNDS

Although mutual funds have been around for more than seven decades, they have experienced a plethora of popularity in the 1990s. There are now some 9,000 funds on the market, which is roughly twice the number of issues on the New York and American Stock Exchanges combined.

You can literally find funds of every flavor, from conservative money market instruments to more aggressive small caps. It's easy to put money to work in a specific sector (like health care and technology), or diversify among a wide range of industries. It's even possible to take advantage of growth in exotic international markets, from Argentina to Zimbabwe, through funds.

The explosion of this industry is nothing short of phenomenal. Total fund assets stood at $500 million in 1940, skyrocketed to $500 billion in 1985 and are approaching $5 trillion today. Assets continue to flow in at a record pace. Furthermore, you can buy funds practically everywhere, from the local bank to your nearby discount broker. There's even a multilevel marketing company offering folks a chance to peddle these investment pools door to door.

The Appeal of Mutual Funds

What led to this sudden popularity? To begin with, people are more concerned than ever about savings. Baby boomers realize that without a carefully crafted investment plan they could fall short when it comes time to retire.

In addition, many businesses, both large and small, use mutual funds to manage employee benefit and profit sharing plans. This is a major growth area for the fund families that will continue to flourish for years to come.

Perhaps the number one reason for the public's insatiable appetite for funds rests with the overwhelming amount of publicity they have received in recent years. There are more than a dozen personal finance magazines currently available, all of which devote a lot of space to mutual fund investing. Moreover, virtually every major newspaper carries a regular column on funds, and financial commentators on radio and television continue to sing their praises.

Aside from all this free editorial space, the mutual fund companies themselves have spent millions educating and enticing the public to send in their hard-earned cash. The message is obviously getting through. New money now comes into funds at the astonishing rate of $1.6 billion a day.

Using Funds

There's no question mutual funds make a great deal of sense, especially for those unwilling to do the research and follow-up necessary to buy individual securities. Funds are most useful for equities. After all, the first rule of successful investing is *diversification*. You certainly don't want to put all your eggs in one basket when dealing with stocks. It is often argued that a rational person never keeps more than 5 percent of his or her money in any single security. Otherwise the risk is overwhelming.

When you buy a stock mutual fund, you automatically achieve instant diversification. Smaller funds, in terms of asset size, spread their money over dozens of companies, while larger ones may take positions in hundreds. Either way, your overall exposure is significantly reduced, though not entirely eliminated.

Funds make the process of investing a breeze. You simply send in a check and, for a small fee, hire a professional manager to make all the decisions for you. What could be easier? It's even possible and advisable to accumulate wealth in funds over time through dollar cost averaging, a method in which you invest on a regular basis regardless of market conditions, enabling you to buy more shares when prices are down, and less when they're up.

Just remember that not every fund is created equal. Roughly 75 percent of all stock funds actually *underperform* the unmanaged market indexes. These are funds supposedly spearheaded by top-notch investment professionals. Plus, with so many choices, picking a fund is about as complicated as sorting through individual stocks. Therefore, the key to success rests with proper selection, which is the focus of Part 2.

The Downside of Funds

There are disadvantages to owning funds. To begin with, they give you little control over exactly how your money is invested. Sure, you can buy a fund full of stocks, but you're not allowed to choose the companies. The fund manager can purchase anything he or she wants, within the guidelines of the prospectus, without regard to your preferences.

Additionally, fund companies can be extremely impersonal. Many are huge organizations that hire scantily trained representatives to answer shareholder questions. That's no problem if you just want to know your account balance or the fund's total return for a given year. However, should you have specific questions about what investments the fund is making or which stocks it recently purchased, you'll probably be out of luck. And you can forget about talking directly with the fund manager. This kind of access is almost unheard of.

Another problem is that good funds tend to grow quite large, which can hamper returns. A fund with $1 billion or more in assets is usually forced to diversify over dozens, if not hundreds, of companies. That makes it difficult to outperform the market, because each stock probably only comprises around 1 percent of total assets. Therefore, when one or two issues double or triple in value, they have little impact on overall results. It's a case of being overdiversified. Furthermore, funds are required to pay out any realized capital gains to shareholders each year, meaning you could have a tax liability even if you sit tight with your shares, and some of these gains will likely be taxed at the higher ordinary income rate. Conversely, when you buy stocks, you don't experience a gain until you liquidate your holdings. If that's more than 18 months after making your initial purchase, your tax rate is capped at 20 percent under current law.

Finally, funds can take some of the fun out of investing. Many people find the process of hunting down stocks and then watching them (hopefully) rise to be quite exciting. It's thrilling to match wits with the market in pursuit of profits. Because fund managers do everything for you, that pleasure is gone.

More on Asset Allocation

Still, mutual funds have a place in most portfolios, particularly for those more eager to spend time on the golf course or at the beach than reading through stock reports and monitoring price movements. If that describes you, simply choose from the following recommendations and relax.

I've divided the funds into four different categories: aggressive growth, growth, growth and income, and international. Aggressive growth funds typically invest in the stocks of smaller companies, making them susceptible to dramatic short-term price swings, but also potentially more rewarding. Growth funds these days generally hold a combination of small, midsize, and large companies, though the selections in this book tend to stick with the bigger names that are global powerhouses. Growth and income funds generally buy dividend paying stocks to create a portfolio that throws off a respectable yield, while reducing overall risk. International funds, as you might guess, invest primarily (and sometimes exclusively) in foreign-based securities of all sizes. While foreign funds are inherently volatile, due to factors such as currency fluctuations and political turmoil, they can actually help to reduce your portfolio's overall volatility, because overseas markets don't necessarily move in tandem with the United States.

Which types of funds should you buy? As a general rule, younger investors and those not requiring immediate income would be wise to focus on the more aggressive selections, while older and more conservative readers may want to pay close attention to the growth and income offerings.

I decided not to include pure bond funds for a couple of reasons. First of all, you can often do better by purchasing bonds, like Treasuries, directly from the government or through a discount broker. Furthermore, when you look at the evidence, one thing is clear: Over time, stocks provide the highest returns. Since 1926, the S&P 500 has compounded at an average annual rate of 11 percent, compared with 5.2 percent for government bonds and 3.8 percent for money market funds. That means it's impossible for your capital to significantly increase without putting a large portion into equities.

Unfortunately, the stock market doesn't always go up, and losses in any given period can be dramatic. Luckily, so can the rewards, as we've seen in recent years.

That's why it makes sense for younger investors to be more heavily and aggressively invested in equities than older ones, although almost everyone should have a respectable exposure to stocks.

There's a rule of thumb that states a person should subtract his or her age from 100 and put that percentage in equities, the rest in bonds. So, under this theory, if you're 40, you would have 60 percent of your assets in the stock market. Nevertheless, Philip Carret, the renowned investment legend who launched what is now called the Pioneer Fund in 1928, called that philosophy, "Nonsense." As he put it in an interview with me prior to his death at the age of 101 in May, 1998, "What difference does age make? That has nothing to do with it. Why, just because I'm 101, should I sell all my stocks and sit on bonds? I still have 75 to 80 percent of my money in stocks." (I interviewed Carret for this book just prior to his passing. You can read more about his recommended stock, Inacom, in Part 1, and more about him in Part 3.)

Even if you need a monthly check to live on, stock funds remain a good choice. You can always redeem a set number of shares each month to produce the required amount of income (it's called a systematic withdrawal plan), while your principal continues to grow.

Though there are no magic formulas, here are some general stock and bond asset allocation guidelines for each age group that might even be considered somewhat conservative. In fact, several of my panelists argue that you should avoid bonds entirely.

Age	Suggested Weighting
Under 40	80 to 100% Stocks, 0 to 20% Bonds
40–50	75% Stocks, 25% Bonds
50–60	65% Stocks, 35% Bonds
60–70	60% Stocks, 40% Bonds
70+	50% Stocks, 50% Bonds

Selecting Your Funds

The next question is how many funds do you need? The consensus varies widely, though if you have less than $10,000 to invest, one or two is probably enough. When you get up to $50,000, it makes sense to buy around five. If your investment capital exceeds $100,000, it's possible to own eight or ten different funds. However, each fund should have a slightly different focus or investment objective. Otherwise, you could end up owning a bunch of funds holding the exact same companies.

A well-rounded collection of stock funds might include one with each of the following objectives: large company growth, large company value, mid-cap growth, small-cap growth, small-cap value, and diversified international. The market tends to favor various groups at different times. By investing in numerous areas, your chances of always making money greatly increase. My experts will offer more advice on this subject in Part 3.

Load versus No-Load

Fortunately, all of the funds listed in this book are offered on a "no-load" basis, meaning you won't pay any sales fees to get in or out, so every cent of your investment goes to work for you. You might ask, "How do the fund companies make any money then?" The answer is by charging an annual management fee, which is reflected in the fund's expense ratio. This is usually under 1 percent for bond funds, 2 percent for those invested in equities. You are never actually billed for this charge. Instead, it is taken directly out of the fund's daily net asset value, which is listed in the business section of most major newspapers.

It's important to note that both load and no-load funds carry management fees. The only difference is that funds with a load cost you up to 8 percent more. The load is simply a commission that comes off the top and goes directly into the pocket of the person who sells it to you, usually a broker or so-called financial planner. The fund companies generally don't get a penny. Therefore, if you do your homework and read books like this one, there's no reason to ever pay a load to buy a fund. In fact, several studies have shown that, as a group, no-loads actually perform better than their loaded counterparts. This means they not only save you money, but are also more profitable in the long run.

Buying Your Funds

After you figure out how many and which types of funds you want, it's time to decide where you should buy them. One option is to simply call the fund company directly to request a prospectus and application. You then merely fill in the blanks, send in a check for the required opening investment and you're in business. Each confirmation slip comes with a coupon, enabling you to easily mail off additional contributions as often as you like, which is helpful for dollar cost averaging.

The latest and perhaps most convenient way to purchase funds is through the various national discount brokers, especially the big three: Charles Schwab, Fidelity Investments and Jack White & Company. All offer no-transaction-fee programs, enabling you to buy hundreds of no-load funds from many different families without ever paying a commission. The brokers make their money through a service charge paid by the mutual fund companies. It doesn't cost you a penny more than if you were to buy the funds directly.

These no-transaction-fee programs are definitely worth investigating. They have two major advantages. The first is that all of your funds are consolidated on one easy-to-read monthly statement, which is very convenient. What's more, you can purchase shares and make trades on a specific day through your broker with a simple phone call. This saves you the hassle of writing out a check and mailing it in and enables you to direct exactly when you want the trade to take place. With the postal service, it could take up to three weeks for your check to arrive.

At the end of each profile, if a fund can be purchased through any or all of these programs, this will be listed in italics. For more information on opening an account, just call the discount broker of your choice. They are all accessible through the following toll-free numbers and Internet addresses:

Charles Schwab & Co.	(800) 845-1714	www.schwab.com
Fidelity Investments	(800) 544-9697	www.fidelity.com
Jack White & Co.	(800) 233-3411	www.jackwhiteco.com

I have also included the Internet address for each fund that has one. By the way, I wrote an entire book on how to take advantage of these no-load fund super-markets called *Buying Mutual Funds for Free* (Dearborn Financial Publishing). It shows you how to construct a winning portfolio using funds offered through these programs, compares each of the participating brokers, gives past performance statistics for every available fund, and includes several model portfolios featuring the very best of more than 1,000 available choices. You should be able to find this book at your local bookstore.

About the Recommendations

What follows are some specific picks for 1999 from the world's leading mutual fund authorities. There are three aggressive growth, three growth, three growth and income, and two international selections. Each description lists the fund's primary objective and investment focus (to help you construct a diversified portfolio), along with its past performance record, expense ratio, top holdings, management profile, and contact information. As you read through this, remember that "past performance is no guarantee of future results." Keep in mind there are a lot of dogs in the mutual fund world, so stick with these gems, and savor the rewards.

BARON SMALL CAP

Michael Stolper
Stolper & Company

Manager: Cliff Greenberg
Style: Small-Cap/Growth

Fund Profile

It's not often that investors are given access to the talents of a seasoned hedge-fund manager for as little as $2,000. But that's exactly what you get with the Baron Small Cap fund. Manager Cliff Greenberg spent 12 years with HPB Associates, working alongside successful hedge-fund manager Howard Berkowitz, before joining Baron Capital at the end of 1997. "The hedge-fund mindset, which has been retained solely to increase the wealth of a very demanding clientele, is clearly ingrained in Greenberg," says Michael Stolper of Stolper & Company. "Investors in Baron Small Cap are getting that same intense dedication."

Although Greenberg has a law degree from Columbia, he has been interested in investing since his early teens, when he worked summers at his grandfather's investment firm. He majored in securities law and really got turned on to stocks after taking an investment course at Columbia taught by Jim Rogers, the colorful TV commentator and former colleague of George Soros at the Quantum Fund. "It's unusual for an investment professional to leave a thriving hedge fund, as Greenberg did, for a mutual fund environment, where results are posted daily, investment options are far more restricted, and the portfolio manager is not entitled to pocket 20 percent of the annual appreciation," Stolper concedes. "But Greenberg feels most comfortable investing in publicly traded stocks, and HPB was increasingly making direct investments in private companies."

Greenberg works closely with boss Ron Baron, who manages Baron Asset and Baron Growth & Income, both of which have been featured in previous editions of *Wall Street's Picks*. "Greenberg shares Baron's approach to selecting growth stocks," Stolper shares. "They found that out more than a dozen years ago when they were calling on—and often buying—some of the same names. They want to own companies with expanding businesses, such as specialty retailers, restaurant chains, assisted living homes, and child-care companies. Baron Small Cap just opened at the end of 1997, and I expect Greenberg will hold an average of 50 names in the portfolio. He likes companies that double in size every three or four years, and he'll hold on to them as long as they come through."

Noticeably absent from Greenberg's portfolio, and Baron's as well, are technology companies. "They admit to not knowing much about technology," Stolper says. "They like to stick with what they understand. They do very thorough analytical research. These are guys who really get to know their companies. And they won't buy any foreign stocks either." Because Greenberg and Baron have similar tastes in companies, there is some overlap in holdings from one fund to another. The difference is that Greenberg's fund will hold smaller names than Baron's other two offerings. "The overall portfolios will be very different, for Greenberg is more attracted to fallen angels and special situations than Baron is," Stolper observes. "You can trace that back to his hedge-fund days. Greenberg is an assiduous prospector for unappreciated growth companies and he knows what price to pay for them. Greenberg has total freedom in the management of the fund and serves as a senior analyst for Baron's other two offerings. Investors in Baron Small Cap are hiring a talented and educated moneymaker."

Reason for Recommendation

That's what it ultimately comes down to for Stolper. When selecting a fund, he looks for the manager he thinks will give him the greatest return over time. Stolper says it's especially hard to find a small-cap manager capable of generating consistently superior performance in the long run. But he believes Greenberg has a good shot at it, given his impressive background. "This fund comes to me with a whole series of endorsements behind it," Stolper says. "I've always tried to stair-step relationships in this business. I found Ron Baron about 12 years ago, after he was highly recommended by another manager who retired. When Baron hired Greenberg, I took notice. He worked with Berkowitz, who is known for his legendary skills. Greenberg came from the hedge-fund business, which has a much different view of the world. He's 40, which is the perfect age for a manager. And he was given an ownership stake in Baron's company. Once I personally met Greenberg, that sealed the deal. He's got the right look and feel. He's smart, and I think the fund is going to be a real winner."

As for Greenberg, he hopes to double his shareholders' money every three to five years. "We set our sights on long-term performance, because thinking long-term enhances our returns," Greenberg contends.

Minimum Initial Investment: $2,000

(Available without a transaction fee from Schwab, Fidelity, and Jack White)

Contact Information: Baron Small Cap Fund
767 Fifth Avenue
New York, NY 10153
(800) 992-2766
www.baronfunds.com

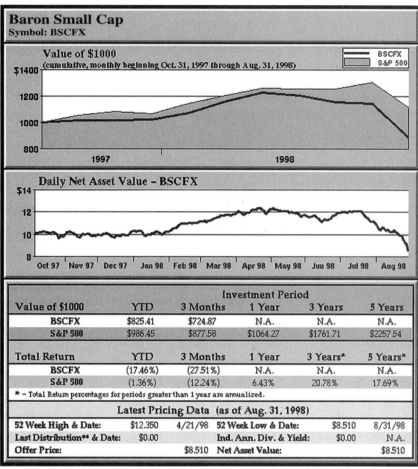

Baron Small Cap
Symbol: BSCFX

Source: IDD Information Services

Top 10 Holdings	Key Statistics	
Centennial Cellular CIA	Sales Load (max)	0.00%
Iron Mountain	Redemption Charge (max)	0.00%
Premier Parks	Expense Ratio	N/A
Culligan Water Technologies	Management Fee	1.00%
Metro Networks	12b-1 Marketing Fees	0.25%
AMF Bowling	PE Ratio	33.30%
Universal Outdoor Holdings	Dividend Yield	N/A
Counsel	Turnover Ratio	N/A
United Stationers	Beta Factor	N/A
Choicepoint	Total Assets	$571 mil.

FIRST EAGLE FUND OF AMERICA

Stephen Savage
Value Line Mutual Fund Survey

Managers: Harold Levy and David Cohen
Style: Mid-Cap/Value-Oriented

Fund Profile

While you may not have heard much, if anything, about the First Eagle Fund of America, Stephen Savage of the *Value Line Mutual Fund Survey* predicts that you soon will. "It has a great track record and, eventually, that's going to get discovered," he says. "The managers don't take a lot of chances, yet they've generated some good returns."

First Eagle has been managed by Harold Levy and David Cohen since its inception in 1989. "They work as a team and do some really solid research," Savage says. The fund is advised by the New York investment banking boutique Arnold and S. Bleichroeder, a successor corporation to two German banking houses whose roots date back to the 1800s. "Overall, we see ourselves generally as mid-cap value investors who do not use traditional value models to find attractive stocks," Levy and Cohen say. "Our process starts with a reason for wanting to own a company based on a positive change happening that causes us to think we can make money. We look for potential catalysts that signal corporate change. These can be management changes, share repurchases, acquisitions, divestitures, litigation controversies, strategies to enhance value, technological breakthroughs, liquidation of nonperforming assets, or changes in a company's strategy." In addition to investigating the fundamentals of any business they invest in, Levy and Cohen also like to interview a company's management, employees, customers, suppliers and competition.

"What's interesting about this fund is that it has a bit lower risk profile than the typical aggressive growth fund and it takes a more mixed approach to stock selection," Savage observes. "That's unusual since you normally see more of a growth bias in this category. These guys are trying to determine the value of a company based on cash flow. They look at how well a company generates free cash, rather than focusing on earnings. Then they try to find ways the company can use that cash to increase the stock price."

The fund's average market capitalization is around $8 billion, and the 60 stock portfolio features a lot of household names like IBM, Lockheed Martin, Finova Group, NationsBank, Mirage Resorts, Amgen, U.S. Surgical, Allstate, and H&R

Block. There are also plenty of more obscure holdings, like Aavid Thermal Technologies, Allegiance, TIG Holdings, and Millennium Chemicals. Noticeably absent are some of the Dow stocks, like General Electric and Gillette, which have run up to huge multiples in the past few years. While Cohen and Levy admit these are all fine companies, they don't believe their high prices are justified.

"Let's look at how our search-for-change strategy is illustrated by one of the fund's largest and most successful holdings—BankBoston," Cohen and Levy offer. "After a new CEO took over the bank in 1995, the fund began buying shares. The bank had a pretty good corporate business with a very attractive franchise in Latin America, but lacked a strong retail operation in the home market. The new executive pruned the company's low-return assets, strengthened the bank's retail presence through a merger with BayBanks, and repurchased stock." The value of the BankBoston shares have since more than doubled.

As for the fund's sell discipline, Levy and Cohen say they monitor and review every company in the portfolio daily to make sure the premise of their purchase is still valid. "We sell to rebalance positions to reflect our conviction to the price," the managers explain. "We scale out of a stock as our perceived value is recognized. We also sell to drive out old ideas and replace them with more compelling ideas, or if the premise changes."

Reason for Recommendation

In a category where fund managers are notorious for running extremely volatile portfolios and producing roller-coaster-like returns for shareholders, Savage contends that First Eagle is a refreshing change. "The managers of this fund have been in place for a long time and have an established record of success," he says. "The fund also has a small asset base, which is going to swell once this fund gets discovered."

Savage admits the fund does have two negatives: A relatively high expense ratio (1.42 percent) and a history of paying out hefty capital gains distributions. This makes it more attractive as part of an IRA than a regular taxable account. Nevertheless, he believes First Eagle is a real standout that should shine in 1999. "Trust me, you're going to hear a lot more about this fund in the years to come," he predicts. "It is a great choice for relatively conservative aggressive growth investors."

Minimum Initial Investment: $5,000 ($2,000 for IRAs)

(Available without a transaction fee from Schwab, Fidelity, and Jack White)

Contact Information: First Eagle Fund of America
1315 Avenue of the Americas
New York, NY 10105
(888) 482-5667

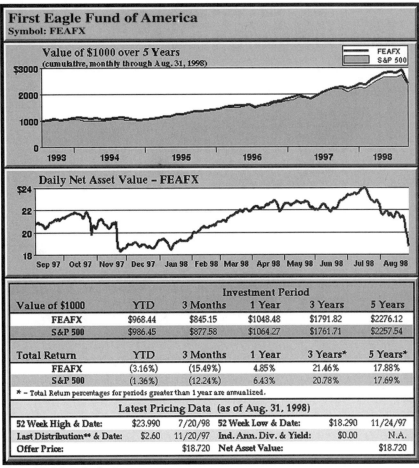

First Eagle Fund of America
Symbol: FEAFX

Value of $1000 over 5 Years
(cumulative, monthly through Aug. 31, 1998)

FEAFX
S&P 500

Daily Net Asset Value – FEAFX

Value of $1000	YTD	3 Months	Investment Period 1 Year	3 Years	5 Years
FEAFX	$968.44	$845.15	$1048.48	$1791.82	$2276.12
S&P 500	$986.45	$877.58	$1064.27	$1761.71	$2257.54

Total Return	YTD	3 Months	1 Year	3 Years*	5 Years*
FEAFX	(3.16%)	(15.49%)	4.85%	21.46%	17.88%
S&P 500	(1.36%)	(12.24%)	6.43%	20.78%	17.69%

* – Total Return percentages for periods greater than 1 year are annualized.

Latest Pricing Data (as of Aug. 31, 1998)				
52 Week High & Date:	$23.990	7/20/98	52 Week Low & Date:	$18.290	11/24/97
Last Distribution** & Date:	$2.60	11/20/97	Ind. Ann. Div. & Yield:	$0.00	N.A.
Offer Price:		$18.720	Net Asset Value:		$18.720

Source: IDD Information Services

Top 10 Holdings	Key Statistics	
BankBoston	Sales Load (max)	0.00%
Tele-Com TCI Group Cl A	Redemption Charge (max)	0.00%
FINOVA Group	Expense Ratio	1.70%
Storage Technology	Management Fee	1.00%
Comcast Special Cl A	12b-1 Marketing Fees	0.00%
Biogen	PE Ratio	24.67
Ceridian	Dividend Yield	0.00%
Amgen	Turnover Ratio	98.00%
Gulfstream Aerospace	Beta Factor	0.85
General Dynamics	Total Assets	$351 mil.

RYDEX NOVA

Paul Merriman
Paul A. Merriman & Associates

Manager: Thomas G. Michael
Style: Enhanced Index

Fund Profile

You're no doubt familiar with S&P 500 index funds, which have become favorites with investors in recent years. One reason is that they whipped the socks off of actively managed funds in both 1996 and 1997. Now there's a way for you to invest in the S&P, with a high-octane twist. Rydex Nova is a fund that seeks to provide a return that's 150 percent greater than what you would get being in the plain vanilla S&P 500 index. It does this by engaging in a speculative investment technique known as leveraging. "What they do is use derivatives as a way of imitating a return that's one and a half times that of the S&P 500," explains Paul Merriman of Paul A. Merriman & Associates. "It's definitely a large-cap growth fund, but the portfolio is made up of derivatives, not individual stocks." The derivatives include stock index futures contracts, options on stock index futures contracts, and options on securities and stock indexes.

Rydex Nova's portfolio in the latest reporting period consisted solely of S&P futures contracts and S&P 500 call options. There are so few holdings, the list takes up less than half a page in the fund's annual report. Why would you be interested in such a fund? It's really quite simple. If you are bullish on the outlook for the stock market, and specifically those companies found within the S&P 500 index, this fund is a perfect choice. If it works like it's supposed to, it will give you a return much greater than you would get from simply buying a standard S&P 500 index fund. Of course, if the market goes down, this fund will go down even more. So the risk, like the potential reward, is theoretically one and a half times greater than the index itself.

"Another interesting thing about this fund is they actually encourage market timing," Merriman notes. "Rydex likes to see people switch around through its various funds." This is something other index fund sponsors, like the Vanguard Group, abhor. Actually, fund families in general normally despise market timers. They can wreak havoc on money flows, increase transaction fees and ultimately hurt all shareholders in the long run. That's why some fund families, and most discount brokers, impose fees on investors who trade frequently, in an effort to quell this practice. Not Rydex. The company caters to market timers, like Merriman, by offering a series of funds similar to Nova, but with different objectives. For example, Rydex offers what it calls the Ursa fund. It's objective is to generate a return that's 150 percent in the opposite direction of the S&P 500. This means that in bear markets, Ursa should be a shining star. Ursa engages primarily in short selling, and its portfolio consists mostly of puts and calls on the S&P 500. The idea is that if you're a market timer, you can switch from Nova to Ursa when you turn bearish, and back to Nova once you turn bullish again. (I will remind you, however, about something I already mentioned in Part 1 of this book about market timing: It simply can't be done accurately over time. Most people who time the market fail and wind up making less money than they would by simply buying and holding.) That being said, Merriman is a believer in market timing. He admits it can hurt your returns, but he's convinced it also reduces risk over time. So if you, too, want to time the market, this fund is perfect for you. When you're bullish, you can load up on shares of Nova. When you change your mind, you can switch into something else. This is a practice Merriman engages in himself.

Reason for Recommendation

But Merriman concedes there's an even better way for most investors to use Rydex Nova, which is why he recommends it. "It's a wonderful investment for people who are believers in corporate America, particularly within their IRA," he says. "You can't go out and borrow in your IRA to have leverage. By buying this fund, you can have leverage inside your IRA without borrowing. Assuming U.S. stocks are going to grow and achieve a higher rate of return than any other investment instrument, here's a way to leverage that growth in the greatest equity market in the world." Merriman further points out that Rydex Nova is a perfect fund for dollar-cost-averaging in over both bull and bear markets. "What I teach young folks is that you want bear markets," he notes. "When the market goes down, it gives you the chance to purchase more shares at a lower cost."

However, there are a number of negatives for you to consider as well. First, it goes without saying that this is among the most volatile funds you will come across. You shouldn't buy it unless you're either emphatically bullish or willing to endure some severe voiatility. Second, the fund's expense ratio of 1.16 percent is extremely high for an index fund, especially considering how uncomplicated it is to manage. Finally, if you purchase the fund directly from Rydex, the minimum initial investment is a hefty $25,000. You can lower this amount to as little as $2,500 for a regular account, and $1,000 for IRAs, by purchasing shares through select discount brokers, although you will have to pay a commission on the transaction.

Minimum Initial Investment: $25,000 (less through some discount brokers)

Contact Information: Rydex Nova Fund
6116 Executive Blvd., Suite 400
Rockville, MD 20852
(800) 820-0888

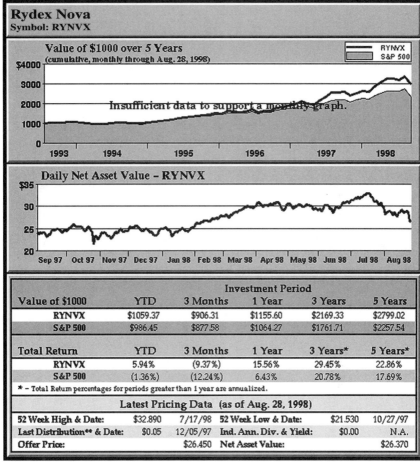

Rydex Nova
Symbol: RYNVX

Value of $1000 over 5 Years (cumulative, monthly through Aug. 28, 1998)

Insufficient data to support a monthly graph.

Daily Net Asset Value – RYNVX

Value of $1000	YTD	3 Months	1 Year	3 Years	5 Years
RYNVX	$1059.37	$906.31	$1155.60	$2169.33	$2799.02
S&P 500	$986.45	$877.58	$1064.27	$1761.71	$2257.54

Total Return	YTD	3 Months	1 Year	3 Years*	5 Years*
RYNVX	5.94%	(9.37%)	15.56%	29.45%	22.86%
S&P 500	(1.36%)	(12.24%)	6.43%	20.78%	17.69%

* – Total Return percentages for periods greater than 1 year are annualized.

Latest Pricing Data (as of Aug. 28, 1998)

52 Week High & Date:	$32.890	7/17/98	52 Week Low & Date:	$21.530	10/27/97
Last Distribution** & Date:	$0.05	12/05/97	Ind. Ann. Div. & Yield:	$0.00	N.A.
Offer Price:		$26.450	Net Asset Value:		$26.370

Source: IDD Information Services

Top 10 Holdings	Key Statistics	
S&P 500 Index (call) @ 775	Sales Load (max)	0.00%
S&P 500 Index (call) @ 440	Redemption Charge (max)	0.00%
S&P 500 Index (call) @ 790	Expense Ratio	1.11%
S&P 500 Index (fut)	Management Fee	0.75%
	12b-1 Marketing Fees	0.00%
	PE Ratio	N/A
	Dividend Yield	0.00%
	Turnover Ratio	N/A
	Beta Factor	1.54
	Total Assets	$923 mil.

RAINIER CORE EQUITY PORTFOLIO
Larry Chin
No-Load Fund Analyst

Manager: James Margard and Team
Style: Large-Cap/Growth at a Reasonable Price

Fund Profile

It's not often that you come across a fund which manages to outperform the S&P 500 consistently quarter after quarter, year after year. Rarer still is when such a fund remains relatively unnoticed by the masses and the media. But that's exactly what you get with the Rainier Core Equity Portfolio. "It's an all-cap fund, meaning they will buy companies of any size, but it predominately contains large-cap stocks," notes Larry Chin, senior editor of the *No-Load Fund Analyst*. The fund has been around since 1994 and has consistently outperformed its benchmark, the S&P 500 index. Even more impressive, according to Chin, is Rainier's private account track record, which goes back more than a decade. "They have consistently been good performers, beating the S&P 500 over the past three, five and ten years," he points out. "The fund's lead manager is Jim Margard, although he works with a team of three other people." What's even more amazing is that they have posted such impressive numbers while holding an extremely diversified portfolio and not making any big bets.

Margard and Team practice an investment discipline known as GARP, or growth at a reasonable price. In other words, they look for companies likely to experience above-average earnings growth selling at attractive valuations. "They start the process of looking for stocks by doing multiple quantitative screens," Chin says. "They look for companies with earnings consistency over time and a strong balance sheet cash flow selling at low prices. They pretty much cover all the bases with this first screen. Then they do some qualitative screens, looking at each company's competitive strategy, products, and management. They especially want to see a shareholder-oriented management team with a significant ownership position in the stock. After the screens have been done, they throw in their own personal judgment and are constantly tinkering with the formula to make sure it works."

Margard and his team avoid over- or under-weighting any sector relative to the S&P by spreading their assets over as many as 150 names. With so many holdings, it's impossible to personally visit each company they invest in. Nevertheless, Chin says they do whatever due diligence is necessary before taking a position to confirm what they learn from the screening process. "They meet with or at least call on companies they feel they need more information about," he maintains. "This is generally done on an as-needed basis. This is yet another thing that's unusual about Rainer. I like managers who are very bottom-up and do a lot of tire kicking. They don't do that. But they keep on top of their companies in other ways."

Before joining Rainier, Margard was a portfolio manager with Value Line Mutual Funds. "He comes from an unusual, eclectic liberal arts background," Chin notes. "Margard and his team came together very quietly. They ran the investment arm of Rainier National Bank, where they managed private portfolios. Then they decided to split off from the bank and go out on their own." Today, Rainier Investment Management oversees some $4 billion in assets for various clients from its Seattle headquarters.

You might think that being so far away from Wall Street might be a disadvantage. At one time, that might have been true. "But not anymore, especially with technology being the way it is," Chin maintains. "It really doesn't matter where you physically manage money from. In fact, I think it's refreshing that they work away from New York. It helps them to think more clearly."

Reason for Recommendation

Chin loves to invest in top-performing funds that are ignored by the public. In this case, he's convinced Rainier hasn't received the attention it deserves because the company does almost no advertising. They also haven't been all that savvy when it comes to public relations. Nevertheless, *Barron's* ranked Margard among the 100 best fund managers in the nation in 1997 for both Rainier Core Equity and its sister portfolio Rainier Small/Mid-Cap, which is now closed to new investors. "The other thing is that not too many publications have gone back and researched his separate account record, which is just as impressive as the fund's," Chin adds. "Another positive about Rainier is that it will close a fund the minute it feels its performance will be compromised by an overflow of assets. They already did it with the small-cap fund, and I am convinced they would close Core Equity too if they felt it was necessary. This firm has a lot of integrity in that regard. They are just the epitome of managers who have succeeded using a discipline that has been perfected over a long period of time."

One thing to keep in mind is that if you purchase shares directly from the fund, you will have to make a minimum initial investment of $25,000. However, if you buy your shares through one of the NTF programs at Schwab, Fidelity, or Jack White, you can get in for as little as $2,500.

Minimum Initial Investment: $25,000 ($2,500 through NTF programs)

(Available without a transaction fee from Schwab, Fidelity, and Jack White)

Contact Information: Rainier Core Equity Portfolio
601 Union Street, Suite 2801
Seattle, WA 98101
(800) 248-6314

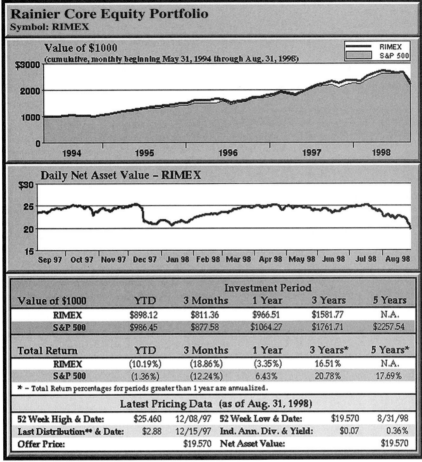

Rainier Core Equity Portfolio
Symbol: RIMEX

Value of $1000
(cumulative, monthly beginning May 31, 1994 through Aug. 31, 1998)

RIMEX
S&P 500

Daily Net Asset Value – RIMEX

Value of $1000	YTD	3 Months	Investment Period 1 Year	3 Years	5 Years
RIMEX	$898.12	$811.36	$966.51	$1581.77	N.A.
S&P 500	$986.45	$877.58	$1064.27	$1761.71	$2257.54

Total Return	YTD	3 Months	1 Year	3 Years*	5 Years*
RIMEX	(10.19%)	(18.86%)	(3.35%)	16.51%	N.A.
S&P 500	(1.36%)	(12.24%)	6.43%	20.78%	17.69%

* – Total Return percentages for periods greater than 1 year are annualized.

Latest Pricing Data (as of Aug. 31, 1998)				
52 Week High & Date:	$25.460	12/08/97	52 Week Low & Date:	$19.570	8/31/98
Last Distribution** & Date:	$2.88	12/15/97	Ind. Ann. Div. & Yield:	$0.07	0.36%
Offer Price:		$19.570	Net Asset Value:		$19.570

Source: IDD Information Services

Top 10 Holdings	Key Statistics	
Microsoft	Sales Load (max)	0.00%
Merck	Redemption Charge (max)	0.00%
Mobil	Expense Ratio	1.14%
Bell Atlantic	Management Fee	0.75%
United Technologies	12b-1 Marketing Fees	0.25%
Household International	PE Ratio	27.52
Marsh & McLennan	Dividend Yield	0.28%
Bristol-Myers Squibb	Turnover Ratio	119.88%
Pepsico	Beta Factor	0.94
WorldCom	Total Assets	$812 mil.

SELECTED AMERICAN SHARES

Michael Hirsch
Freedom Capital Management

Manager: Chris Davis
Style: Large-Cap/Growth

Fund Profile

Investing is truly a family affair at Selected American Shares. Not only is the fund managed by a father-son team, but they have millions of their own money invested in it. "This fund is now in its third generation, if you will," notes Michael Hirsch of Freedom Capital Management. "Chris Davis is currently the lead portfolio manger. He has been comanaging the fund with his dad Shelby Davis since 1994 and was promoted to manager in February 1997. Shelby is now involved in an ancillary role. Before that, Shelby's dad and Chris's grandfather, was a renowned insurance stock analyst and investor on Wall Street, who had amassed a fortune of some $800 million by the time he died in 1994."

Shelby Davis is a former *Wall Street's Picks* panelist and has one of the most distinguished records in the business. He managed the Davis New York Venture fund for almost thirty years, producing some amazing returns. If you had put $10,000 into New York Venture 20 years before Shelby turned it over to Chris in 1997, you would have seen your investment grow to $360,000, compared to $160,000 for the S&P 500. "I have been investing in Venture for a long time," Hirsch says. "It's on my honor roll. It's one of the funds I've used since I started in this business in 1975."

Selected American has a colorful history. It was launched in 1933 and has been through a series of managers over the years. Shelby Davis was tapped to take it over in 1993. From day one, he crafted the portfolio to look almost like a no-load clone of New York Venture. Unfortunately, Venture has a hefty 4.50 percent sales load. "Selected is a bit more concentrated, but that's the only major difference," Hirsch offers. The portfolio is full of blue chip names, which manager Chris Davis, like his father, hopes to buy with the idea of marrying growth with value. He looks for stocks one company at a time and views himself as a partner in the business once he makes a purchase. "The kinds of businesses we want to own have such characteristics as first-class management, high returns on capital, a lean expense structure, a dominant or growing share in a growing market, products or services that do not become obsolete, a strong balance sheet, and successful international operations," Chris says. "In terms of how much to pay, we want to buy stocks of those businesses for considerably less than they are worth. No business is a good buy regardless of the price."

The Davises are also famous for using a "thematic" approach to investing. "They look for broad themes and then seek out individual companies that can benefit from those themes," Hirsch explains. "For example, they considered the 1990s to be the decade of financial service stocks." As a result, Selected American's portfolio has been top heavy which such names as American Express, Wells Fargo, Travelers Group and BankAmerica. In fact, before coming to Selected American, Chris Davis managed a financial services fund for his father's fund family. "They have been right on target being in financials so far," Hirsch observes. "What happens when the financials play out? I think Chris will be adaptive enough to move on to the next theme. And based on past history, he'll be there before everyone else realizes it. He's proactive, not reactive."

Reason for Recommendation

Hirsch calls Selected American Shares nepotism working. "Why is it working?" he asks. "I don't know if it's a genetic thing or not. It certainly proves that a large part of successful investing is having a discipline. Chris is using a proven methodology that worked for his grandfather, then his dad, and now him. He's not trying to reinvent the wheel. The Davis's stick to their knitting."

Looking ahead to 1999, Chris Davis continues to seek out ideas, although he's sounding somewhat cautious these days. "We expect to see a much greater emphasis on old-fashioned investment basics, rather than on new-era thinking," he says. "Fundamentally, we remain optimists, but we believe that investors must moderate their expectations. In fact, between 1966 and 1997, the Dow Jones Industrial Average, excluding dividends, compounded at only 7 percent, a rate far below what many would guess. Yet even if this modest growth rate were sustained for the next 30 years, the Dow would trade at 64,000. So more moderate expectations need not be cause for despair."

And in a volatile market environment, Hirsch maintains this is the perfect fund to own. "They follow an investment style that has proven itself in a variety of market environments—up markets, down markets, high inflation, low inflation—and their methodology has always worked," Hirsch adds. "If you want to talk about certain funds that absolutely must be in your portfolio, this is definitely one of them."

Minimum Initial Investment: $1,000

(Available without a transaction fee from Schwab, Fidelity, and Jack White)

Contact Information: Selected American Shares
124 East Marcy Street
Santa Fe, NM 87504
(800) 279-2279
www.selectedfunds.com

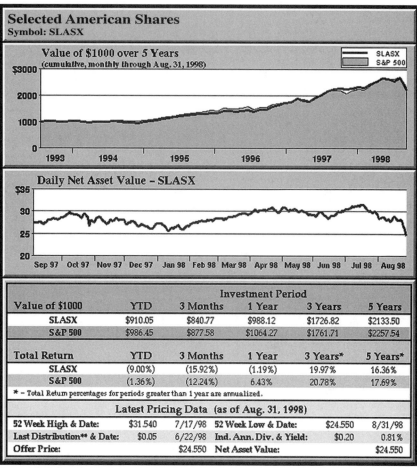

Selected American Shares
Symbol: SLASX

Value of $1000 over 5 Years (cumulative, monthly through Aug. 31, 1998)

Daily Net Asset Value – SLASX

Value of $1000	YTD	3 Months	Investment Period 1 Year	3 Years	5 Years
SLASX	$910.05	$840.77	$988.12	$1726.82	$2133.50
S&P 500	$986.45	$877.58	$1064.27	$1761.71	$2257.54

Total Return	YTD	3 Months	1 Year	3 Years*	5 Years*
SLASX	(9.00%)	(15.92%)	(1.19%)	19.97%	16.36%
S&P 500	(1.36%)	(12.24%)	6.43%	20.78%	17.69%

* – Total Return percentages for periods greater than 1 year are annualized.

Latest Pricing Data (as of Aug. 31, 1998)

52 Week High & Date:	$31.540	7/17/98	52 Week Low & Date:	$24.550	8/31/98
Last Distribution** & Date:	$0.05	6/22/98	Ind. Ann. Div. & Yield:	$0.20	0.81%
Offer Price:		$24.550	Net Asset Value:		$24.550

Source: IDD Information Services

Top 10 Holdings	Key Statistics	
American Express	Sales Load (max)	0.00%
Wells Fargo	Redemption Charge (max)	0.00%
Travelers Group	Expense Ratio	1.96%
Morgan Stanley/Dean Witter	Management Fee	0.65%
Hewlett-Packard	12b-1 Marketing Fees	0.25%
IBM	PE Ratio	24.48
General Re	Dividend Yield	0.59%
McDonald's	Turnover Ratio	26.00%
Halliburton	Beta Factor	1.01
BankAmerica	Total Assets	$2.7 bil.

TWEEDY, BROWNE AMERICAN VALUE
Janet Brown
DAL Investment Company

Managers: Chris Browne, Will Browne, and John Spears
Style: Mid-Cap/Value Oriented

Fund Profile

The management company running Tweedy, Browne American Value has a history dating back to 1920. One of the brokerage division's original clients was none other than Benjamin Graham, author of the 1934 book *Security Analysis* and the 1973 classic *The Intelligent Investor*, both of which are often viewed as the bibles of value investing. It should come as no surprise then that the managers at Tweedy, Browne employ the same approach outlined in Graham's books when picking stocks for their portfolios. Their primary emphasis is on preserving capital, while at the same time seeking to generate a respectable rate of return.

One way they attempt to do this is by examining what they call a "two-tier price structure" for publicly traded corporations. First is the stock market value, which is what a stock trades for on the exchange. Second is what they refer to as "intrinsic value," which is the amount a company would be worth if it were sold or liquidated on the open market. Once they figure out a company's intrinsic value, they check to see how it compares with the price on the exchange. Their ideal stock is one that can be purchased for at least a 50 percent discount to intrinsic value. The stock is then sold once that price gap closes, and the proceeds are reinvested in another undervalued company. Most investments in the portfolio have one or more of the following characteristics: low stock price in relation to book value, low price-to-earnings ratio, low price-to-cash-flow ratio, above-average dividend yield, low price-to-sales ratio compared to other companies in the same industry, low corporate leverage and high insider ownership.

During the runaway bull market of the past several years, in which investors chased many growth stocks to levels not seen before, value investors like the folks at Tweedy, Browne have not made the top of any performance lists. But that's precisely why Janet Brown, president of DAL Investment Company, thinks Tweedy, Browne American Value is a perfect fund to own in 1999. "I think that given how strong the market has been over the past four years, it's possible we could see some weakening this year," she predicts. "If that happens, I believe this fund will hold up better than most. Its strict value discipline leads the managers to a pretty eclectic

139

group of stocks. They have a terrific long-term track record and tend to do well when the market falls."

Tweedy, Browne American Value is run by three managers, Will Browne, Chris Browne, and John Spears. They seek long-term growth by investing in a diversified portfolio consisting primarily of U.S. equities, although up to 20 percent can be placed in foreign securities. In an effort to further reduce volatility, all international holdings are hedged to protect against possible currency fluctuations. (Incidentally, the firm also runs a global fund following the same strategy, which was highlighted in *Wall Street's Picks for 1996*.) "They don't care about the size of the companies, and their value bias does occasionally lead them to small-caps," Brown notes. "I would say this is really more of a mid-cap growth fund than anything else. They screen a list of about 10,000 companies, narrow down the list of candidates and go on to perform a detailed analysis." Their broad diversification discipline mandates that no one company accounts for greater than 4 percent of the portfolio, and no more than 15 percent of net assets will be invested in any one industry. "Diversification through the principle of the law of large numbers, which is utilized by insurance companies, not only reduces risk, but also increases the probability that a particular investment strategy will work," the managers have said. Since inception, Tweedy, Browne American Value has slightly underperformed the S&P 500, although it has done so by taking much less risk. "That is really fabulous considering the type of market environment we've been in," Brown adds.

Reason for Recommendation

"I am really convinced the tide will turn from growth to value this year," Brown forecasts. "It always has in the past and I am banking that it will do it again. If I'm right, this is a fund that will do well in that kind of environment. Regardless, I believe value outperforms growth over time anyway. This is a fund you could hold on to through various market environments." Brown is also impressed that the fund's three managers eat their own cooking. "They have all of their own money in the fund," she observes. "That's always a good sign." In late 1997, the partners at Tweedy, Browne sold their firm to the publicly traded Affiliated Managers Group for $300 million in cash. Nevertheless, Brown is convinced the managers will maintain their commitment to increase the wealth of shareholders. Should you decide to pursue an investment in this fund further, be sure to ask Tweedy, Browne for a free copy of their booklet *What Has Worked In Investing* when you call for a prospectus. It includes the results of 44 different studies showing various value-oriented investment strategies that have been effective over time.

Minimum Initial Investment: $2,500 ($500 for IRAs)

Contact Information: Tweedy, Browne American Value Fund
                               52 Vanderbilt Avenue
                               New York, NY 10017
                               (800) 432-4789

Tweedy, Browne American Value
Symbol: TWEBX

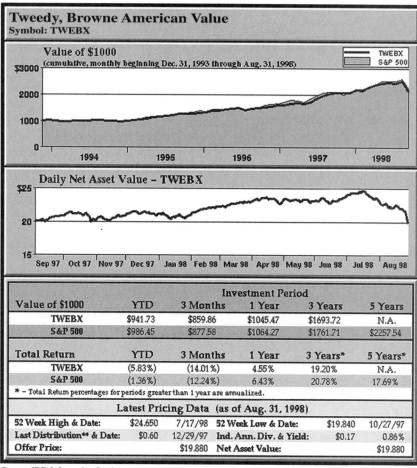

Value of $1000			Investment Period		
	YTD	3 Months	1 Year	3 Years	5 Years
TWEBX	$941.73	$859.86	$1045.47	$1693.72	N.A.
S&P 500	$986.45	$877.58	$1064.27	$1761.71	$2257.54

Total Return	YTD	3 Months	1 Year	3 Years*	5 Years*
TWEBX	(5.83%)	(14.01%)	4.55%	19.20%	N.A.
S&P 500	(1.36%)	(12.24%)	6.43%	20.78%	17.69%

* – Total Return percentages for periods greater than 1 year are annualized.

Latest Pricing Data (as of Aug. 31, 1998)					
52 Week High & Date:	$24.650	7/17/98	52 Week Low & Date:	$19.840	10/27/97
Last Distribution** & Date:	$0.60	12/29/97	Ind. Ann. Div. & Yield:	$0.17	0.86%
Offer Price:		$19.880	Net Asset Value:		$19.880

Source: IDD Information Services

Top 10 Holdings	Key Statistics	
McDonald's	Sales Load (max)	0.00%
Philip Morris	Redemption Charge (max)	0.00%
Chase Manhattan	Expense Ratio	1.39%
Pharmacia & Upjohn	Management Fee	1.25%
American Express	12b-1 Marketing Fees	0.00%
FHLMC	PE Ratio	21.79
UST	Dividend Yield	0.71%
Lehman Brothers Holdings	Turnover Ratio	6.00%
GATX	Beta Factor	0.76
Popular	Total Assets	$1.2 bil.

BARR ROSENBERG MARKET NEUTRAL

Peter Brown
Evensky, Brown, Katz & Levitt

Manager: Team Managed
Style: Market Neutral

Fund Profile

Imagine a fund that would allow you to make money in both bull and bear markets with little risk, yet had much more upside potential than bonds or other fixed-income investments. Sound too good to be true? Maybe it is. But the fund industry is betting it can be done through what's being dubbed a "market neutral" strategy. First out of the box with such a fund was Barr Rosenberg, the Orinda, California quantitatively driven investment firm, run by a man of the same name. Dr. Rosenberg is an acknowledged expert in the modeling of complex investment processes and was a former professor of finance before starting his financial consulting firm. Once his fund was up and running, several other fund families came out with similar offerings.

The concept behind market neutral funds is simple, although in practice the strategy is quite complex. The goal is to come up with a portfolio composed of promising long stock positions that are hedged by an equally well-researched group of shorts. The hope is that both sides will record gains. At the very least, however, any big losses should be counteracted by gains from the other side. So if the market goes up, the shorts will lose money. But the hope is you'll make even more on the long side. Conversely, if the market takes a tumble, if you've done a good job at stock selection, your shorts should provide impressive profits to counter any losses in the longs. Are you with me so far?

Financial planner Peter Brown sure is. He feels the Barr Rosenberg Market Neutral fund is perfect for the conservative growth and income portion of a portfolio, especially in a toppy market environment like the one he thinks we're in right now. "Barr Rosenberg's management team tries to identify what it considers to be the most undervalued stocks with the most appreciation potential on the long side," Brown explains. "Then, on the other side of the spectrum, they look for stocks they feel are overvalued and should fall. Let's say the portfolio has $1 million. They'll take that $1 million and buy what I'll call the 'good stocks.' Then they'll go out and short $1 million of the 'bad stocks.' They'll put the proceeds from the short sales in a money market fund, which should throw off a little interest. If the market keeps rising, even the shorts will go up, meaning the portfolio will lose money on the short side. But if their analysis is correct, they will make more money on the longs than they lose on the shorts, plus they'll have made a money-market return on part of those investments. If the market tanks, they expect the shorts to fall a lot more than the longs, thus, producing a larger return." Does it make sense now? Like I said, it's really not that complicated, but your stock picking prowess has to be outstanding in order for this to work.

Barr Rosenberg certainly has a great track record. The firm's other funds, most of which specialize in small-cap stocks, have been top performers over time. The Market Neutral fund holds mostly small- and mid-cap stocks. It is extremely diversified, with most positions making up 1 percent or less of the entire portfolio.

One reason you haven't heard about funds like this before is that until the Taxpayer Relief Act passed in 1997, they were illegal. "There used to be a regulation applying to funds called the short-short rule, which said funds could get no more than 30 percent of their income from short-term gains," Brown explains. "By definition, in a market neutral fund, you're going to have a lot of short-term gains. The other problem is that until the law changed, funds couldn't short half of their portfolio like they can now." While Barr Rosenberg doesn't have much of a track record with market neutral funds, it has run private accounts using this strategy going back to 1989. During that period, such accounts returned an average of 8.04 percent a year, lousy compared to stocks, but better than the 5.34 percent return from three-month U.S. Treasury Bills. As Rosenberg refined its process, the returns improved. For the three-year period ending November 30, 1997, the market neutral strategy generated an average annual return of 17.66 percent, compared to 5.33 percent for T-Bills. The fund's stated target is to provide a return that's 6 percent better than what you could get from a T-Bill.

Reason for Recommendation

"I like this fund because I'm kind of antsy about the market right now," Brown admits. "I have faith it will give me an equity-like return even if the market falls. This is a fund that really takes the market out of the equation." Keep in mind that if the market goes way up, this fund will likely be a weak performer, relatively speaking. But if the market moves sideways or goes down, it should be a real standout, assuming the system works as planned. Two more caveats: Expect a lot of year-end taxable distributions (meaning it makes more sense for use in an IRA) and notice the fund's above-average expense ratio of 2.50 percent.

Minimum Initial Investment: $2,500 ($2,000 for IRAs)

(Available without a transaction fee from Schwab, Fidelity, and Jack White)

Contact Information: Barr Rosenberg Market Neutral
3435 Stelzer Road
Columbus, OH 43219
(800) 447-3332
www.riem.com

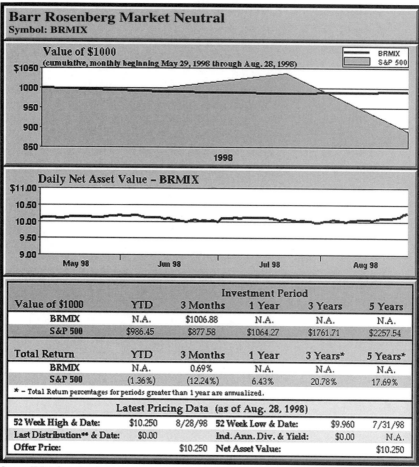

Barr Rosenberg Market Neutral
Symbol: BRMIX

Value of $1000 (cumulative, monthly beginning May 29, 1998 through Aug. 28, 1998)

BRMIX / S&P 500

Daily Net Asset Value – BRMIX

Value of $1000	YTD	3 Months	Investment Period 1 Year	3 Years	5 Years
BRMIX	N.A.	$1006.88	N.A.	N.A.	N.A.
S&P 500	$986.45	$877.58	$1064.27	$1761.71	$2257.54

Total Return	YTD	3 Months	1 Year	3 Years*	5 Years*
BRMIX	N.A.	0.69%	N.A.	N.A.	N.A.
S&P 500	(1.36%)	(12.24%)	6.43%	20.78%	17.69%

* – Total Return percentages for periods greater than 1 year are annualized.

Latest Pricing Data (as of Aug. 28, 1998)			
52 Week High & Date:	$10.250	8/28/98	
52 Week Low & Date:	$9.960	7/31/98	
Last Distribution** & Date:	$0.00		
Ind. Ann. Div. & Yield:	$0.00	N.A.	
Offer Price:	$10.250		
Net Asset Value:	$10.250		

Source: IDD Information Services

Top 10 Holdings	Key Statistics	
Whirlpool	Sales Load (max)	0.00%
Unisys	Redemption Charge (max)	0.00%
Woolworth	Expense Ratio	N/A
Amerada Hess	Management Fee	1.90%
Storage Technology	12b-1 Marketing Fees	0.50%
Tandy	PE Ratio	22.20
Liz Claiborne	Dividend Yield	N/A
Union Camp	Turnover Ratio	N/A
Kansas City Southern Inds.	Beta Factor	N/A
General Instrument	Total Assets	$54 Mil.

J.P. MORGAN TAX-AWARE U.S. EQUITY

Sheldon Jacobs
The No-Load Fund Investor

Manager: Terry Banet
Style: Large-Cap Growth/Tax-Sensitive

Fund Profile

Now that Congress has decided to be a little more generous to investors by lowering the maximum tax rate on long-term capital gains to 20 percent, Sheldon Jacobs feels we need to be more conscious about taking advantage of it. "I think tax awareness is going to be the coming mantra," says the editor of *The No-Load Fund Investor*. "If you haven't factored it into your investment thinking, you should." As I told you earlier, one downside to funds is that they are required to pay out any realized dividends and gains to shareholders at the end of each year, meaning you could have a tax liability even if you simply hold on to your shares. And funds that do a lot of trading during the year can rack up a hefty list of short-term gains, which are taxed as ordinary income with no cap. "Now that we have such a big difference in tax rates, running from 39.6 percent down to 20 percent, people should be taking this into account," Jacobs insists. "Under the current tax law, it really pays to minimize taxes."

Jacobs refers to a study from J.P. Morgan Investments that gives some eye-popping numbers to illustrate the importance of keeping taxes on your investments as low as possible. "If you're in the top 39.6 percent federal bracket, and take all your profits in less than a year (either from dividends or short-term capital gains), $1 will grow to $10.44 over a 40 year period," he notes. "If you hold on to your aggressive growth fund for more than 12 months, qualifying for the 28 percent capital gains rate, your dollar grows to $16.14, assuming you have no ordinary income. If you sell your fund after 18 months, qualifying for the 20 percent capital gains rate, your dollar grows to $22.03, again assuming you have no ordinary income." The effects of this compounding are even greater if you hold on for a longer period of time. After 40 years of no gains, and then paying the 20 percent top rate, your $1 becomes $36.41. If you instead leave this security to your heirs when you die, after 40 years the dollar would be worth $45.26. "And we haven't even considered the impact of state or local income taxes," Jacobs adds. "These differences are certainly big enough to get everyone's attention."

147

There are two ways you can implement a tax-aware investment program. One is by looking for funds that have historically paid out small annual distributions, and there are a few of them out there. Most have very low annual turnover, like index funds. But now you can also buy so called tax-efficient funds, such as J.P. Morgan Tax-Aware U.S. Equity. "Tax-aware managers, like those at J.P. Morgan, follow six primary guidelines," Jacobs points out. "One, they seek stocks they are comfortable holding long term, to avoid realizing taxable gains. This often means investing in growth industries. When they do take gains, they want them to be long term. Two, they prefer capital gains to dividends, which means their portfolios can be more volatile than those that emphasize dividend-paying stocks. Three, they avoid concentrated initial positions, because they have the potential to grow in such size as to make the portfolio dangerously underdiversified. Four, they try to avoid rebalancing the portfolio, because this realizes gains. Five, they 'harvest' losses. In other words, they are quick to take losses so they can be used to offset gains. Six, their decision making includes taxes. Sophisticated managers have a capital gains 'budget.' They restrict realizing capital gains to the extent they can add value by switching."

Jacobs is quick to point out there are some negatives to the restrictions of a tax-aware strategy. "First, there is a clear temptation not to sell deteriorating stocks quickly enough," he notes. "Also, it is possible to become overexposed in specific asset classes or sectors, because rebalancing is restricted. Over the short run, tax-aware strategies may reduce performance. In addition, keep in mind that heavy redemptions by other shareholders can force the fund to realize capital gains, which will then be distributed to the remaining shareholders." It further goes without saying that if you sell out of one of these funds before the 18-month holding period has passed, you will have to pay taxes on any short-term gains.

Reason for Recommendation

J.P. Morgan Tax Aware U.S. Equity keeps its portfolio fully invested at all times. Manager Terry Banet ranks stocks in each sector according to relative value, using a proprietary model, and seeks to maintain a sector-neutral portfolio of undervalued companies. "The fund holds about 86 stocks," Jacobs says. "Consequently, it will be more volatile and hopefully achieve better results than an index fund. It is not sector neutral, meaning that the manager does overweight or underweight specific sectors."

Minimum Initial Investment: $2,500

(Available without a transaction fee from Schwab, Fidelity, and Jack White)

Contact Information: J.P. Morgan Tax-Aware U.S. Equity Fund
522 Fifth Avenue
New York, NY 10036
(800) 521-5411
www.jpmorgan.com

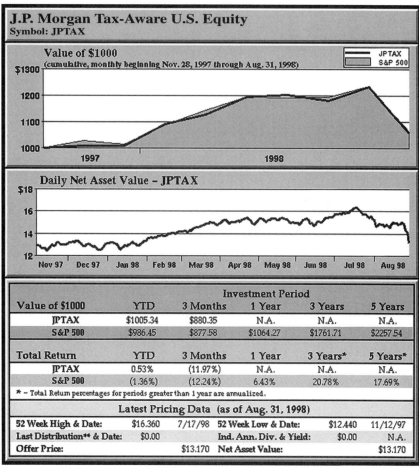

J.P. Morgan Tax-Aware U.S. Equity
Symbol: JPTAX

Source: IDD Information Services

Investment Period					
Value of $1000	**YTD**	**3 Months**	**1 Year**	**3 Years**	**5 Years**
JPTAX	$1005.34	$880.35	N.A.	N.A.	N.A.
S&P 500	$986.45	$877.58	$1064.27	$1761.71	$2257.54

Total Return	YTD	3 Months	1 Year	3 Years*	5 Years*
JPTAX	0.53%	(11.97%)	N.A.	N.A.	N.A.
S&P 500	(1.36%)	(12.24%)	6.43%	20.78%	17.69%

* – Total Return percentages for periods greater than 1 year are annualized.

Latest Pricing Data (as of Aug. 31, 1998)				
52 Week High & Date:	$16.360	7/17/98	52 Week Low & Date:	$12.440	11/12/97
Last Distribution** & Date:	$0.00		Ind. Ann. Div. & Yield:	$0.00	N.A.
Offer Price:		$13.170	Net Asset Value:		$13.170

Top 10 Holdings	Key Statistics	
Warner-Lambert	Sales Load (max)	0.00%
EMC/Mass	Redemption Charge (max)	1.00%
Procter & Gamble	Expense Ratio	0.85%
Mobil	Management Fee	0.45%
Exxon	12b-1 Marketing Fees	0.00%
Fannie Mae	PE Ratio	29.09
Bristol-Myers Squibb	Dividend Yield	0.59%
IBM	Turnover Ratio	N/A
Allied Signal	Beta Factor	N/A
Wal-Mart Stores	Total Assets	$73 Mil.

MARSICO GROWTH & INCOME

Bob Markman
Markman Capital Management

Manager: Thomas Marsico
Style: Large-Cap/Growth

Fund Profile

When Tom Marsico left his high-profile job at the Janus Group at the end of 1997, media speculation abounded as to the reason behind his decision. Marsico had successfully managed the $6 billion Janus Twenty fund to a 22.38 percent annualized return from January 31, 1988 to August 7,1997. That compared favorably to an 18.20 percent return for the S&P 500. He also posted stellar returns with the Janus Growth & Income Fund, which began on May 31, 1991. From that date to August 7, 1997, Janus Growth & Income grew at 21.19 percent annually, compared to 18.59 percent for the S&P 500.

Investment manager and fund analyst Bob Markman says from his perspective, the reason for Marsico's departure is pretty straight forward. "I think he just wanted to run his own shop," Markman contends. "There are a lot of very strong, good people at Janus. Money management is no different than any other personality-oriented business. There can only be one lead dog in the sled. If you're not the lead dog, the scenery never changes. Janus is so rich in incredible talent that I think Marsico decided he could either remain part of a talented team, or leave and have his name on the door. In this kind of business, having your name on the door is quite attractive, and that's the decision Marsico made. I don't think it was any more complicated than that."

Once Marsico struck out on his own, he created two new funds that look like clones of his previous offerings at Janus. That gives investors, in Markman's opinion, a chance to enjoy some great wine served up in a fresh new bottle. "There are few things I like better than new funds run by experienced managers," Markman says. "The manager won't always tell you this because they have other agendas. However, any objective observer will confirm that, all things being equal, a new fund is a much more potent vehicle than an existing fund. You have better cash inflows, relative to outflows, and you don't have any dead wood stakes in the portfolio. You're starting with a fresh slate, and the portfolio tends to be sharper because of that." Besides, Markman says, Marsico clearly knows what he's doing. "What makes his performance at Janus stand out even more is that he was running

151

some very large funds. To be able to make the kinds of gains he did with that much money is pretty impressive. You take that same brain power and management skill and use it on a new fund, where he's got the flexibility to buy and sell whatever he wants, and I think you have a very potent mixture."

Of Marsico's two offerings, Markman especially likes Growth & Income. "I would put the words growth and income in very small type," Markman says. "Roughly 25 percent of the portfolio is supposed to be in securities with income-producing potential. But for all intents and purposes, this is a growth-oriented fund. It is one of the racier entrants in the category." The portfolio will normally contain around 40 stocks, sporting a mixture of large-cap brand names with strong franchises and global reach. Marsico favors stocks with earnings growth potential not recognized by the market at large. He also likes managements that aren't afraid to institute change, if it will help to improve the overall business.

Another leg of Marsico's investment approach is to choose stocks based on broad themes. "We seek to invest with, and not against, the major social, economic and cultural trends taking place in the world," Marsico notes. "Once an idea has emerged, we look for companies that are well positioned to capitalize on it. We subject these to a disciplined process of analysis, designed to move quickly to a decision. This process involves both top-down and bottom-up elements. From the top, we examine the environmental factors—economic, social, and political—that support a particular company's ability to grow. From the bottom, we analyze fundamentals to determine the present future value of the company as an investment." Marsico will sell a position when there is a change which negates his reason for buying it in the first place, or whenever there is an adverse event that puts the company's competitive position in jeopardy.

Reason for Recommendation

In addition to Marsico's proven track record and the perceived "new fund" advantage, Markman favors Marsico Growth & Income because of its large-cap bias. "Even though I'm very bullish on the market, and expect a rising tide to lift all boats, I would rather be in a big boat than a small boat right now," Markman says. "I think we've entered a long-term era where large companies will dominate. That shouldn't be much of a surprise if you work backwards and think in terms of our global economy. The companies that are going to do best are those with operations all over the world. This fund is perfectly positioned to benefit from this."

Minimum Initial Investment: $2,500 ($1,000 for IRAs)

(Available without a transaction fee from Schwab, Fidelity, and Jack White)

Contact Information: Marsico Growth & Income Fund
P.O. Box 3210
Milwaukee, WI 53201-3210
(888) 860-8686
www.marsicofunds.com

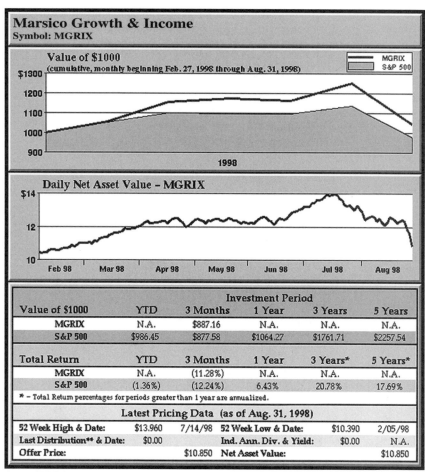

Marsico Growth & Income
Symbol: MGRIX

Value of $1000
(cumulative, monthly beginning Feb. 27, 1998 through Aug. 31, 1998)

MGRIX
S&P 500

1998

Daily Net Asset Value - MGRIX

Feb 98   Mar 98   Apr 98   May 98   Jun 98   Jul 98   Aug 98

Value of $1000	YTD	3 Months	Investment Period 1 Year	3 Years	5 Years
MGRIX	N.A.	$887.16	N.A.	N.A.	N.A.
S&P 500	$986.45	$877.58	$1064.27	$1761.71	$2257.54

Total Return	YTD	3 Months	1 Year	3 Years*	5 Years*
MGRIX	N.A.	(11.28%)	N.A.	N.A.	N.A.
S&P 500	(1.36%)	(12.24%)	6.43%	20.78%	17.69%

* – Total Return percentages for periods greater than 1 year are annualized.

Latest Pricing Data (as of Aug. 31, 1998)

52 Week High & Date:	$13.960	7/14/98	52 Week Low & Date:	$10.390	2/05/98
Last Distribution** & Date:	$0.00		Ind. Ann. Div. & Yield:	$0.00	N.A.
Offer Price:		$10.850	Net Asset Value:		$10.850

Source: IDD Information Services

Top 10 Holdings	Key Statistics	
Ford Motor Co.	Sales Load (max)	0.00%
Dell Computer	Redemption Charge (max)	0.00%
Pfizer	Expense Ratio	N/A
Warner-Lambert	Management Fee	0.84%
Citicorp	12b-1 Marketing Fees	0.25%
Merrill Lynch	PE Ratio	N/A
Delta & Pine Land	Dividend Yield	N/A
Time Warner	Turnover Ratio	N/A
Volkswagen	Beta Factor	N/A
Northern Telecom	Total Assets	$149 Mil.

AMERICAN AADVANTAGE
INTERNATIONAL EQUITY

Tricia O. Rothschild
Morningstar Mutual Funds

Manager: Team Managed
Style: International/Value-Oriented

Fund Profile

What does an airline know about running a mutual fund? Not much. That's why the folks at American Airlines hire outside managers at leading investment firms to oversee their family of mutual funds. You might be wondering how American got into the fund business in the first place. The airline's AMR Investments unit is a multibillion dollar asset management firm that has long overseen the pension funds for American's employees. A few years ago, it realized it could branch out even further by starting a series of funds and making them available to the public. Some funds even offer mileage points in American's frequent flyer program.

Now that you have some background information, let's talk about Tricia Rothschild's favorite fund for 1999. It's the American AAdvantage International Equity Fund. Like all offerings in the American family, International Equity is a value-oriented fund. It is run by leading managers from Hotchkis and Wiley, Morgan Stanley Asset Management, and Templeton Investment Counsel. "This is what I call one stop shopping for a trio of great international managers," Rothschild says. "Each investment firm gets to run one-third of the portfolio. So you have the skills of three top-notch managers combined in one portfolio." Specifically, the managers include Sarah Ketterer of Hotchkis and Wiley International, Dominic Caldecott of Morgan Stanley International Equity, and Gary Motyl of Franklin Capital Accumulator.

While I mentioned that all three of these managers have a value orientation in running their own funds, Morningstar's Rothschild notes that they each pursue value in different ways. "The other thing is they tend to stick only with the developed markets and rarely venture into emerging regions," she adds. "This is truly a large-cap international fund." In fact, by prospectus, the managers are limited to investing in the following countries: Australia, Austria, Belgium, Canada, Denmark, Finland, France, Germany, Hong Kong, Ireland, Italy, Japan, Malaysia, Mexico, the Netherlands, New Zealand, Norway, Portugal, Singapore, South Korea, Spain, Sweden, Switzerland, and the United Kingdom. Individual securities are selected based upon a country's economic outlook, market valuations and potential changes in currency exchange rates. Every manager looks for undervalued companies with above-average growth expectations. "The overall allocations are pretty typical for a foreign stock fund," Rothschild observes. "It has roughly 60 percent in Europe, which I like. The changes taking place in Europe are really fundamentally progressive. There's a revolution going on. I think the market there could be very promising for several years to come. Another 10 percent of the fund is in the Asian Pacific, with an additional 10 percent in Japan." The highly diversified portfolio normally contains some 300 securities.

At least 80 percent of the fund's holdings will be kept in overseas stocks at all times, with the remainder in highly rated non-U.S. debt securities. The fund can also trade forward foreign currency contracts, which are derivatives. This would be done when managers wanted to hedge their exposure to currency fluctuations.

Reason for Recommendation

Although this fund has an impressive record of its own, Rothschild points out that each manager has posted pristine performance at their respective firms as well. "Buying this fund is like combining three of the best international funds into one," she says. "What's more, you would have to pay a load to buy the Templeton fund, and the Morgan Stanley fund is only available to institutions. This is a way for individuals to still get access to these managers in a no-load vehicle."

One more thing: American offers funds in three separate classes, including PlanAhead, Mileage, and Institutional. The class Rothschild recommends is PlanAhead. This one has the lowest expense ratio. The mileage class allows you to earn one mile in American's frequent flyer program for every $10 you have in the fund, but you wind up paying steeper expenses for that privilege. "You can get your miles some other way," Rothschild offers.

Rothschild further recommends that investors consider owning three separate foreign funds. One would be like this one, which concentrates primarily on the developed markets. The others would be a small-cap international, and an emerging markets fund. "The performance between large and small-caps overseas is incredible," she adds. "There are risks to a plan like this. But over time, you'll get returns that compensate you for those risks. Just remember you will likely need to keep your money in these funds for at least five and probably ten years to fully reap the rewards of this valuable diversification."

Minimum Initial Investment: $2,500

(Available without a transaction fee from Schwab, Fidelity, and Jack White)

Contact Information: American AAdvantage International Equity Fund
P.O. Box 419643
Kansas City, MO 64141-643
(800) 388-3344
www.aafunds.com

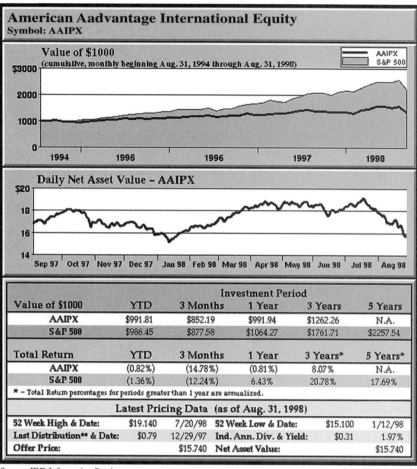

American Aadvantage International Equity
Symbol: AAIPX

Value of $1000
(cumulative, monthly beginning Aug. 31, 1994 through Aug. 31, 1998)

Daily Net Asset Value - AAIPX

Value of $1000	YTD	3 Months	Investment Period 1 Year	3 Years	5 Years
AAIPX	$991.81	$852.19	$991.94	$1262.26	N.A.
S&P 500	$986.45	$877.58	$1064.27	$1761.71	$2257.54

Total Return	YTD	3 Months	1 Year	3 Years*	5 Years*
AAIPX	(0.82%)	(14.78%)	(0.81%)	8.07%	N.A.
S&P 500	(1.36%)	(12.24%)	6.43%	20.78%	17.69%

* – Total Return percentages for periods greater than 1 year are annualized.

Latest Pricing Data (as of Aug. 31, 1998)				
52 Week High & Date:	$19.140	7/20/98	52 Week Low & Date:	$15.100	1/12/98
Last Distribution** & Date:	$0.79	12/29/97	Ind. Ann. Div. & Yield:	$0.31	1.97%
Offer Price:		$15.740	Net Asset Value:	$15.740

Source: IDD Information Services

Top 10 Holdings	Key Statistics	
Nestlé	Sales Load (max)	0.00%
Elf Aquitaine	Redemption Charge (max)	0.00%
ING Groep	Expense Ratio	1.14%
Akzo Nobel	Management Fee	0.10%
Telefonica	12b-1 Marketing Fees	0.00%
BTR	PE Ratio	24.95
Groupe Danone	Dividend Yield	1.67%
CGU	Turnover Ratio	15.00%
B-A-T Industries	Beta Factor	0.53
Philips Electronics (NV)	Total Assets	$44 Mil.

T. ROWE PRICE INTERNATIONAL

Earl Osborn
Bingham, Osborn & Scarborough

Manager: Martin Wade
Style: International Growth

Fund Profile

T. Rowe Price International Stock is one the oldest and most broad-based funds of its kind. "It's a real core international holding," says Earl Osborn, partner at the investment management firm Bingham, Osborn & Scarborough. "An investor who wants to have participation in the world securities markets can simply buy and hold this fund."

The portfolio is managed by Martin Wade and a team of analysts through a joint venture between T. Rowe Price and the London-based Fleming Group. This gives Wade access to Fleming's extensive global network of experts, which have firsthand knowledge of local markets around the world. "The portfolio managers have the ability to effectively deal in a much wider range of countries," Osborn notes. "I firmly believe that in order for an international manager to be successful, he must have a presence in the country he's investing in. The Price-Fleming partnership makes that possible. You can't do this kind of work by sitting in an office in New York and simply reading a foreign newspaper. You've really got to have links to local investment and brokerage firms, which this fund has."

Unlike some of its peers, T. Rowe Price International generally focuses on larger established companies, with proven track records and a history of earnings. Nevertheless, like any international fund, its daily share price will be volatile. All international investing involves special risks, including political uncertainty, unfavorable currency exchange rates, and market illiquidity. Still, Osborn is convinced that devoting up to 25 percent of your portfolio to international investments will help to increase your returns while lowering your risk over time. "Some say you are seeing evidence of an increasing correlation between the U.S. and foreign markets, but I disagree," he says. "In fact, we're witnessing today that overseas markets are moving in the opposite direction, especially in Japan and the Pacific Rim. You see more correlation between Europe and the U.S., but it's not perfect there either. The one correlation argument that I think has validity is that when the U.S. collapses, it tends to pull everything else with it. But absent a major collapse here, I don't think you're seeing an increased correlation." Besides, he adds, nearly two-thirds of the world's stock market value is located overseas.

While it's true that over long periods of time foreign markets as a whole have outperformed the U.S., that hasn't been the case recently. In fact, T. Rowe Price International has returned an average of 10.61 percent annually over the past decade, compared to 18.1 percent for the S&P 500. Osborn has a good explanation for that. "The primary reason for this underperformance is that Japan has been an absolute disaster over this period, in terms of stock investing, and that has pulled down all international funds," he says. "Just remember we've seen this in reverse before. We saw it in the 1970s, when international markets did better than the U.S. Those are the days when John Templeton made his fame. And I believe we could start seeing that again soon, especially considering the high levels the U.S. market is at now."

T. Rowe Price International currently has about 62 percent of the portfolio invested in Europe, followed by Japan at 21 percent, Latin American and the Far East at 7 percent each, and 3 percent everywhere else. These weightings tend to stay pretty consistent. In Europe, Wade has concentrated much of his money in the United Kingdom, France, Germany, Switzerland, and the Netherlands. "In Europe, we have seen an encouraging picture of improving economic growth, rising exports and currencies that have now stabilized against the U.S. dollar," Wade reports. "Valuations in Europe look reasonable, and there is the added interest of corporate restructuring as companies position themselves for the European Monetary Union. Turning to the Far East, clearly the prospects are less certain, and it will take some time for the less-developed economies of Asia to put themselves back on sounder footing. The important point here is that stock markets always tend to overdo things, and taking a longer-term view, attractive valuations are beginning to emerge. The stock market there lists some of the best-managed companies in the world, and we believe it is right to take advantage of current weakness by adding to our favorites."

Reason for Recommendation

In addition to his conviction that investors need to have some money overseas this year, Osborn singles out T. Rowe Price International for three primary reasons. First, it has a low expense ratio of 0.85 percent, compared to around 1.4 percent for the average international fund. Secondly, it has a very low annual turnover rate of around 16 percent. Finally, the fund has a great deal of consistency in its management structure. "It has never been a high turnover fund, never had high expenses, and maintains a consistent set of world allocations," he observes. "And it holds a lot of stocks, which reduces your risk."

Minimum Initial Investment: $2,500 ($1,000 for IRAs)

Contact Information: T. Rowe Price International Stock Fund
100 East Pratt Street
Baltimore, MD 21202
(800) 225-5132
www.troweprice.com

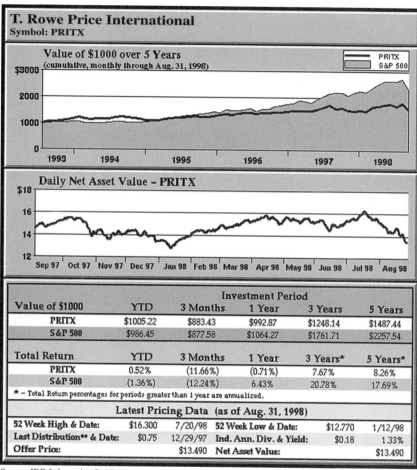

T. Rowe Price International
Symbol: PRITX

Value of $1000 over 5 Years
(cumulative, monthly through Aug. 31, 1998)

PRITX
S&P 500

Daily Net Asset Value – PRITX

Value of $1000	YTD	3 Months	1 Year	3 Years	5 Years
PRITX	$1005.22	$883.43	$992.87	$1248.14	$1487.44
S&P 500	$986.45	$877.58	$1064.27	$1761.71	$2257.54

Total Return	YTD	3 Months	1 Year	3 Years*	5 Years*
PRITX	0.52%	(11.66%)	(0.71%)	7.67%	8.26%
S&P 500	(1.36%)	(12.24%)	6.43%	20.78%	17.69%

* – Total Return percentages for periods greater than 1 year are annualized.

Latest Pricing Data (as of Aug. 31, 1998)

52 Week High & Date:	$16.300	7/20/98	52 Week Low & Date:	$12.770	1/12/98
Last Distribution** & Date:	$0.75	12/29/97	Ind. Ann. Div. & Yield:	$0.18	1.33%
Offer Price:		$13.490	Net Asset Value:		$13.490

Source: IDD Information Services

Top 10 Holdings	Key Statistics	
Reserve Investment	Sales Load (max)	0.00%
Natl. Westminster Bank	Redemption Charge (max)	0.00%
Royal Dutch Petroleum	Expense Ratio	1.85%
SmithKline Beecham	Management Fee	0.35%
Nestlé	12b-1 Marketing Fees	0.00%
Wolters Kluwer	PE Ratio	32.22
ING Groep	Dividend Yield	1.25%
Diageo	Turnover Ratio	15.80%
Glaxo Wellcome	Beta Factor	0.64
Kredietbank	Total Assets	$10.5 Bil.

part

3

UP CLOSE
WITH THE
EXPERTS

GETTING TO KNOW WALL STREET'S FINEST

As always, this is my favorite part of the book. Now that you've read about the many stocks and mutual funds my distinguished panelists are buying in 1999, it's time to learn a little bit more about what makes them so great. What follows are complete biographies of each expert, presented in alphabetical order. You'll find a picture (so you can see they're not only savvy, but also good-looking), followed by a brief overview of what they do and how they got where they are. Every profile ends with thoughts on the biggest mistakes investors make and strategies for success in the stock market. Also included is the panelist's occupation, birth date, educational background, market outlook, and the best and worst investments they've ever made.

Each luminary has a different way of choosing stocks and/or a unique field of expertise, so you will get a truly diversified list of disciplines and techniques to help you become a better buyer and seller of both stocks and mutual funds.

I'm often asked what characteristics the world's greatest investors share. After doing some careful analysis, I came up with five traits they all seem to have in common. First, they have adopted very specific strategies that they consistently follow, regardless of what's happening with the overall market. Clearly, there isn't just one technique that works all the time. Nevertheless, if you develop a system you understand and heed without fail, over time you will make a lot of money. Second, the pros are highly suspicious of "hot tips" and anything recommended by a stockbroker. Many go as far as to say people should avoid taking the advice of a broker altogether, because most are mere salespeople who don't know much about the market to begin with. Third, the masters don't pay attention to what they see and hear on the news. Instead, they ignore the day-to-day direction of the Dow and focus on uncovering new ideas while closely following the holdings in their own portfolios. Fourth, the wealthiest investors avoid market timing. They are always fully invested, although the specific stocks and funds they hold might change depending on their outlook for such things as interest rates and the economy. Fifth, and this should come as no surprise, the gurus all agree that diversification is the secret to achieving long-term investment success.

It's interesting to note that only a handful of these experts actually majored in business or planned to invest other people's money for a living. I guess that goes to show you don't need a Harvard MBA to become a first-class portfolio manager. It's also striking how open and easygoing most of these living investment legends are. Even though they work in a fast-paced, often frenetic industry, these folks have a great deal of confidence and faith in their decisions. They aren't constant traders, yet are willing to accept both success and failure, and aren't afraid to move on when they're wrong. Without question, they understand the true essence of what makes the stock market work.

In addition to giving you a lot of insight into who these people are, the profiles will teach you how to pick stocks and mutual funds, when to sell, and what to expect from your investments in the future. You are sure to uncover valuable advice you can profit from for decades to come.

One last observation I will leave you with is that going into 1999, most of my panelists remain optimistic, but wouldn't be surprised to see some sort correction during the year. More importantly, they warn that stock market returns are likely to be more in line with their historic norms of between 8 and 10 percent for the foreseeable future. In other words, it's time to lower your expectations. If my panelists are on the money again, as they have been in the past, careful stock and fund selection will be of vital importance. Now let's hear from them about how to properly pick your investments now and into the future.

JOSEPH BATTIPAGLIA

Gruntal & Co.

Joe Battipaglia may be the most bullish investment strategist on Wall Street today. He's telling Gruntal & Co.'s aggressive clients to keep 100 percent of their assets in equities this year. But that's nothing new for Battipaglia. He's been positive on the market since getting into the investment business back in 1982. "There are really three reasons I feel so good about stocks," he explains. "In descending order, you have diminishing inflation, the fact that economic activity has been on an upswing, and a consumer confidence level that keeps improving. These conditions merit that investors have a substantial exposure to equities."

Battipaglia was introduced to the stock tables in *The Wall Street Journal* by his father at a young age. But after getting an MBA from the Wharton School, he went into the corporate world, as a financial analyst with Exxon. "My initial position was to work on five-year business plans," he says. "I learned what it meant to be in a pyramidal organization, where you were expected to advance only in your particular discipline." He wanted to explore other opportunities though. He was investing his own portfolio in stocks on the side and decided that might be fun to do full-time. "I liked the entrepreneurial and risk-taking aspects of the investment industry, plus structurally investment firms are pretty much on a horizontal plane," he adds.

So Battipaglia got on the phone and started calling some of his classmates and contacts from Wharton. Within a few days, he had offers to become everything from an odd-lot bond trader to an institutional salesman. "In 1981, I took a position with a small broker-dealer out of Philadelphia called Elkins & Co.," he says. "I was a man of many hats. I did some analysis, helped out in the underwriting of investment banking, and worked on the roll-out of an IRA product. As the bear market we were in at the time started to wither and die, Elkins decided to sell out to Bache, which viewed everyone at the firm as either a salesman or overhead. It was clear to me I had to tell them I was a salesman in order to keep my position. So I spent one year as a broker, thinking that would give me enough time to figure out what my other choices were."

In his search for new opportunities, he came across Gruntal & Co., which had just 300 brokers in the New York area and was looking to establish a presence in Philadelphia. "The firm wanted to build up its research department, which consisted essentially of two people," Battipaglia notes. "I joined as the third person and started following anything that was interesting. My first recommendations included AT&T, Centocor, and Vanity Fair Corporation." In 1986, Gruntal asked him to come to New York, and four years later he was named director of research and given a larger staff of analysts. "I became head of our in-house money management business in

1993," he adds. "Then, in early 1997, I was named chief investment strategist and am now a partner as well."

There are two main focuses of Battipaglia's job now. First, he gives an overall recommendation as to how much exposure clients should have to equities. As you know, for those willing to accept the volatility, he thinks that percentage should be quite high. And he doesn't expect this bullish environment to end anytime soon. "In fact, we are at a point now where inflation is running at an even lower level than the best expectations, and will continue to do so, spurred on by a recovery in Europe, ultimate recovery in Asia, good economic performance out of China, and a revitalized U.S. consumer," he predicts. What about the argument that stocks are overvalued, given the market's meteoric rise? Battipaglia doesn't buy it. "I think you've got to take a top-down approach to looking at markets and flip it over," he insists. "The indexes are giving an unrealistic view of what's going on with the entire market. If you look at the individual stocks that make up the Dow 30, for example, you will see the PE ratio of the individual stocks is much lower than the overall index. Besides, capital flows to where returns are the best. I would argue that because conditions are so good, money will continue to flow into U.S. equities. Admittedly, when the fundamentals change, you'll see a rapid flow out of stocks. But I don't see that happening in the foreseeable future."

The second thing Battipaglia does is look for specific companies that clients of the firm should consider investing in. His favorite themes currently include pharmaceuticals, transportation, financial services, and telecommunications. "When evaluating individual stocks, I'm looking for what I would call an anomaly in the market," he shares. "That is the market's valuation of the stock is not on point with the company's true fundamental condition. This could be caused by investors not realizing how strong the company's franchise is, an event that causes it to temporarily stumble, or a positive unexpected new product or development."

Occupation: Chairman of Investment Policy, Gruntal & Co.
          New York, New York
Birth Date: October 29, 1955
Education: BA, Boston College, 1976
          MBA, University of Pennsylvania, Wharton School, 1978
Biggest Mistake Investors Make: "Becoming too emotionally attached to the investments they have made."
Best Investment: Buying pharmaceutical stocks in the 1970s and holding on.
Worst Investment: Never investing in Microsoft.
Advice: "Have a clear sense of the broad fundamentals and stay focused on the creation of company value."
Market Outlook: Bullish.

ALAN BOND

Bond Procope Capital Management

In Alan Bond's mind, there's only one word to describe the stock market environment U.S. investors have enjoyed over the past several years: "incredible." Nevertheless, he claims he's still finding plenty of good ideas for his money. "We are always out buying on the pullbacks," he says.

It was a vacation to Disney World at the age of ten that first set the stage for Bond's successful career on Wall Street. After returning home to Queens, New York from the trip, his parents gave him the responsibility of deciding which stocks his $3,000 college fund would be invested in. "We had just been to Disney World, the place was packed, so I said, 'Let's buy some Disney,'" he remembers. "I also thought we should buy some Delta Airlines, since it was the preferred provider of transportation to Disneyland." He rounded out his portfolio with shares of GM. "Those three stocks helped to pay for Dartmouth College and the Harvard Business School," he says.

After Harvard, Bond joined Goldman Sachs and pursued his goal of being involved with the stock market full time. "I was what's called a research salesman on the institutional desk," he explains. "I would advise portfolio managers on what they ought to buy or sell. But ultimately I wanted to be the trigger puller and make those investment decisions myself, as opposed to telling others this is what I really think you ought to do." That opportunity came almost three years later with W.R. Lazard & Co., which brought Bond on board to develop its equity management division. By 1991, however, he longed for something different. "The firm was changing course and had many different divisions," he recalls. "I told the founder I loved what I was doing so much that I wanted to pursue it without the distractions of other divisions and so forth. I wanted to start my own firm."

Bond went out on his own at the age of 30 and now manages more than $500 million for institutions and wealthy clients. He admits starting his own firm today would be much more difficult. "There are so many firms and mutual funds that it makes it hard for someone new to stand out," he observes. While Bond has never invested professionally during a bear market, he expects that eventually he will. "I think there is something to the 'New Era' thinking, in that productivity enhancements in the last five years have really driven what I call USA, Inc., to be more efficient," he surmises. "But this can't go on forever, and there are all kinds of unforeseen crises that can hit at any time."

Still, Bond feels the opportunities for individual investors have never been greater. "I've got to believe you have more people following the stock market now than ever in history," he maintains. "That's probably due to a lot of factors, including people being more worried about their retirement benefits than past generations. Plus, with the market making double digit gains year after year, they're looking at passbook interest rates and opting for another alternative that's more compelling, and that's the stock market."

Bond manages portfolios following three different objectives: aggressive growth, large-cap growth, and mid-cap growth. "I start my screening for stocks based on a set of quantitative criteria," he shares. "If I can find companies trading at a discount to their growth rate, I zero in on those first. I look for earnings growth of better than 15 percent over a three- to five-year period. I look for a beta of typically less than 1.5. I want the return on equity to be better than 15 percent. I also prefer a price-to-cash flow ratio of less than ten."

With his ideas in hand, Bond crafts his portfolios. "I think of these stocks as lumps of clay and then begin to decide what to do with them," he offers. "I rank them based on relative valuation, earnings strength, and profitability. I'm trying to identify companies that are, for example, growing at 20 percent, yet selling for ten times earnings."

After the numbers have been crunched and filtered, Bond performs fundamental analysis, what he calls the "meat" of the process. "I'll go out and talk with top company executives and see how happy and enthusiastic the workers are," he says. His sell discipline is equally rigid. "Typically, once I've achieved a 25 to 30 percent return on a holding, I'll take some profits," he says. "I also generally get out of a stock whenever it declines 15 percent from my cost. Another test I now perform is I take the stock's 52-week high and my cost, add both numbers together, and divide by two. This is my threshold of pain for my winners. If the price falls below that magic number, I'll sell."

Bond is now preparing to teach his own two young children the same investment lessons his father taught him more than two decades ago. "My six-year-old daughter already asks me each day how the market did," he says.

Occupation: President, Bond Procope Capital Management
New York, New York
Birth Date: August 8, 1961
Education: BA, Dartmouth College, 1983
MBA, Harvard Business School, 1987
Biggest Mistake Investors Make: "Staying with stocks for too long, and not having the discipline to sell."
Best Investment: Lucent Technologies (Bought the stock as an IPO for $25 in 1996. Today it trades above $120 a share.)
Worst Investment: CML (Purchased it for $15 in 1991, rode it to $30, sold it for $11, and watched in go down to $3 in less than two years.)
Advice: "Establish an investment discipline and stick with it."
Market Outlook: Bullish.

JANET BROWN

Janet Brown will tell you what die-hard indexers have been preaching for years: the brilliance of a top-performing mutual fund manager rests solely on being in the right place at the right time. "There are lots of great stock pickers, but there is a tremendous variance in their returns from year to year," she observes. "That's why I believe your best chance for beating the market is by following the leaders."

Brown and her former boss, Burton Berry, devised a unique strategy for selecting funds in the late 1970s. They call it "upgrading." The results of their research are printed each month in *NoLoad Fund*X*, a newsletter published by Brown's firm. "The first thing we do is classify the funds in our database by risk," she explains. "We then look at current performance over the past twelve, six, three, and one month periods. Next, we take a simple performance average during those four periods, give funds in the top 15 some bonus points, and rank each one by its performance-based score." It's a purely quantitative process, which calls for blindly purchasing funds based on returns alone. The best five funds in each risk category are recommended for purchase. When a fund's performance drops, thus booting it out of the top five, Brown recommends switching into another winner.

The logic behind this system is pretty straightforward. Every fund manager has a certain investing style which works well in some environments and poorly in others. "For instance, large-cap growth stock pickers have been doing well over the last few years, because that's where the market leadership has been," Brown says. "But there will be periods when small-cap managers do better. There are also certain sectors that come and go out of vogue. Investing is quite cyclical, because of changing economic fundamentals. It's easy to identify areas of outperformance after the fact, but they're impossible to forecast."

Brown's discipline calls for staying fully invested at all times. If it works as designed, you'll always be in the right place at the right time. "The system should continually keep in you those funds that have gotten it right, either because they're in the best stocks or sectors. They might be in cash if the market's going down," she adds. "The system may even steer you to international funds. Unlike most asset allocators, I don't believe you should always keep a certain percentage overseas. I would only invest outside of this country when foreign markets are doing well." An outperforming fund usually maintains its momentum for an average of six months, though Brown says some have stayed in the spotlight for as long as two and a half years.

Following the leaders means paying capital gains taxes each time you make a trade. In retirement accounts, that's not a concern. But in taxable portfolios, Brown admits it doesn't always make sense to switch around so much. "You really have to look at whether upgrading will result in enough increased performance to make the trade pay off," she admits. "To be truthful, in the last few years it often hasn't, since you've been able to get good results in almost all domestic market environments."

Brown entered the fund business through a rather unconventional channel. After graduating from college with a degree in architecture and art, she went off to Brussels with a friend. She needed a job and wound up working for a large insurance brokerage firm as a fund administrator. "The company sold mutual funds, mostly to U.S. servicemen," she recalls. "In order to do my job, I had to get licensed. I began to study investments, and particularly funds. I quickly concluded that no-loads were the way to go." Unfortunately, her European employer only peddled load funds, which carried steep 8.5 percent sales charges. Brown moved back to San Francisco three years later and thought about becoming a stockbroker. "I knew I wanted to be in the investment business, but found brokers did more sales work than investment management," she says. "I also felt there was a conflict of interest between the broker and the client, since it was a commission-based relationship. Then a friend of mine introduced me to Burt Berry, who had started an investment firm using only no-load funds. He hired me as his assistant in 1978 when we had less than $10 million under management. The two of us developed this upgrading strategy." Last year, Berry sold most of the firm to Brown and her partners, although he still helps out with some of the fund research.

Brown's upgrading system seems to be effective. *The Hulbert Financial Digest* reports that the *NoLoad Fund*X* conservative growth portfolio has managed to beat the S&P 500 by about 2 percentage points annually. "It's not complicated, but it really does work," she says.

Occupation: President, DAL Investment Company
San Francisco, California
Birth Date: November 10, 1950
Education: BA, California State University, Hayward, 1974
Biggest Mistake Investors Make: "Being too conservative and not taking a longer-term view."
Best Investment: SAFECO Growth Fund (Bought three years ago and has just held on. Since then, it's up more than 175 percent.)
Worst Investment: Matthews Korea (Purchased in mid-1996, and sold out a month later at a 15 percent loss.)
Advice: "Take a long-term view and stay with investment managers who are doing well in the current market environment."
Market Outlook: Cautious.

PETER BROWN

When Peter Brown was growing up in New Jersey during the 1950s, his parents told him he had to become a doctor, lawyer, or, at worst, an engineer. "Engineering was the least unpalatable alternative," he concluded. "So I wound up going to MIT and getting a chemical engineering degree." He worked for Allied Chemical for about four years before going back to school for an MBA. "I wanted to learn more about operations research and statistics," he explains. "I went on to do long range planning for both Kraft Foods and Celanese Chemical. I used to run linear programming models on computers that would take eight hours to run. Today, using an Excel spreadsheet, you can do the same thing in less than a minute."

In the early 1970s, Brown got a call from Harold Evensky, his wife's cousin. Evensky told him he should come check out Florida. Evensky was working in construction with Brown's father-in-law and was able to coax him into making the move. "Harold and I eventually decided to start our own building business," Brown recalls. "Harold did the building, and I did the financial work."

But then Brown got involved with a Colorado alternate energy company called Bio-Gas. "It was founded by some friends of mine," he says. "I helped them prepare the prospectuses for a couple of private offerings. When the company went public, they asked me to come run it. The building business was starting to get lousy anyway because interest rates were going through the roof, so I moved my family to Colorado." After four years, Brown got homesick, since his entire family lived on the east coast. By then, Evensky had become a stockbroker in Florida. He coaxed Brown into starting a financial planning firm with him. "In 1985, we set up a broker-dealer, because we felt that was the only way we could make any money," Brown says. "We didn't have hopes of making big dollars in financial planning."

In a period of six months, Brown got all the securities licenses he could. However, he and Evensky (a former *Wall Street's Picks* panelist) worked on commission and weren't making much money. Then along came a new program from discount broker Charles Schwab, which enabled independent planners to manage money on a fee basis using no-load funds. Evensky and Brown immediately switched over. "We decided we had to evolve out of the commission business," Brown explains. "We were never comfortable with the commission concept, and the only worse salesperson in the world than Harold is me."

With a lot of hard work and hustling, Evensky, Brown, and their two new partners have managed to grow the business from $5 million in assets in 1992 to more than $300 million today. Their minimum client account is $2 million. On the fixed-income side of a portfolio, Brown buys individual bonds, since he feels that's a more cost-effective way to go. But when it comes to equities, he believes in funds all the way.

"The theory I have is that you can't be an expert on everything," he reasons. "I don't have the expertise to select securities in the various areas of the market, be it large-cap, small-cap, or international. That's why I spend my time looking for managers who can do a much better job for a low fee." In the early days of his business, Brown bought actively managed funds almost exclusively. He now feels his clients are better off in index funds. "I got tired of the mixed performance," he rations. "Our clients want pretty much market-like returns with low expenses, and that's what we're offering. We set the allocation policy and build the portfolio around that. On the equity side, we start with a core fund tied to the S&P 500. We also use institutional passively managed funds to cover other areas of the U.S. and the international markets."

However, Brown will still occasionally use active managers for specialized sectors, such as small-cap growth and the emerging country markets. "One thing I look for is style consistency," he adds. "If a small-cap manager tells me he's working on a momentum basis, I want to make sure he's holding stocks that fit in with that philosophy. I also look at past performance and volatility. My clients have high net worths. Their biggest concern is not losing money. They want to stay ahead of inflation and get a decent return. We're not going to produce returns consistent with an aggressive growth strategy. Then again, I suspect our clients will lose less when the market goes through some bad times."

Brown keeps his portfolios fully invested at all times, rationalizing that it's impossible to make good market timing decisions. "When you do that you're making a guess about an economy that's a sample of one," he says. "There are just too many different exogenous factors out there for you to ever be right."

Occupation: Principal Partner, Evensky, Brown, Katz & Levitt
                 Coral Gables, Florida
Birth Date: March 29, 1940
Education: BS, Massachusetts Institute of Technology, 1962
               MBA, New York University, 1968
Biggest Mistake Investors Make: "Going after the winners."
Best Investment: Starting his financial planning business (He invested just $200 of his own money, borrowed the rest, and today makes a pretty penny managing some $300 million.)
Worst Investment: Managers Intermediate Mortgage Fund (Bought it six years ago, and when interest rates spiked up, lost 15 percent of his investment.)
Advice: "Stay the course. Select your investment policy and stick with it."
Market Outlook: Cautious, but turning more bearish all the time. "We're beyond all of the historical norms," he warns.

SUSAN BYRNE

Westwood Management

Could it be that Susan Byrne is going from portfolio manager to supermodel? When I called to chat with her recently, her assistant told me she was out on a day-long photo shoot for *Money* magazine. Once Byrne and I finally caught up, she admitted to not even being sure what the story was all about. "I don't know if I'm going to be on the cover or exactly what they have in mind," she said. This celebrity treatment afforded to fund managers is a relatively new phenomenon. "When I first started out in this industry, you dealt in a much quieter institutional setting," Byrne explains. "If your name was mentioned in the paper, clients usually frowned on that. But with this incredible bull run we've been having, the whole stock market has become an industry unto itself."

Growing up in Pasadena, California, Byrne didn't even know what Wall Street was. Following her short-lived first marriage, she headed for New York at the age of 24 with her 4-year-old son and a lot of ambition. "I thought New York would be a neat place to go and start my grownup life," she recalls. "I had my choice of three secretarial jobs, and the one that paid the most was with E.F. Hutton." By always volunteering, overselling her abilities, and yearning to make more money, she eventually was able to talk her way into a job as a research editor at another brokerage firm. "It wasn't a very glamorous job," she admits. "I took all of the material from the analysts and edited it into proper English."

From there, she became a member of the investment team, specializing in political economics, an area she studied in college. "I loved this job and felt I had really found something that I not only enjoyed, but also could make a contribution in," she shares. "I was also encouraged by my clients. They would say, 'Based on the way you look at things, Susan, you should really consider managing money.'" One thing led to another, and in 1977, she was hired as an apprentice portfolio manager by Banker's Trust. Two-and-a-half years later, she was offered a chance to work as an assistant treasurer and in-house pension fund manager at GAF Corporation. "This job gave me the opportunity to clearly demonstrate an ability to manage money. In the bank you had committees and guidelines. Here I was on my own," she recalls. "I was with them for almost four years, and with their blessing, started my own firm, Westwood Management, on April 1, 1983." GAF was her first client.

Byrne pauses at this point to note that her journey must sound awfully unconventional. But she maintains it's simply a function of the fact that she's over 50 and female. "There was a horrible bear market in the early 1970s, and the securities industry wasn't attracting a bunch of people," she explains. "My first five years in the business were from 1970 to 1975. These were terrible times, and there wasn't a lot of competition. Today the firms want to see a certain type of person from the best and brightest schools."

Still, Byrne admits she started her own company because she knew that was the only way she'd ever become a big player in the business. "I was waiting for these firms to come knock down my door and make me a partner, which was clearly not happening," she explains. "So I decided to start my own company and demonstrate to myself and my peers that I had a talent for managing money." She started with $35 million and today has grown to more than $2 billion in private accounts and mutual funds.

You don't gather that much money unless you know how to make it multiply, and Byrne has clearly proven she does. Her first rule of investing is to avoid losing your capital. "That may sound silly, but it's one of those things people sometimes forget," she says. "I begin with a top-down viewpoint, by looking at what's happening with inflation. If the environment seems right for financial securities, I look at a combination of the expected 12- to 18-month economic cycle, along with the outlook for corporate profits, interest rates, inflation, and the dollar."

She then chooses stocks by searching for a catalyst that can drive a company's share price higher. Once she's found that, she looks at what other analysts are saying about the stock, and will only buy if she thinks they are underestimating its potential. "This sounds easier than it is, because we only own about 40 stocks out of a universe of 6,400. So you can see that we agree with other analysts 95 percent of the time," she notes. "We'll only invest in those companies that we have a high degree of confidence will come through with a positive earnings surprise." Every stock in her portfolio has a price target based on her estimated forward-looking growth rate. Byrne says her primary goal is to buy value stocks that ultimately turn into high growers.

Occupation: President and CIO, Westwood Management
Dallas, Texas
Birth Date: August 5, 1948
Education: Attended but didn't graduate from the University of California at Berkeley
Biggest Mistake Investors Make: "Trying to time the market; if it's long-term money, just put it in the market and forget about it."
Best Investment: Dell Computer (She bought it for a split-adjusted $3.50 a share in 1994 and sold out for $80 in 1997.)
Worst Investment: Trying to buy options some 25 years ago.
Advice: "Set up an investment program and stick to it."
Market Outlook: Cautious.

PHILIP CARRET

Carret and Company

Warren Buffet once said Philip Carret had "the best long-term investment record of anyone in America." He also had one of the longest. This celebrated Wall Street veteran, who passed away in May, 1998, at the age of 101, traced his interest in the profession back to 1919. Having graduated from Harvard and served in the Army Signal Corps, Carret took a job as a bond salesman. He didn't make much money at that, so he talked his way into a writing position at what is now known as *Barron's*. When the head of the Massachusetts Investment Trust came by to chat with the paper's managing editor one day about his concept for forming a mutual fund, a nosy Carret eavesdropped on the conversation. "I got very interested," he recalled. "A short time later, I used money from my family and a few friends to start my own fund."

That was just a few months before the crash of 1929, an event he vividly remembered. "At first it was seen as blowing the froth off the boom, just a temporary setback that really didn't mean anything," he said. "That was a great mistake, but a lot of very important people thought that." Carret's fund, appropriately named Pioneer, went down some 50 percent before the bloodbath was over. Needless to say, it was virtually impossible for him to attract any investors for a number of years after that. He was forced to take other jobs to earn a living, while continuing to run Pioneer on the side.

Carret eventually sold the fund's management company in 1963 to what today is called The Pioneer Group. However, he stayed on as lead manager until 1983. One study shows that a $10,000 investment in the fund on March 1, 1928, with dividends reinvested, is worth more than $69 million today. Carret continued to work three or four days a week as a portfolio manager at the New York investment firm he founded, Carret and Company, up until his death. I was honored to be one of the last writers to interview him prior to his passing.

This Wall Street veteran told me things had certainly changed over the past seven decades, with both the stock market and America in general. "Life was much simpler back then," he shared. "In the 1920s, investing was a very easy affair. There was the New York Stock Exchange, which had a few hundred securities, and that was the market. We now have thousands of securities along with many other exchanges and a huge over-the-counter market."

Caret kept a majority of his financial assets in stocks to the end and conceded the secret to his success was simple. "Part of it has to do with being a contrarian," he said. "In other words, if everybody is all hot and bothered by a particular kind of stock, I leave it alone. If nobody likes it, and the figures are good, I buy it." He never used a computer, except the one in his head, and maintained that common sense was the most important requirement for unearthing good companies. "Find a product that seems to be exceptionally good, find out who makes it and then look at the figures," he revealed. "If the balance sheet looks good and the company has a quality product, you've probably got a bargain."

That's how he found what became his greatest investment ever. He was staying in a Boston hotel in the 1970s and liked the soap in his room, which was made by Neutrogena. "I discovered it was a public company, so when I was in Los Angeles a year or so later, I went to the see the company's officers," he shared. "It sounded pretty good to me so I bought the stock." He paid $1 a share and sold out for $35.75 when Johnson & Johnson agreed to buy the company in 1994. "I find it very difficult to sell stocks I own," he pointed out. "I like to hold them as long as possible. If a company looks overpriced, or I figure I made a mistake, I'll sell it. Or if it gets taken out, like Neutrogena, that's fine too. But I never set a price target. That's crazy."

Long life was a characteristic of Carret's family. His father died at 82 and his mother lived to 87. His wife of 63 years, Elisabeth, passed away 12 years before him. They had three children, and spawned a chain of 12 grandchildren and 16 great-grandchildren. "It's amazing," Carret quipped. "I was an only child." Carret's only health complaint prior to his death was that his eyesight was beginning to fail, which was frustrating since he had always been a voracious reader. He continued to travel around the world to view total eclipses until the end and was never a fan of physical exercise. "I am not a worrier, and that's a major necessity for getting old," he conceded. He also looked forward to his favorite annual trip: Going to the Berkshire Hathaway meeting in Omaha to meet up with his old friend Warren Buffett. "I first met him when he was just a young boy at his father's brokerage firm," Carret said. "We've been close ever since."

Occupation: Founder and Chairman, Carret and Company
          New York, New York
Birth Date: November 29, 1896
Education: BA, Harvard College, 1917
Biggest Mistake Investors Make: "Following the crowd and not understanding how to interpret balance sheets."
Best Investment: Neutrogena (Bought for $1 a share in the 1970s, and sold it for $35.75 in 1994.)
Worst Investment: Bank of New England debentures (Purchased thousands of dollars worth of them in the 1980s for 10 cents on the dollar. When he sold out, he only got 50 cents for every $100 he owned.)
Advice: "Be patient."
Market Outlook: Cautious.

LARRY CHIN

No-Load Fund Analyst

What's the perfect job for a guy who likes cartooning, philosophy, and being creative? Analyzing mutual funds, of course. At least that's the case for Larry Chin, a former subscriber turned senior editor of the *No-Load Fund Analyst* newsletter. The San Francisco native majored in marketing in college and went directly into the advertising business after graduation. "I worked for several agencies both here and on the east coast," Chin says. "I was somewhat of a radio specialist near the end and won a lot of awards for my work in that area. But I did a little bit of everything."

Chin first thought about investing in the late 1980s. He was in a serious relationship, contemplating marriage, and decided he better plan for his financial future. "I started to read magazines, books, and anything I could get my hands on," he says. "I looked at everything from the very simplest primers on money to different newsletters. I just kind of felt my way through the process. Before long, I began to see patterns and started to identify track records." Using no-load funds, he reasoned, was the only way to go. "It was common sense," he insists. "Coming from the outside and having no background in investing meant the smart thing to do was let a professional pick the stocks and do the day-to-day work on my portfolio."

Through his reading, he kept stumbling across quotes from Ken Gregory, an investment manager who started the *No-Load Fund Analyst* newsletter. "I liked what he had to say, so I called the number and got a sample of the publication," Chin says. "I thought the quality and detail of his work was excellent." Chin soon became a dedicated paid subscriber. Then along came an article which Chin disagreed with. "I wrote Ken a letter questioning some of the points he made in a fund review," Chin says. "He gave me a call and thought I had some interesting opinions. At the time, I had no idea he had a job opening. A couple of months later, there was an ad in the newsletter looking for a junior analyst to help out with some small freelance projects." Chin called Gregory to see if he could help out. "I was still working in advertising when I started the freelance work," he recalls. "To be honest, I didn't take it that seriously. I just wanted to give it a shot. Before long, Ken offered me a full time job." That was in 1994. Chin has been there ever since.

The *No-Load Fund Analyst* has a small but dedicated subscriber base heavily composed of serious investors and financial advisers. The publication is known for doing detailed reports on its favorite funds. "To find the best ideas, we first look for a track record of some length," Chin reveals. "We like at least four years, but the longer the better. Furthermore, we want this record to be superior, in terms of return and risk compared to similar funds. We're not necessarily looking for the top performer. Instead we want those funds with a track record that consistently performs better than its composite."

Once the numbers have been checked, Chin and his colleagues dig a little deeper. "We go directly to the fund and get as much information about the investment approach as we can," he says. "If the manager has a separate account record outside of the fund, we'll try to get a hold of that too. We then figure out if the manager is experienced over several market cycles, if they think independently, and if they are passionate about their work."

Chin also likes to personally interview managers, both to get a better sense of how they operate, and also so he has someone to hold responsible in both good and bad times. "I like to interface with them in their native environment whenever possible," he adds. "It's good to see what kind of support they have." Chin also keeps a close eye on how much money the manager is overseeing, to make sure they don't take on more than they can successfully chew.

Of course, even with all of this research, you can never guarantee a fund won't turn out to be a turkey. That's why Chin gives the boot to any investment that slips in performance compared to its peers, even after as little as one year. He'll also pull the trigger if the manager changes their style or investment approach. "If the fund's asset base gets too big, especially for small-cap funds, I may also move on if I think that will impede the manager's ability to remain successful going forward," he says. "In addition, if a manager has left, I'll usually either sell or follow the manager to his new job. New funds from experienced managers are some of my favorite things."

Despite his love for funds, Chin concedes that if investors are willing to do their homework, they'll probably make more money using individual stocks instead. "If you're a good trader, your upside is greater with stocks," he admits. "But if you don't have the time to monitor your companies every single day, a diversified fund portfolio is the way to go."

Occupation: Senior Editor, *No-Load Fund Analyst*
                 Orinda, California
Birth Date: April 24, 1961
Education: BS, San Francisco State University, 1985
Biggest Mistake Investors Make: "Not doing enough research in what they're investing in and trading too much."
Best Investment: Skyline Special Equities Fund (Got in before the fund closed in 1992 and has hung on ever since.)
Worst Investment: Buying a couple of Asian funds in 1996, which fell more than 40 percent the following year.
Advice: "Do your homework."
Market Outlook: Cautious.

ELIZABETH DATER
Warburg Pincus Asset Management

It seems only fitting that Beth Dater would wind up as a panelist on the PBS program *Wall $treet Week* shortly after launching her career in the investment business. After all, she's been a great communicator interested in the performing arts all of her life. As a young girl, she was a dancer who figured she'd probably wind up teaching drama, only because breaking into show business was so tough. But after graduating with a fine arts degree from Boston University in 1966, she decided instead to tour the world as a flight attendant for Pan American World Airways.

Two years into this vocation, she got married, which in those days essentially meant forced retirement from the airline. So Dater hopped on over to a temporary employment agency that specialized in helping former stewardesses find new work. "They sent me to Wall Street working for Lehman Brothers," she recalls. "The first year on the job I sat in Bobby Lehman's office answering phones. He was ill at this point, and I talked to his estate lawyer every day. He told me I should consider a career in this business. I spent a few days on the trading desk with a couple of high pressure institutional sales people and really got into it." Before long, she was working for the department full-time, picking up some accounting and economics courses at night.

As luck had it, Dater began her adventure in investing right at the peak of a roaring bull market. "I then had the unique opportunity of spending the next 11 or 12 years waiting for the next one to come around," she quips. "It got pretty rough in the mid-1970s." Dater left Lehman Brothers in 1971 to become an assistant portfolio manger at Fiduciary Trust Company. "I worked my way up to the research department, where I became an analyst," she says. "I developed a fair amount of expertise in the area of media communications, which was a very underfollowed industry at that point. There were maybe one or two public newspapers and the major television networks. Then there was this funny little business starting up to help improve the reception of TV signals called cable. I was one of the first people to cover that industry."

By the time she left Fiduciary Trust to join Warburg Pincus in 1978, a year after becoming a panelist on *Wall $treet Week*, she was a vice president. "Over the years, I had really broadened out my skills to cover many different areas, including food and beverages, paper and forest products, high technology, and some special situations," she notes. "When I joined Warburg Pincus as a securities analyst, it was very small, with only $300 million under management. Since there were only a few of us here, I viewed it as a real entrepreneurial opportunity, which is why I made the switch." Warburg Pincus's roots are in venture capital, a market Dater was no stranger to. Many of the media companies she followed were little more than tiny upstarts when she began covering them. Today she heads up Warburg's small-cap and post-venture capital effort.

Dater is a growth investor who looks for those tiny, well-managed companies with the potential to become the large blue chips of tomorrow. "If I'm successful, the businesses I follow will have very little recognition when I start investing in them, but a lot by the time I'm ready to sell," she says. "I look for companies with proprietary products and services, along with access to the capital they need to fund their growth. I like companies with low debt to equity and a high return on equity, because these tend to be the most profitable businesses." Most importantly, Dater takes a close look at management, which she believes is essential for determining whether an upstart will succeed or fail. "Management must be able to articulate a clear vision and business plan that I can benchmark them to and watch as it progresses," she explains. "I also like them to have an incentive to hold an equity ownership position, to make sure their interests are aligned with the shareholders."

Since many small-cap companies aren't making much money, it isn't always easy to determine how much they are worth. Dater's rule is that she likes to buy them at a PE ratio below their growth rate. She also is well-diversified among 75 to 85 names to spread out her risk. "I rate each company in my portfolio as either a core holding or changing dynamic," she adds. "At least 75 percent are core holdings. These are companies with the strongest earnings momentum, most unique business models, and best management. The other 25 percent, the changing dynamics, are put on close watch to make sure they grow like I expect. This would include the Internet stocks. If they don't work out, they get replaced."

Occupation: Managing Director, Warburg Pincus Asset Management
New York, New York
Birth Date: May 13, 1945
Education: BFA, Boston University, 1966
Biggest Mistake Investors Make: "Overstaying momentum plays by staying with a stock for too long."
Best Investment: Affiliated Publications (First bought as an IPO in the early 1970s. The company was acquired a couple of times, and she ultimately made 30 to 40 times her original investment.)
Worst Investment: WPP Group (Purchased in 1988 for $12 and wound up selling out for around $3 a few months later.)
Advice: "Focus on the fundamental investment philosophy you have developed for yourself that works over time."
Market Outlook: Bullish, but expecting a lot of volatility.

MICHAEL DiCARLO

DFS Advisors

Mike DiCarlo has just one word to explain why the big blue chips have handily outperformed the faster-growing small-cap stocks he loves so much since 1994—indexing. "It's a self-fulfilling prophecy," he laments. "The S&P 500 funds, which have received huge inflows, rank the companies in their portfolios by market capitalization, just like the index. Of course, the biggest companies get the most money, and the smallest companies get the least. That's why larger stocks have done better."

But the tide appears to be turning, and DiCarlo expects 1999 to be a great year for small-caps. In fact, he thinks they could outshine their larger brethren for some time to come. One reason is that more people appear to be indexing their money to other benchmarks, like the S&P 600, which are comprised of tinier companies. "Small companies are so inexpensive right now, I think we're leading up to another time like 1991–1993 where stocks can double, triple, and quadruple from where they're at today," he predicts. "I also feel the direction of interest rates is in my favor. Plus, if history is any guide, the capital gains tax cut of 1997 should be a big plus for small companies."

DiCarlo has always had a knack for making money. Even as a teen, he had his own business managing a number of local bands. It was a profitable venture, and DiCarlo found himself with an abundance of cash. He reasoned the best place to put it was in the stock market. "Having run my own company, I was familiar with the kinds of things companies faced every day and that helped me to make investment decisions," he says. In college, he prepared for a career in politics. But as graduation day drew closer, he had a change of heart. "The more I saw my politician friends having to go through lots of scrutiny, the more I said that's not for me," he recalls. So he took a job as a bill processor with John Hancock. He worked his way up over the years, eventually taking over management of the top-ranked small-cap Special Equities Fund in 1988 and later becoming the company's chief equity officer. Because he's always been an entrepreneur at heart, it came as no surprise when he left John Hancock in July 1996 to form his own investment firm with two other partners. "It was something I always wanted to do and the timing just felt right," he says. "I had been at John Hancock for 18 years and was looking for a new challenge." DiCarlo continued to manage Special Equities through mid-1998, and also runs a $75 million hedge fund. Both investment pools concentrate exclusively on small-cap stocks, but the hedge fund takes more risk by shorting and buying exotic securities. "I think small-cap companies are interesting because they attack a niche in the market, which is easily definable," he shares. "It's clearly one of the riskiest areas, but if you have a disciplined approach to doing things, you can take out and mitigate some of that risk."

DiCarlo uses four yardsticks to measure his stocks, all of which can be applied consistently in any kind of market or economic environment. "First, I try to find companies that are growing by 25 percent or better before the momentum investors get a hold of them," he says. "Next, I look for companies that are self-financing and in a leadership position in their particular market. Finally, and most importantly, I look for a management that's focused on generating shareholder gains. You've got to sit down with the managers and grill them about their business, what their margins and new products look like, how their competition is doing, and what their exit strategy is. Then you go talk to vendors, distributors, customers, competitors, anyone you can to make sure what you're being told by the top of the house is actually being executed throughout the entire company. You also want to see management have a lot of their net worth tied up in the company."

Most of DiCarlo's companies have market capitalizations between $100 and $750 million when he makes his initial purchase, although he'll hold his winners even if they grow beyond that range. "If a company continues to give me the kind of growth I bought it for in the first place, I'll stay with it even if it exceeds those parameters," he says. "I'll get rid of a stock when it goes down 12 percent from what I paid for it. Also, because I'm always fully invested, if I find a new candidate for purchase, I'll sell one holding to buy another."

DiCarlo maintains there are four things you need to be successful in the investment business, and an MBA isn't one of them. "It takes hard work, skill, luck, and, most importantly, common sense," he says. "We all try to make this job, for whatever reason, sound more complicated than it really is."

Occupation: Founding Partner, DFS Advisors
              Boston, Massachusetts
Birth Date: March 6, 1952
Education: BA, University of Massachusetts at Boston, 1980
Biggest Mistake Investors Make: "Not getting rid of their losers."
Best Investment: Infinity Broadcasting (Started buying as an IPO, and it was eventually taken over by Westinghouse.)
Worst Investment: Hunter Environmental (Paid up to $5 a share for the stock several years ago, and it dropped down to $1 in one day.)
Advice: "When it comes to investing, always reassess what you've done, but only after you've given it time to play out as you expected."
Market Outlook: Bullish, especially on small-cap stocks.

AL FRANK

The Prudent Speculator

Al Frank isn't afraid to admit he's a naturally cheap guy. "I'll still go to a discount gas station a mile away to save three or four cents a gallon," he concedes. "I like to get things on sale, and when I travel, I always look for the lowest fare." He's even having a hard timing finding a new research assistant, since he doesn't want to pay a very high salary. Frank traces his frugality back to his childhood. Both of his parents were uneducated tailors who never had a lot of cash.

As a youngster, Frank was bored with school and wanted to do nothing more with his life than work at a print shop. "I had no intention of going to college," he admits. "I was a very mediocre student. I graduated in the lowest quartile of my high school class." But because all of his buddies enrolled at Los Angeles City College, Frank decided to join them. "It was the best educational institution I ever attended," he contends. "I was still planning to be a printer and thought I'd take a business major for two years to learn how to run my print shop. But when I got there, I decided I didn't want to be a business major after all." So he transferred to UCLA with dreams of becoming a cinematographer. He practically flunked out and enlisted in the Army instead. After his discharge, he hitchhiked to New York, working briefly for the *New York Times*. He then married his first wife and came back to California to earn a bachelor's degree at UC Berkeley. Next, he moved to Las Vegas, then back to New York, and over to Europe, before returning to California to get his master's degree and work toward a Ph.D. at UCLA.

Frank is unquestionably a man who loves adventure. But his search for what to do with his life ended one day after his mentor at UCLA introduced him to the stock market. He quickly developed a passion for it. "I was studying the stock market, while working as an assistant professor," he recalls. "In 1977, one of my friends suggested that I write a newsletter, and another wanted me to manage money. I decided to register with the SEC and started *The Pinchpenny Speculator*, which is the original name of *The Prudent Speculator*." It was just a hobby at first. Frank mailed out around 100 letters and managed some $65,000. That all changed in 1983, when *The Hulbert Financial Digest* crowned his publication the year's number one performer. "All of a sudden I had 1,000 subscribers and then 6,000," he exclaims. "Before long, I was grossing $2 million a year." Everything was going great until the Crash of 1987 came along. Frank was fully margined, and his model portfolio lost more than 55 percent of its value in one day alone. "I personally had a $2 million portfolio," he dreadfully recalls. "After the crash, it was worth $400,000. I made the money back in two years, but most of the subscribers I lost never returned."

The performance of Frank's newsletter is back on top and so is he. He now works out of his home in Santa Fe, New Mexico, and maintains an office in Laguna Beach, California, where his partner John Buckingham does most of the actual stock research these days. He also started his own mutual fund last year. Frank follows about 850 companies at any given time and pays close attention to such fundamental factors as price-to-book value, price-to-cash flow, price-to-sales, and PE ratios, along with debt and return on equity. "In the beginning, when I was doing this myself, I just used *Barron's*. Twenty years ago you could find stocks selling for six times earnings, 60 percent of book value, and yielding 6 percent," he remembers. "They were called 'The Triple Sixes.'"

His computerized database is much more sophisticated now, but stocks that cheap are hard to find in today's market. Nevertheless, Frank's overriding goal remains the same: to uncover stocks that he expects to double within three to five years. "Once I spot a company that looks promising, I send for 10-Ks and 10-Qs," he adds. "I then estimate a value for each stock, and if the current selling price is below 50 percent of my target, it's a buy." Frank rarely visits a company or talks with management. "I've never found a chief executive who didn't see the problems at his corporation as anything but opportunity," he notes. Frank is a big believer in diversification and has learned a lot from studying the work of his mentor, Benjamin Graham. "His was one of the first books I ever read," Frank reveals. "His idea that you should buy undervalued stocks because they provide a cushion of safety is very impressive to me." Frank readily admits that about 25 percent of the stocks he recommends are never profitable. "But the other 75 percent range from barely profitable to exceptionally profitable," he claims.

Occupation: Publisher, *The Prudent Speculator*
Laguna Beach, California
Birth Date: April 19, 1930
Education: BA, UC Berkeley, 1956
MA, California State University, Los Angeles, 1962/1965
Biggest Mistake Investors Make: "Being impatient and panicking out before the market realizes the value of a corporation."
Best Investment: SunAmerica (Bought for a split-adjusted 38 cents a share in 1980, and sold for $50 in 1997.)
Worst Investment: A couple of savings and loans that were forced out of business and went down to zero in the 1980s.
Advice: "Realize that if you have a good system, you'll be right about your investment decisions about 75 percent of the time. But if you're right just two out of four times, you'll make a great return."
Market Outlook: Cautious (Worries that we'll get a major correction sometime during the year.)

ANTHONY GALLEA

Smith Barney

Anthony Gallea made a killing in the stock market before the age of 12. Unfortunately, his buy and sell orders never left his living room. "I used to look at the stock tables and paper trade," he remembers. "That was in the early 1960s. I didn't know it at the time, but the U.S. was in the middle of a great bull market. I would pick out stocks at random in the paper and they would all go up. I learned at a very early age not to confuse brains with a bull market." While Gallea's fascination with the market continued as he got older, he took a slight detour after college to teach high school English. "After three years, I decided teaching wasn't for me," he says. "I didn't want to spend the rest of my life disciplining kids, and I really didn't see a commitment on their part to learn. That frustrated me."

He then joined Shearson Loeb Rhoades as a broker and has been with the firm ever since. (It was eventually purchased by Smith Barney.) "I immediately liked the independence you have in this business," he says. "I also enjoy the excitement of the markets and the whole idea of investing." Gallea has since gone from being a retail broker to being named senior director of a portfolio management team overseeing $640 million in assets.

Gallea's investment style is a lot like his own personality. "I have always been a skeptic and bargain hunter," he says. "I tend not to believe the obvious, and usually think a little bit deeper than most." It follows then that Gallea naturally drifted to a contrarian investment style once he began choosing stocks for his client's portfolios. "I also read David Dreman's two books in the early 1980s," he adds. "Those were a seminal influence on my life. His contrarian beliefs resonated with me and I've held on to them ever since." (Dreman, incidentally, was a member of my panel in *Wall Street's Picks for 1998*.)

Gallea recently co-authored a book on the subject, called *Contrarian Investing*. In it, he codifies all of the strategies he follows when hunting for attractive ideas. "Contrarian investing tends to work very well when you're buying depressed assets," he explains. "I'm looking for stocks that are down 50 percent or more from their 52-week highs. I use that as a proxy for contrarian sentiment. So if a stock goes from $40 to $18, for example, I'm interested. From there, I like to see insiders buying the stock. I treat them as analysts. When they're buying, they're telling me that the company's prospects are still promising." He doesn't want to meet these managers though, since he says the numbers are more valuable to him than what some chief executive might say. "I'm frail and weak, and most of those guys are too smart for me," he contends. "They can fool me, which is why I never go visit them. I don't want to talk with management. I just want to know what they're doing with their money."

Gallea also likes to see good fundamentals and a clean balance sheet, although he admits that looking at an injured company too closely can often cause a contrarian trouble. "I know that if I dig deep enough, I'll see all of the ugliness that has scared everyone else away from the stock," he says. "That's why the down 50 percent rule tends to work so well. It shows you that much of the risk has already been squeezed out. The bottom line question you have to ask before buying is, 'Does this investment make sense?'"

Furthermore, Gallea prefers that every stock have at least two of the following four characteristics: a PE ratio of less than 12, a price-to-cash flow ratio below 10, a price-to-book value ratio of less than 1, and a price-to-sales ratio below 1. "I generally find my ideas by turning on my computer each morning and doing a screen of around 10,000 stocks," he says. "I then come up with a list of names that are down 50 percent or more. From there, I begin to dig deeper. I should also point out that once I buy a stock, I want everybody to agree with me about it so the price will go up. Therefore, 99 percent of the time I really don't want to be a contrarian."

When it comes to selling, Gallea has two hard and fast rules. He'll get rid of a stock if it drops 25 percent or more from his initial purchase price, or if it gains at least 50 percent. "When it goes up 50 percent, that doesn't mean you have to sell everything, but it's often smart to start paring back your position. In fact, one study by John Howe at the University of Kansas showed stocks tend to start underperforming for a period after experiencing such a large gain," he points out. "I further recommend keeping no more than 5 percent of your money in any one stock, which means to be properly diversified you need a portfolio of at least 20 companies. You should also put no more than 20 percent in any one industry to reduce risk."

Occupation: Senior Vice President, Smith Barney
                Rochester, New York
Birth Date: August 5, 1949
Education: BA, University of Rochester, 1974
Biggest Mistake Investors Make: "Not understanding themselves."
Best Investment: Buying deep discounted 8 percent Ginnie Mae's in the early 1980s when they sold for around 60 cents on the dollar.
Worst Investment: Overthrust Resources (Bought for around $5 in the early 1980s and it ultimately went to zero.)
Advice: "Spend more time controlling risk. Also, concentrate more on figuring out when to sell than when to buy."
Market Outlook: Bullish, assuming interest rates don't go up.

SETH GLICKENHAUS

Glickenhaus & Co.

What bothers Seth Glickenhaus right now isn't the direction of the market or whether his favorite companies will meet their next earnings reports. Instead, he's concerned about a potentially serious medical problem. "New research shows that bacteria which cause such disease as Tuberculosis and staff infection are evolving to the point where many strains are unfortunately resistant or impervious to treatment by antibiotics," he points out. "This problem of antibiotics losing their efficacy could become an even bigger problem than AIDS. I'm trying to get a broad program going in this country to face up to it. The sooner we do something, the more lives we can save."

It's only natural for Glickenhaus to become interested in a scientific subject of this nature. After all, he once had dreams of becoming a medical doctor. But, the call of Wall Street was stronger. When Glickenhaus graduated from Harvard some 64 years ago, he was convinced by Herbert Salomon of Salomon Brothers to give up a chance to go to law school in favor of working as a broker. "I agreed to take a job with him for three months under the condition that if it didn't work out, I'd go back to school," Glickenhaus recalls. "It worked out, but I left in 1938 because I was generating about $25,000 a week in profits for the firm, though they were paying me just $48."

He managed to earn his law degree by going to night school, and went on to work for a little brokerage shop that folded a few months after he joined it. "The owner was a disposmaniac," Glickenhaus contends. He first thought it served him right for leaving what could have been a cushy future at Salomon. But then Glickenhaus and one of his colleagues had an idea. They convinced the defunct brokerage shop's principals to let them take over, after promising to return the $25,000 the principals had invested in the company. "They agreed, and in a few months we had paid them back and turned it into our own firm," he recalls. "We ran it through 1946, although I went off to war for awhile, and my partner took over until I came back." That was when Glickenhaus started what, in effect, was the first hedge fund. "If someone had invested $10,000 with us, by the time we wound the fund up 13 years later, they would have walked away with something on the order of $300,000."

Glickenhaus made out much better, since he and his partner were entitled to 50 percent of the fund's profits. By that point, he was a multimillionaire and figured his performance to this point would be a tough act to follow. That brings us to the scientific connection. Glickenhaus next decided to become a medical doctor at the age of 46. "I did my premed work at Columbia and was admitted to the Einstein Medical School," he says. "The lure of Wall Street got to me again. I quit school and started my own firm, Glickenhaus & Co. All I did at first was trade for my own account. This went on for about ten years."

Then some rich friends asked him to manage their retirement accounts, and he agreed. Since that time in 1972, his firm has grown to overseeing some $6 billion. Over the past ten years, his average equity account has returned an annualized 19.9 percent, compared to 18.1 percent for the S&P 500, placing him in the top 1 percent of all investment managers in the nation.

Glickenhaus calls himself a cautious investor who is more concerned about downside risk than the quality of earnings. "When I look for a stock, I want to find outstanding management," he reveals. "I'm also very price conscious. I love overlooked companies that have come down in value for one reason or another that I feel is invalid. I also like companies with a lot of cash flow that will be used to buy back the stock." Furthermore, he seeks out names that are either industry leaders or low-cost producers, and he wants to buy them for less than intrinsic value, or what a reasonable person would pay for the entire business. "I look for stocks selling for very low price-earnings multiples," he adds. "I also examine a company's dividend policy and profit margins."

Glickenhaus deals almost exclusively with large-cap stocks. He has several strict sales disciplines. "Let's assume I buy a stock and I think it's going to go up 80 percent in two years," he offers. "If it does that, and it's not a bargain any more, I'll sell it. Another reason is if a stock goes up too much too fast, I'll get rid of it to avoid losing my gain."

This 84-year-old investor admits the current market is like none he's ever seen before and he credits the public for realizing that equities are the place to be. "The market will keep going up until this money stops coming in," he predicts.

Occupation: Senior Partner, Glickenhaus & Co.
New York, New York

Birth Date: March 12, 1914

Education: BA, Harvard College, 1934
LLB, New York University Law School, 1938

Biggest Mistake Investors Make: "Investing without professional guidance."

Best Investment: Global Marine (Bought for around $2 six years ago, now it's worth more than $20.)

Worst Investment: An entertainment company (he forgets the name) that went from $23 to zero in 1994.

Advice: "Get a good money manager. If you can't find one, just put your money in two-year government bonds."

Market Outlook: Bullish, although he points out the overall market is no bargain.

MICHAEL HIRSCH

Freedom Capital Management

Michael Hirsch is gratified to see how popular mutual funds have become. After all, he was investing in them long before they were cool. "I started managing money using funds in 1975 and remember getting a 45-minute interview with the assistant pension officer at Chrysler to convince him to let me manage some of their money," he says. "I spent the first 30 minutes of that time explaining to him what a mutual fund was. He had no idea."

Today it seems everyone knows about funds and how they work. Hirsch was one of the first to show the world they could build an entire portfolio using nothing but carefully selected funds. "I saw what was happening with the market even in the 1970s, in terms of volatility and whatnot, and realized funds were an efficient way to diversify," he recalls. His underlying thesis was that, because institutional investors constantly change their preferences for sectors and styles, one must be ready to shift around at any time, and funds offer the most flexibility. When Hirsch started out, there were just 125 funds. Today there are more than 8,000 in the United States alone. "There are too many in my opinion," he contends. "Funds are becoming like commodities, and that confuses the hell out of the public. It's become so bad that people truly need professional help. I think the same due diligence investors always had to perform on individual stocks is now required for mutual funds as well."

That really is to Hirsch's benefit, since he manages the FundManager family of funds. These are mutual funds that invest in other mutual funds. The idea is an investor can buy just one FundManager fund and let Hirsch do the picking for them. "It's a trend that's really catching on. We even have our own fund-of-funds association," he notes. "Mutual funds are the way to go because the markets are moving more rapidly, and the individual has no way to effectively compete with the institutions by going directly into stocks. What bothers me is the naiveté that's out there. The problem is most people are new to funds and expect the market to keep going up. They have unrealistic expectations and will bail out at the first sign of trouble."

When choosing funds, Hirsch always prefers the tortoise over the hare. "Slow but steady wins the race," he maintains. "I get nervous when one of my funds winds up in the top 10 percent." He looks at what he calls his "three Ps" when evaluating individual funds: performance, people, and the process. "I want consistent performance over the long term, not spectacular performance over the near term," he explains. "If you only look at funds that have stayed in the top half of their peer group for the last three years, that will knock out 90 percent of all candidates."

Next comes people. "I like funds run by individuals, not committees," he says. "I believe investing is an art, not a science. You can't paint the Mona Lisa by committee. I want strong-willed individuals with demonstrated investment manage-

191

ment talents who are putting their reputations on the line each day." Hirsch points out that the major difference between managers who oversee private money and those with funds is that a fund manager's record is on public display each day. Private managers are only accountable to their clients, and even then it's not always clear-cut how well they're doing. Additionally, he wants fund managers who can describe their investment style and discipline in 25 words or less, and he demands that they do their own research, instead of being dependent on analysts from other brokerage firms. "People who rely primarily on third-party research are doomed to mediocrity," Hirsch insists.

The final "P" is the process. "I have to satisfy myself that each manager is bringing a different area of expertise to the totality of our clients' portfolios," he says. "I don't look at labels. I look at the investment approach. That's how you build in the downside protection, because any particular investment will fail at some point."

Hirsch works out of both New York and Israel. His wife and two youngest children live in Tel Aviv year-round, and Hirsch flies back and forth to be with them. "We felt Israel was a better environment for our family," he shares. "It's a society that really revolves around the children." He believes an investment port-folio can easily have 30 to 40 different stock funds and five to ten bond funds without being overdiversified. "That's because I'm trying to create safe, steady returns," he maintains. "I do believe that more is better." Hirsch concedes that such an approach prevents him from ever being at the top of the charts, in terms of performance, but insists he'll look like a genius during the next bear market. "I do make sure each fund owns different stocks, and I stay in regular contact with all of my managers," he adds. "I'll sell a fund when assets get too big, and the manager can't deal with it anymore."

Occupation: Portfolio Manager, Freedom Capital Management
New York, New York
Birth Date: February 7, 1945
Education: BA, Brooklyn College, 1966
Biggest Mistake Investors Make: "Going for yesterday's hot fund. Novice investors look at who has had the best fund over the past few months and blindly rush into it."
Best Investment: Won't say to avoid offending any of his managers.
Worst Investment: Won't reveal this one either for the same reason.
Advice: "Invest for the long term. Buy a good basket of funds, and stick with them."
Market Outlook: Bullish.

SHELDON JACOBS

The No-Load Fund Investor

How long will the seemingly nonstop growth of the mutual fund industry continue? Sheldon Jacobs has the answer. "Until the next bear market comes along," he says. "Then we'll probably get a fairly sizable amount of consolidation." One reason Americans are in love with funds, Jacobs surmises, is because there's really no better financial alternative available right now. "Real estate returns were great through the 1970s and part of the 1980s, but that's not true anymore," he explains. "In a real sense, the stock market's the only game in town."

Before becoming one of the nation's leading observers of the fund industry, Jacobs spent 25 years predicting which shows people would watch on television for both ABC and NBC. But once he discovered no-load funds in the early 1970s, he was instantly hooked. He wrote his first book, *Put Your Money in Your Pocket*, in 1974, and began publishing a quarterly no-load fund newsletter from his kitchen table five years later. When the bull market took off in 1982, Jacobs walked into his boss's office at NBC, just four years shy of his scheduled retirement, and quit his job. His new mission in life was to teach others how to successfully invest in funds. His *No-Load Fund Investor* newsletter now has 20,000 subscribers. He also publishes two annual mutual fund guides and manages some $400 million in discretionary accounts, along with partner Bob Brinker, host of the popular ABC radio weekend program *Moneytalk*.

Jacobs is clearly a big believer in funds. "I don't own any individual stocks, and I'm a professional in this field," he maintains. "All I own for my personal portfolio is mutual funds." He notes that funds have two distinct advantages: diversification and professional management. There is, however, one exception to his all-fund rule. "You should buy equities through a mutual fund unless you know more about a stock than Wall Street does," he offers. That doesn't mean getting a hot tip from a broker or the Internet. Instead, he's referring to the inside information one gains through working for a particular company or industry. As he puts it, "Everybody owns IBM, so there's no edge for the individual investor. There's only one negative to buying mutual funds instead of individual stocks. You can't control the tax situation. You're at the mercy of when the portfolio manager decides to take his capital gains. Other than that, I don't think there's any reason to buy individual stocks." He also argues that almost everyone should have a significant equity component in their portfolio. "If you're wealthy and don't need the money, you should keep a minimum of 60 to 70 percent in stocks, no matter what your age," he insists.

Jacobs admits that funds are less advantageous as a vehicle for purchasing Treasuries, although he believes junk bonds should always be bought through funds because of the diversification they provide.

What's the best way for investors to select individual funds? "You start with past performance, then you adjust it for other factors, such as where you think the market's going, which stock groups will be hot, the size of the fund, things like that," he says. "You've got to get beyond the numbers." But Jacobs admits it was a lot easier for him to pinpoint which television shows would be popular in his former career than picking which funds will act best in the future. "If I just had to do a guesstimate, I could have probably made a run-of-the-mill prediction on television audiences with an error rate of maybe 2 or 3 percent," he says. "On mutual funds, if I get within 25 percent, I'm doing great."

Jacobs concedes he failed to predict how enormously popular funds would become when he entered the business full-time in 1979. "I bought an existing newsletter when I started *The No-Load Fund Investor*," he recalls. "The man who sold it to me said that the mutual fund newsletter would never be as big as his other publication, which focused on stocks, because more people buy stocks than funds. He was wrong. I think funds are the only sane way to go. If you do it on your own now, you're competing against all of these professionals. It makes more sense just to hire them. Plus, they'll do a better job. Over and above their picking prowess, they'll diversify properly, and they'll be there every day."

Although he expects to see a bear market or two along the way, Jacobs predicts the market's future direction from here will remain up. As for his own career, he's only willing to look out for the next three years or so. "I've been telling everybody that I'll consider retirement in the year 2001," he says. "But I honestly don't have any firm plans either way right now."

Occupation: President and Editor, *The No-Load Fund Investor*
                 Irvington-on-Hudson, New York
Birth Date: January 29, 1931
Education: BA, University of Nebraska, 1952
              MBA, New York University, 1955
Biggest Mistake Investors Make: "Being stuck in the past and not open to change."
Best Investment: "Marrying my wife, Lisbeth. She's provided priceless returns."
Worst Investment: "I can't remember any major disasters."
Advice: "Stay in the stock market, but don't bet the ranch on it."
Market Outlook: Bullish. "We're going to get a bear market at some point. I just don't know when."

ROBERT KERN

Kern Capital Management

In Bob Kern's eyes, small is beautiful. He was one of the first money managers to begin successfully investing in tiny companies on a full time basis. But Wall Street wasn't always his passion in life. He originally became an engineer, working for General Electric in Boston right out of college. "I had been interested in stocks since college and always thought about getting into the business," he says. "I began self-educating myself by reading various investment books. I eventually tried to get a job with a bank or insurance company while I was at GE, but was unsuccessful in convincing anyone that an engineer could be effective in the investment field."

He instead went off to Huntsville, Alabama, and joined Boeing, although the investment bug kept getting stronger. Kern ultimately decided to risk his future by quitting to attend graduate school at New York University. He didn't really plan to get a degree. Instead, he wanted to show potential employers he was serious about becoming a professional investor. "I interviewed with Chase Manhattan Bank after my first semester in 1965," Kern recalls. "It had a pretty large research department at the time, and I was offered a job as a junior research analyst for less than half the salary I was making as an engineer. It was the only offer I got, so I took it." Chase originally planned to have Kern cover retail stocks. But after he pointed out his background in engineering, he was assigned to the electrical equipment industry.

It was at one of his first analyst meetings that Kern realized small stocks were his true calling. "I went to hear the people from General Electric speak," he says. "There must have been 100 analysts there. I looked around the room and noticed everyone was older and much more experienced. I tried to figure out how I was going to add value, in terms of competing with them. GE also had a group of four investor relations people, so it was hard to get access to top management. I left that meeting and decided to instead start looking for smaller companies within the areas I followed."

In 1969, Chase started a small company investment area and put Kern in charge of it. Unfortunately, he didn't get off to the best start. "I was down 10 or 15 percent in the first six months because small stocks were having a difficult time," he admits. "Luckily, things began to improve. In fact, small-cap stocks had one of their best periods ever from 1975 to 1983."

Kern's universe of companies began to get even smaller in 1982, when one of his clients, Bechtel Corporation, wanted to do venture capital investing in their profit sharing program. "The company had a problem since money flows came in and out once a month," he says. "You can't get valuations for venture capital funds on that basis. So Bechtel asked me if there were smaller companies on the public

195

market with venture capital characteristics. The answer was absolutely yes. I created a separate product for Bechtel containing nothing but these very tiny companies. I think it's fair to say that was the beginning of micro-cap investing at the institutional level."

Micro-cap, in Kern's mind, means the bottom 5 percent of all stocks, in terms of market valuation. "Roughly 90 percent of publicly traded companies with market caps above $10 million are in my universe, which means I have about 5,000 names to choose from," Kern notes. "I think there's a definite advantage to investing in micro-caps. The potential to add value through fundamental research is greater where the markets are less efficient. Even the small-cap market has become more efficient than it was 20 years ago. Therefore, the market inefficiency has shifted down to the micro-caps."

In 1986, Kern and most of his immediate colleagues left Chase to build a small-cap equity department for Morgan Grenfell. That's when he began following micro-caps even more religiously. He finds his ideas from both screening, internal research, and working with investment analysts across the country. "Most people think you do research to find winners, and that's true," he says. "But I will tell you a key part of success for small- and micro-cap investing is to minimize your mistakes. We not only do the financial analysis, but also visit with management to understand their business. In addition, we're sensitive to valuation, even for the best companies." To figure out a fair price to pay, he looks not only at current growth, but also at how sustainable it is. Then he figures out what the business is really worth. Kern's turnover runs between 80 and 90 percent a year. He'll sell if the fundamentals deteriorate, valuations become too excessive, or the stock grows out of his market cap universe.

Kern left Morgan Grenfell in 1997 and, with son, David, started his own firm specializing in small- and micro-cap investing. He also continues to manage the Fremont U.S. Micro-Cap Fund, which was launched in 1994.

Occupation: President and CEO, Kern Capital Management
New York, New York
Birth Date: January 2, 1936
Education: BSME, Purdue University, 1960
Biggest Mistake Investors Make: "Not understanding the companies they invest in, especially the key factors that contribute to a firm's success or failure."
Best Investment: Cisco Systems (Bought as an IPO in 1990 and sold out a couple of years later with a huge gain. Sadly for Kern, the stock has gone up about 20 times more since then.)
Worst Investment: Network Equipment Technologies (Purchased in the late 1980s, held on for several years, and finally sold out at a loss.)
Advice: "Understand the business of the company you're investing in."
Market Outlook: Cautious.

FRED KOBRICK

Kobrick Cendant Funds

Imagine two teenage boys attending high school together in the 1950s. These lads become friends and talk about seemingly everything but investing. As adults they go their separate ways, and both become legendary mutual fund managers who garner worldwide recognition for their stock picking prowess. Is this the plot for yet another exciting novel on the world of finance? No, it's the true story of Peter Lynch and Fred Kobrick. "Peter and I went to Newton High School in Boston together," Kobrick says. "Back then I wanted to be a doctor, and I think Peter just wanted to play golf. I had never even read an economics book."

Kobrick has always looked for ways to make extra money though. "As a kid, I used to mow lawns, shovel snow, and sell garden seeds," he remembers. "I was also interested in stocks. When I opened the newspaper, I used to wonder what made them go up and down. I have always been very curious. I think that's the most important tool an investor can have." Kobrick bought his first stock at the age of 14. With a broker's help, he chose General Motors. The stock promptly went up, and he felt like a genius. Nevertheless, Kobrick's passion was medicine. He went off to the University of Chicago as a biology major. Everything went well until his second year of classes. "I saw a cadaver and realized I couldn't stand the sight of blood," he recalls. "I knew at that moment I didn't want to become a surgeon. I didn't know what to do. So I quit school and shocked everybody by joining the Navy."

Navy life was nothing to write home about. Kobrick's major responsibilities were washing dishes and cleaning toilets. So he opted to become a Navy photographer, and wound up working on a cruiser destroyer flotilla in the Mediterranean. "I decided to build a library in the photo lab and ran across this economics book," he shares. "It really got me supercharged. I loved it. When I got out of the Navy, I went to Boston University and graduated first in my class in economics. I then went off to Harvard Business School and graduated first in investment management." Kobrick wound up taking a job with Wellington Management out of Harvard, working with people like former Windsor Fund manager (and *Wall Street's Picks* panelist) John Neff, plus Vanguard Group chairman Jack Bogle. "I learned so much from them," Kobrick says. "At Wellington, I spent half of my time learning portfolio management and the rest as an analyst. My core industry was the airlines, but I looked at a lot of different things. I met with all kinds of management and began to learn the patterns they used when talking to the Street."

Kobrick really wanted to manage a mutual fund, and it was clear Wellington wasn't going to give him that chance anytime soon. The firm had him work on pension and private accounts instead. Then State Street Research offered him an opportunity to create an aggressive growth area for the company in 1985. It came with the promise he could manage several funds, including State Street Research Capital. During his 12 years at the firm, he built his division up from $18 million to $4 billion in assets. But as the culture at State Street began to change, Kobrick longed to do something on his own. He quit his job in August, 1997, and began to figure out how to start a new company. That's when he hooked up with Cendant Corporation president Henry Silverman and worked out an agreement to start a joint venture that would put Cendant in the fund business, with Kobrick managing the portfolios. Thus the Kobrick Cendant Capital and Emerging Growth funds were born.

"I have three buy disciplines that all have to be in place for me to purchase any stock," he explains. "I buy companies with high earnings growth, either in the absolute or relative to the market. I buy companies with compelling valuations using several disciplines beyond PEs, including price-to-book, price-to-sales, cash flow, and growth in shareholder's equity. Most importantly, I buy companies with managements that can execute. My mind has been trained to listen to not only what they say, but also to what they don't say."

There are likewise three reasons he'll sell a stock: If it reaches his target price and becomes fully valued, if management changes its strategy, or if the people in charge fail to execute as promised. "I learn from my mistakes and admit them quickly," he insists. "I'm a big believer in risk control. I'll sell a stock when it falls a few dollars, as opposed to letting it crash and burn, even if that means having to buy it back later at a higher price. The greatest remark John Neff ever said to me was, 'If you don't risk adjust, the market will do it for you.' I'm always thinking about where risk is coming from and am willing to accept higher volatility in high growth stocks if I feel I have the right company."

Occupation: Portfolio Manager, Kobrick Cendant Funds
          Boston, Massachusetts
Birth Date: August 6, 1943
Education: BA, Boston University, 1969
          MBA, Harvard University, 1971
Biggest Mistake Investors Make: "Just taking notes when management is talking and not asking the right questions; if you ask great questions, you get great answers, and you make great profits with great answers."
Best Investment: Cisco Systems (Bought for around 50 cents in 1990 and still owns it.)
Worst Investment: Sunglass Hut (Purchased for $8 in 1992, rode it to $36, then wound up selling out at $15.)
Advice: "Be patient, but check (on your holdings) frequently."
Market Outlook: Bullish.

KEVIN LANDIS

Firsthand Funds

If your investment horizon is 20 years or more, Kevin Landis believes most of your portfolio should be filled with technology stocks. That's where he has all of his money. "I would advise you to put all you have the stomach for in technology," he offers. "Technology in general is such a strong proposition that it just has to keep moving forward. You're creating new ways to make people's lives better every day."

It's no surprise that Landis talks this way. After all, he manages three mutual funds which specialize in technology stocks. His Technology Value Fund produced chart-topping returns during its first two years out, rising more than 60 percent in both 1995 and 1996. He's had a more difficult time lately, given that the market has been rough on tech stocks in general. Landis was born and raised in California's Silicon Valley, home to many of the world's leading high-tech names. He studied electrical engineering and computer science in college, before getting his MBA and landing a job as a semiconductor analyst for a technology-oriented market research firm. "I learned how to rigorously analyze fast-changing markets," he says. "But I got itchy to dive back into technology. So I went to work for a chip company called S-MOS as their new products marketing manager."

While at S-MOS, Landis began dabbling in stocks on the side and soon realized he was making more money from trading than working for a living. "I determined my true calling was to be investing in technology," he claims. "So I left S-MOS in the summer of 1993, and my partner and I started this new company." His partner, Ken Kam, owned a medical-device company and was also new to the investment management business. The two have been friends ever since forming an investment club together in 1987. "Stock picking had been a passion of ours for many years," Landis says. "We sat down over Christmas at the end of 1992 and decided to start an investment firm. It took awhile for us to get up and running, since neither of us had any direct experience in the industry."

Because the two wanted to make their investment services available to a large number of professionals in the technology field, they decided to launch a mutual fund. Their fledgling company, renamed Firsthand Funds last year to reflect their firsthand knowledge of the high-tech industry, has grown into a family of five funds specializing in both electronics and medical technology. Landis manages those on the electronic side, while Kam is in charge of picking medical stocks.

Unlike most technology managers, who are willing to pay dizzying multiples for fast-growing companies, Landis compares himself to the likes of Warren Buffett and Peter Lynch. "I favor companies with substantial growth prospects, but want to avoid paying high multiples for them," he says. In other words, he wants to buy high growth on the cheap. "I look for securities that are mispriced," Landis explains. "I pay attention to all of the normal value statistics, like price-to-earnings, price-to-sales, and the total market capitalizations for companies that aren't making any money. But it's not only the historical PE that I look at. It's price-to-what-earnings I think the company could make in the foreseeable future. In other words, what will this company earn a few quarters out? The standard for a lot of chip stocks is that you can get 30 times next year's earnings."

Management is also important, although Landis contends that when it comes right down to it, customers don't buy managers or PEs—they buy products. "Companies that demonstrate they can come up with the right products at the right price points at the right time are the real winners," he maintains. "So I find my favorite companies and then have a patient eye for value, meaning I will only buy when I can get a stock at the right price." He is also willing to give his investments time to make their products successful.

"There are two good reasons to sell a stock," Landis offers. "One is simple outrageous appreciation, to where you can't make a case for buying or even holding it anymore. Another is when you are incorrect in your initial analysis and realize a stock is not worth owning in the first place."

As for those hot high-tech IPOs you've read about over the past few years, Landis tends to stay clear of them unless he can get in for a reasonable price up front. "I value IPOs just like any other stock. If it's a good value today, it should be a good value tomorrow. Therefore, I don't think anyone should buy an IPO if they're trying to make fast money by flipping them for a fast buck on the first day of trading," he insists. "That's silly. It's speculating, not investing."

Occupation: Portfolio Manager, Firsthand Funds, Inc.
San Jose, California
Birth Date: April 28, 1961
Education: BS, University of California at Berkeley, 1983
MBA, Santa Clara University, 1988
Biggest Mistake Investors Make: "Trying to time the market."
Best Investment: Iomega (Bought in late 1994 for a split-adjusted $4 a share, and sold out for between $35 and $48 within six months.)
Worst Investment: Silicon Valley Research (Purchased in 1996 for $4 to $5, and it dropped down to $1 within a few months.)
Advice: "Don't let market volatility discourage you from investing in the technology sector."
Market Outlook: Bullish. "Technology will change your life for the better, and somebody will get rich because of it."

BOB MARKMAN

Markman Capital Management

Bob Markman has never been more bullish. "This is the world we were too embarrassed to even hope for. The stars are totally aligned," he exclaims. "Our planet is going through a productivity and technological explosion, with hardly any inflation on a global basis. What's more, we have a regulatory environment that's more benign than ever. And even though Washington is using phony numbers, we've got a budget that's basically in balance and likely to go into surplus. Any one of these things could have been the catalyst for a bull market. But we've got them all together at the same time. I don't think anyone can possibly predict how high this market will go."

If all that weren't enough, Markman also notes that the country's demographic makeup favors a continued rise in equity prices for some time to come. "We have this huge bulge of baby boomers moving through their 50s," he observes. "As everybody knows, that's when most people start saving for retirement more aggressively. This is only adding fuel to an already hot fire."

And with this continuing market rise Markman foresees will no doubt come an endless array of new mutual funds for him to follow. While funds used to be a simple alternative to investing in individual stocks and bonds, today there are some 9,000 to choose from. This has led to a proliferation of what are known as "fund-of-funds"—mutual funds that invest in other funds. Instead of choosing ten different stock funds on your own, for example, you can simply put your money into a fund-of-funds and let the manager research and select the underlying funds for you. Markman runs three such funds of his own.

"The fund-of-funds concept is starting to catch on, but it's taking a while for both the public and media to figure out what this stuff is," he says. "People don't know whether it's just another fund for their portfolio or a substitute for professional management." Markman views it as a little of both. "It's for the do-it-yourself investor who wants some help," he says. "It lets them buy professional management without entering into a marriage contract." Markman also notes that to hire him directly, it takes at least $500,000. But you can get into one of his funds for much less.

If things had been different, Markman might be managing the futures of some big Hollywood stars instead of mutual fund portfolios. After graduating from Northwestern University, he worked at the William Morris Agency before leaving to pursue a career in advertising. In 1980, he became fascinated with the financial planning field, which at that point was still in its infancy. So he took a job selling load funds with Private Ledger. The idea of charging his customers a commission each time they purchased a fund never made sense to him, especially after the crash of 1987. "It occurred to me that, even if someone had shown me *The Wall Street Journal* two weeks in advance, and I could have known there was a crash coming, I couldn't have done anything about it," he reflects. "I had all my clients' money in load funds and didn't have the discretion." That prompted him to go out on his own, managing money through no-load funds on a fee-only basis.

Portfolio building for Markman revolves around what he calls the "daisy" concept. In the center of the daisy, which accounts for roughly 60 percent of the overall total, he selects a few long-term, reliable performers with good managers. The remaining petals consist of more speculative funds that may be traded with greater frequency. The whole process begins by uncovering the best places to be invested. "I look at my fund portfolio as a team of players with different roles," he explains. Once he's determined which roles need to be filled, he searches for the best players. This usually calls for finding funds with strong current relative strength compared to their peers. He then digs a little deeper to see if that performance can be sustained.

Unlike some of his colleagues, Markman spends little time interviewing individual fund managers, although he concedes the person pulling the trigger is important. "The dirty secret of this business is that it's rare to find a manager who is a real jerk," he reveals. "They are all very sharp guys. The benefits of interviewing managers might be outweighed by the risk of falling for a relationship with them." Markman invests all of his own personal money in funds, noting that the last stock he bought 11 years ago went bankrupt.

Occupation: President, Markman Capital Management
Edina, Minnesota
Birth Date: August 20, 1951
Education: BA, Northwestern University, 1973
Biggest Mistake Investors Make: "Taking too much risk and not diversifying enough."
Best Investment: Mutual Discovery Fund (Bought when it first came out in 1993 and still owns it.)
Worst Investment: Benham European Government Bond Fund (He purchased it in September 1992, 48 hours before the European exchange rate mechanism fell apart. The investment lost about 9 percent of its value in three weeks.)
Advice: "Diversify, cancel your *Wall Street Journal* subscription, and spend more time with your kids."
Market Outlook: Bullish.

CAPPY McGARR

McGarr Capital Management

Maybe it really is true that everything's big in Texas. After all, over the past 14 years, Dallas hedge fund manager Cappy McGarr has showered his partners with annual returns of 29.75 percent, compared to 18.09 percent for the S&P 500. And he's done it without employing some of the exotic strategies used by some of his colleagues. Not bad for a guy who had no career goals growing up, let alone a desire to invest. "In San Angelo, Texas, where I was raised, I don't think we'd ever heard of stocks," he quips.

McGarr wound up on Wall Street almost by accident. He majored in both journalism and government in college, but found the jobs he was qualified for didn't pay much. So he went back to school for an MBA and landed a job with Goldman Sachs after graduation. After spending a year in New York, the firm transferred him to Dallas. Four years later, he decided to go into business for himself. Today, it takes at least $1 million to get into his hedge fund, which now has around $220 million in assets.

When he originally went out on his own, McGarr raised money for various private business deals. He launched his fund in 1984. Despite having the freedom to do whatever he wants, McGarr avoids speculating in currencies, commodities, futures, or derivatives. Instead, he invests his concentrated portfolio of 10 to 15 names primarily in large-cap, household name stocks, which have an average market capitalization of $11 billion. He likes these big companies because of the liquidity they provide. He tried starting a concentrated small-cap-oriented hedge fund last year and found it just didn't make sense. "You have to be more diversified in that area of the market," he concluded.

The most adventurous thing McGarr does is short anywhere from 5 to 40 percent of his portfolio, although he maintains it always makes sense to have a bias toward the long side. "Over time, managements get up every day to make money for their shareholders," he says. "They may execute a wrong strategy, be in a bad business, or be unintelligent. But if they have integrity and are trying to do what's right, the only goal management should have is to increase shareholder value."

McGarr believes earnings are what ultimately drive stock prices. But the people in charge are also important. That's why he checks to make sure the executives of any potential investment have their own personal wealth on the line. "I spend a lot of time looking at management and what they own of their own company," he says. "I want to see what options they have and how much stock they are mandated to own. That's very important because if management owns stock, they're obviously going to have the same interests as the shareholders because they are shareholders."

In addition, a strong financial standing and reasonable share price are essential. "A solid cash flow and earnings growth rate is very important to me," McGarr explains. "If you can find a company selling below its growth rates, by definition you're buying a stock that's cheap. So I obviously try to purchase stocks that are selling below their growth rates. In other words, their PE sells at a discount to their growth rate."

A final requirement for every stock McGarr owns is that it must be a proven leader. "I like companies that have a dominant market share and are number one or two in the areas they deal in," he says. "I find all of this out by constantly pouring over research, reading periodicals, and running computer screens." These elements are so essential because of the few names McGarr keeps in the portfolio. "Over time, this strategy has helped me to substantially outperform the S&P without ever having a down year," he points out. "I try to earn a 20 percent net return for my investors each year. In order to achieve that goal, I attempt to make sure each stock in the portfolio can go up at least 25 percent in a year."

On the short side, McGarr does intense research looking for companies that are doing something wrong. "I will only short a company outright if its balance sheet doesn't make sense, or management is doing something that I don't consider to be forthright," he shares. "I don't do many outright shorts. When I do, I make sure I've done my homework."

Away from the office, McGarr's other full time job his taking care of his wife and two teenage daughters. "My older girl wants to be a sportscaster, and the younger one will either be President or a stand-up comic," he says. Both girls may have inherited their oratory skills from their father. In college, McGarr used to do some 35 different voices for a radio show. Today, he claims, the only voice he uses on a regular basis is his own.

Occupation: President, McGarr Capital Management
Dallas, Texas
Birth Date: August 1, 1951
Education: BA, University of Texas at Austin, 1973/1975
MBA, University of Texas at Austin, 1977
Biggest Mistake Investors Make: "Having a lack of patience."
Best Investment: Dell Computer (Bought in 1990 for under $10 a share and still owns it.)
Worst Investment: PageNet (Purchased in 1996 for $19 and finally sold out several months later for half that amount.)
Advice: "Have a long-term approach. Invest in good companies with outstanding fundamentals and management."
Market Outlook: Bullish, as long as inflation stays in check, interest rates remain low, and U.S. companies continue to make money.

PAUL MERRIMAN

Paul A. Merriman & Associates

Calling Paul Merriman an early bird is a major understatement. "I normally get to the office each morning by 4 a.m.," he tells me. "I've got about 12 hours of work to do every day. With a six-year-old at home who goes to bed at 7 p.m., if I don't get out of here by 4 p.m., I don't see her. On weekends I get up at 3 a.m. and work for four hours on both Saturday and Sunday. The rest of my time is for my family." Merriman has always been a workaholic. But he only began this crazy schedule about four years ago, after he and his wife adopted a little girl from a Chinese orphanage.

It was Merriman's second crack at fatherhood. He admits to spending little time with his two older kids when they were growing up and vowed to do a better job this this time around. "I wanted to make sure our new daughter didn't have to compete with my work," he says.

A lifelong entrepreneur, Merriman started his own small importing business in high school. After college, he became a stockbroker, although he didn't keep that job for very long. "I made a lot of money," he says. "I just couldn't deal with the conflicts of interest. You were really in a position where you had to keep pushing stocks. In 1969, I believed stocks were going to tank, and I was right." He left the brokerage industry that same year to start a distribution business and later took over management of a struggling public company, which he successfully turned around. "As I interviewed investment managers to run the profit-sharing plan for our employees, I was introduced to market timing," he reflects. "When I found out no-load funds would allow you to move in and out of the market without commissions or spreads, it was like magic."

That revelation prompted him to build his own money management firm around the concept of using no-loads to time the market. Today, he runs more than $150 million, both through private accounts and a series of "fund-of-fund" market timing mutual funds. He also publishes a monthly newsletter and operates the Internet site www.fundadvice.com. Everything he does is based around one simple philosophy: "I believe 100 percent in mechanical systems," he explains. "If you're going to beat the market, you cannot let emotions be part of the decision-making process."

As a result, all of his work is computer-based. He monitors four different trend-following models and traditional moving averages to decide whether to be in or out of the market. "I look at things like the direction of the Nasdaq, up and down volume, the number of new highs and lows, things like that," he says. "The only thing these mechanical models indicate is that once a trend is broken, the odds are it will continue in that direction long enough for you to either sell out your position at a profit or buy it back at a lower price."

The system isn't perfect. In fact, the performance of Merriman's funds has consistently fallen below that of the S&P 500 in recent years. But he claims his strategy works well over time. "From 1965 to 1982, almost any simple trend-following system knocked the socks off of a buy and hold strategy," he says. Besides, Merriman contends that market timers are trying to reduce risk and are willing to settle for lower returns as a trade-off, especially in roaring bull markets. "The people I work with are very uncomfortable with the emotional damage a bear market causes," he says. "My goal is to figure out the lowest risk way to make whatever return my clients need."

For his market timing portfolios, Merriman uses actively managed funds exclusively. "I am looking for those funds with good relative strength," he notes. "This shows me the manager owns those stocks that are moving with the market. I don't care about ten-year performance because I'm only going to be in the market for maybe six months at a time." But when it comes to his buy-and-hold portfolios, Merriman won't buy anything other than index funds. "I honestly can't come up with one argument in favor of actively managed funds for the long haul," he maintains.

In terms of global diversification, Merriman recommends keeping fully half of your portfolio invested overseas. "Academics would say you're crazy to keep all of your money in only one country, including the U.S.," he rations. "Just look at the Japanese. Don't you think they felt safe in the 1980s? They questioned why anyone would have money in other countries since they had the strongest banks. Look at what happened."

And if you think operating on Merriman's hectic schedule will help to pump up your investment returns, he cautions you to think again. "One thing I try to impress on people is that working harder does not make you more money in this business," he shares. "In fact, all the studies show that working harder on your investments tends to hurt you more than it helps."

Occupation: President, Paul A. Merriman & Associates
                 Seattle, Washington
Birth Date: October 18, 1943
Education: BA, Western Washington State University, 1966
Biggest Mistake Investors Make: "Not identifying either their need for return or their tolerance for risk. These two things always go together."
Best Investment: Buying a no-load variable annuity for his grandchildren. (He claims it will turn $10,000 into $20 million by growing at 11 percent per year until they reach age 65.)
Worst Investment: Buying stock in four start-up companies in the 1960s. Three of the companies failed completely. (Fortunately, the fourth was a big winner and gave him enough money to retire at the age of 40.)
Market Outlook: Bullish. "But I can change my mind any day," he warns.

RONALD MUHLENKAMP

Muhlenkamp & Company

Ron Muhlenkamp is convinced that investing is a lot like farming. "I was raised on an 80 acre farm in Ohio. My six brothers and sisters and I helped my mom and dad raise hogs, corn, soybeans, wheat, oats, and hay," he says. "I may be an investment manager now, but I'm still farming. It's just that I farm stocks and bonds instead of corn and soybeans."

As an engineering student at MIT, Muhlenkamp took a few business courses to broaden his education. By the time he graduated, he was married with two kids. He went on to get an MBA at Harvard, intending to gain a better understanding of production for when he became an engineer. "My goal was to eventually make enough money so I could retire and farm and live the way I wanted to," he says. "I wound up studying marketing and corporate finance at Harvard." When he graduated in 1968, he decided the job offers that came his way weren't very interesting. That's when he found out a few of his classmates planned to start an investment firm in New York. For some reason, the idea of joining them sounded exciting. "I had never owned a stock or bond, nor had I taken any investment courses," he says. "That turned out to be quite an advantage." By end of their second year in business, Muhlenkamp and his partners had $3 million in assets. But he felt far down on the firm's totem pole and left to join the research arm of an insurance company.

In the early 1970s, of course, stocks were going down more frequently than they went up. Muhlenkamp decided to find out why. "All of the studies up to this point proved that 4.5 percent was a normal interest rate for bonds and 17 was the normal PE for stocks," he remembers. "As PEs went from 17 to 15 to 7, Wall Street analysts kept telling me about stocks they thought were cheap. I'd ask them what the company was worth, and they couldn't tell me. So I did some basic work to arrive at values for companies. I really wrote another chapter from Ben Graham's book, only my chapter showed how evaluation criteria change with inflation. I've used the same stuff ever since, and it's worked beautifully."

In essence, Muhlenkamp concluded that as inflation changes, there is a lag time before the public realizes it. "When we had high inflation and low interest rates in the 1970s, it was a great time to borrow money," he points out. "That trend reversed in roughly 1981, but all through the 1980s people still believed you could make a lot of money buying a big house with a mortgage. They didn't change their mind about that until 1990. The public fears, if you will, set the attitude of the market-place. Where a guy likes me makes money is by exploiting the difference between these fears and reality." In today's environment of stable inflation and interest rates, Muhlenkamp is convinced that stock prices in the coming years will move solely in line with earnings.

Muhlenkamp began his own investment firm in 1978, running private accounts for individuals. He launched a mutual fund in 1988 and now oversees some $270 million. His goal is to provide clients with the best overall total return, regardless of whether that means investing money in stocks or bonds. "To me, inflation is the rate at which your money is shrinking," he says. "What I'm trying to do is make money after taxes and inflation. I have found over the years that if inflation is 3 percent, I'm not interested in owning bonds unless I can get 3 percent over that, or 6 percent. Similarly, I'm not interested in owning stocks unless it looks like I can get a return of 5 or 6 percent over inflation."

Most of the time, Muhlenkamp's money is in equities. One reason he prefers stocks over bonds is that management works for the shareholder and against the creditor. "You don't know of any company executive who owns bond options," he observes. "Can you name a company you'd rather lend money to than own a piece of?" Muhlenkamp won't buy a stock unless it will give him a return on equity (ROE) of greater than 15 percent. And he wants to buy it for a PE ratio below the ROE. "I say I like to buy Pontiacs and Buicks when they go on sale. I don't want to buy Renault's at any price," he says. "The other thing I'll sometimes do is look for clumps of value. For example, in 1990, all of the banks looked cheap. I concluded any bank that didn't go bankrupt was a buy."

While he's primarily interested in the fundamentals, Muhlenkamp often decides to sell based on technical indicators. "I learned a long time ago that you can't find out the bad news in time for it to do you any good," he says. "So I always set price targets. If one my stocks get fully priced or stops performing and I can't figure out why, it's usually best to start selling some."

Occupation: President and Portfolio Manager, Muhlenkamp & Co.
Wexford, PA
Birth Date: February 9, 1944
Education: BS, Massachusetts Intstitute of Technology, 1966
MBA, Harvard Business School, 1968
Biggest Mistake Investors Make: "Buying stocks the way teenagers buy clothes; in other words, buying based on impulse or the fad of the moment, instead of on research."
Best Investment: Green Tree Financial (Bought in 1990 for $1.50 per share. It was acquired in 1998 for more than $40.)
Worst Investment: In high school he put two summer's worth of work money ($1,100) in an Ohio savings and loan that went bankrupt.
Advice: "Buy stocks the way you would buy a used car. Do your homework, and get something you plan to own for awhile. If you wind up with a lemon, sell out and move on."
Market Outlook: Bullish, but expects it to be a stock picker's market.

LOUIS NAVELLIER

Navellier & Associates

Louis Navellier likes to compare his investment strategy to flying a plane. "I'm on autopilot," he says. "I run my computer-based models every weekend and follow them religiously. The best way to think of it is if I were flying an airplane, I wouldn't look out the window. I would just read my instruments."

It's no secret that professional managers have had a difficult time keeping up with the S&P 500 in recent years. Navellier maintains that's because all but 22 of the stocks in the S&P are efficiently priced, making it tough for any one person to gain a competitive edge. So he's devoted his life to finding those names at the opposite end of the spectrum. "Stocks usually get inefficiently priced because of the flow of funds," he says. "Any time a stock's being discovered or institutionalized for the first time, or when Wall Street hasn't properly discounted the fundamentals, it is inefficiently priced."

The only way you can beat the market, according to Navellier, is by finding and buying those inefficiently priced stocks, which is especially hard to do with large companies. That's why he focuses primarily on small-caps, which are often neglected by the major institutions, although he's currently experimenting with large- and mid-caps as well. He determines whether a stock is inefficiently priced or not by looking at its so-called alpha factor. "A stock's return correlated to the market from week to week over the past year is the beta, and the return uncorrelated to the market is this mysterious alpha factor," he explains. "There are a lot of stocks out there that are totally correlated to the market, and 85 percent of big-cap stocks have alphas at or near zero."

Navellier first began honing his investment skills as a finance student in the late 1970s. He didn't buy the conventional wisdom that the stock market was always efficient. "I knew back then there were money managers beating the market," he recalls. So, with the help of two professors, he developed several computer models to prove he was right. It's a system he has refined over the years and still uses today. "I'm continuously testing and monitoring what works on Wall Street and rebuilding my models," he says. "I'm really more of a modeler than anything else."

In other words, Navellier uses his computer to find out which stocks the majority of investors are in love with at the present time. His theory is that if you want to beat the market, you must buy stocks that aren't simply moving in tandem with it. He puts his database of 7,000 stocks through several bottom-up screens each week. Predictably, he starts off by calculating each company's alpha factor. "I then take the alpha, divide it by a stock's volatility, and get a reward/risk ratio," he says. "The quantitative screens are designed to stack the odds in my favor, and that's what I try to do. The whole process is automated. There's no subjective judgment to it at all."

The computer puts his entire list of stocks through 23 back-testing models, which check various ratios such as price-to-book, dividend discount, cash flow, and PE, along with earnings momentum. "I'm trying to find what Wall Street likes fundamentally (at any given point in time), because what it likes does change," Navellier reasons. "I'm overlaying fundamental anomalies on my high alpha stocks to tilt the odds in my favor." Based on the results of this and the risk/reward ratio calculation, the computer sorts each stock in terms of relative attractiveness, and the top 10 percent form Navellier's buy list.

As a final step, he uses an optimization model to determine how to mix and match the final list of stocks to get the highest returns with the least amount of risk. "The model will often say put 5 percent in this stock, 2 percent in this stock, 3 percent in this stock, and so forth," Navellier reveals. "What it's trying to do is find stocks that complement each other and represent different industry groups, while attempting to lower the overall volatility."

Navellier is always highly diversified and has a strong sell discipline. He keeps his average holding a mere six to eight months. "Typically, when I buy a stock, I'll watch it move up in price," he says. "As it moves up, it tends to become risky. My allocation model will tell me to cut back on it, not because it's a bad stock, but because it's getting increasingly risky and less predictable."

Admittedly, Navellier's strategy is hard for individual investors to follow, because it's based on a proprietary computer model. That's why he publishes his research in his monthly *MPT Review* and manages a series of mutual funds. So what does Wall Street like right now? "High earnings growth and companies that are reinvesting those earnings into their own stock," Navellier shares. "Investors also like growth at the right price. The smoother, steadier the growth, the higher the premium Wall Street will pay for a stock."

Occupation: President and CEO, Navellier & Associates
                Reno, Nevada
Birth Date: November 22, 1957
Education: BA, California State University, Hayward, 1978
                MBA, California State University, Hayward, 1979
Biggest Mistake Investors Make: "Putting all their eggs in one basket."
Best Investment: Tyson Foods (Bought in the early 1990s and it went up 800 percent in four years.)
Worst Investment: Digitran Systems (It suspended trading and ultimately went down to zero.)
Advice: "Be very diversified, take some of your money out of index funds, and instead spread it around."
Market Outlook: Bullish, particularly on small- and mid-cap stocks.

VITA NELSON

The Moneypaper

Do companies that treat their shareholders nice really have better performing stocks? According to Vita Nelson, the answer is a resounding "yes." She publishes *The Moneypaper* newsletter, which specializes in reporting on and analyzing companies with dividend reinvestment plans, or DRIPs. Those with the best DRIPs, she maintains, go on to offer the highest returns. As proof, she points to the results of her MP63 index, which is comprised of the 63 stocks offering what she considers to be the most shareholder-friendly DRIPs. From January 1, 1994 through May 21, 1998, this index returned 255.69 percent, compared to 238.96 percent for the S&P 500.

Nelson's rise to becoming queen of the DRIPs was an unconventional one, to say the least. In fact, she owes much of her success to the word "divine." "When I first graduated from college, I went to work at *Mademoiselle* magazine, which seems as far away from the financial markets as you can get," she concedes. "After being there for about a year, I found myself using the word 'divine,' and it was associated with a blouse. I figured that was enough, and it was time to get out of there." In other words, she felt she wanted to do something more substantial with her life. So she began looking through the help wanted section of the newspaper and was attracted to, of all things, an opening as an apprentice in the municipal bond department at Granger & Company. "I was home sick and kept interviewing over the phone," she remembers. "It was in 1960, and even though the company wasn't expecting to have a woman, I got the job."

She learned the bond business from the ground up at Granger. "My boss had to teach me what an eighth of a point translated to," she admits. "I started out bidding on short-term bonds, and after awhile, I was on my own and had millions of dollars that I had to keep busy in the market." Several years later, when Nelson and her family moved to Westchester County, she decided it wasn't practical to keep her job at Granger, even though the company offered to make her manager of municipals. She instead took some time off to raise her three children and decided to reenter the publishing business in 1969, this time founding *Westchester Magazine*. She sold it in 1980, and began what is now known as *The Moneypaper*.

"It was originally called *A Financial Publication for Women*," she recalls. "I looked for strategies to reduce risk, because I knew women were risk-averse. But it was very hard to market to women using traditional direct mail. I didn't change the focus, but after realizing everything was equally appropriate for men, I changed the title after four years."

What made her especially popular with subscribers was her reporting on DRIPs. "I'm always looking for ways to diversify and minimize risk," she says. "I first found out about dividend reinvestment plans in 1984 in an article in *The*

211

Wall Street Journal. There was a list of companies you could invest in without going to a broker. I started writing about them immediately. In the next issue, I published a portfolio of companies that had these programs and told people what they had to do to enroll in them. It just kept growing from there." Today she also publishes the biweekly *Direct Investing* newsletter and the regularly updated *Guide to Dividend Reinvestment Plans*.

DRIPs allow investors to purchase shares of stock and reinvest dividends directly through the company, without paying a brokerage commission. About 1,100 companies offer such programs today, a number that is quickly growing. The catch is that most plans require you to purchase at least one share of stock through a broker before you can enroll. That's become less of a problem, now that you can trade stock on the Internet for as little as $5 per share. Nelson also has a service that will get you your first share of stock and register you for the DRIP for around $15. The downside, Nelson says, is that some companies are starting to charge fees for their DRIPs, including McDonald's and Walt Disney. She hastens to add most DRIPs remain attractive and there is almost always a no-fee alternative in every industry.

"For people with limited resources, in terms of research and finances, DRIPs give you a way to diversify without having to go into a mutual fund," Nelson notes. "Small investors with just $500 can spread their risk among ten or 20 different companies for only $25 a shot. If you had to pay a commission each time, this would be impossible. DRIPs also encourage people who would not otherwise get into the market to get in, and that's the most wonderful part of it."

Occupation: Publisher and Editor, *The Moneypaper*
Mamaroneck, New York
Birth Date: December 9, 1939
Education: BA, Boston University, 1959
Biggest Mistake Investors Make: "Not knowing what they're doing and blindly following the crowd; when you do that, you're not an investor, you're a gambler."
Best Investment: Phelps Dodge (It's the one stock she trades frequently. She says it has given her a 50 percent return several times.)
Worst Investment: Selling American Express just before it went up 500 percent.
Advice: "Understand the product you're investing in, test it against common sense, read annual reports, and make sure you're making an informed decision."
Market Outlook: Cautious. "I don't think we should expect these meteoric market rises to continue in the future."

EARL OSBORN

Bingham, Osborn & Scarborough

Don't hold it against him, but before getting into the investment business full-time, Earl Osborn was an attorney. "I'd always thought about going to law school," he says. "I enjoyed the precision of the law and was intrigued by the intricacies of the legal system." While working in private practice, he found himself handling a lot of cases in the areas of business, valuation litigation, and securities law. He was also good at working with computers. So when his former Amherst College buddy Bob Bingham suggested the two form their own investment management firm, Osborn jumped at the opportunity.

"I came into this business, not because I was unhappy with law, but because I enjoyed investing more," he says. "When we originally established our company, we used loaded funds. It was the only system set up where you could manage complete portfolios, because you had the brokerage servicing arms of the mutual fund companies." In 1990, when Charles Schwab created a system allowing financial planners to electronically trade no-loads, they switched over and began charging clients on a fee basis. "Schwab allowed people like us, who before had to work on a combination of fees and commissions, to work solely on a pure fee basis," he adds.

Today the firm manages $400 million exclusively through funds, with a minimum entry fee of $1 million. "Our primary belief is that it is the market which determines returns more than the individual fund," he explains. "In other words, let's say you're in a large company fund. Over the past year or so, you're going to have the highest returns of any mutual fund. It may appear that is due to the manager, but it is really due to the fact that your fund invests in large companies, which have been the market's best performers."

Therefore, when putting portfolios together, the first question he asks is, "Where's the best place in the market to be right now?" The answer is often determined by a proprietary computer model he developed. "We'll go back historically and look for those particular forms of diversification or combinations of markets that give us the most efficient portfolios," he explains. "We want to put together a portfolio offering the maximum return for the particular level of risk we're willing to accept." Typically, he keeps at least 30 percent of his clients' money in stocks at all times, both domestic and foreign, but never goes above 80 percent. "That's because once you get a mix of 70 to 80 percent stocks, the last 20 or 30 percent you add historically has not increased returns at all, though it has increased risk," he observes. In terms of global diversification, his current equity model calls for a split of 75 percent in the U.S. and 25 percent overseas.

Once Osborn determines where he wants to be, the next step is finding the right vehicles to get him there. Much of the mix involves index funds. "All of our fixed-income portion is indexed," he reveals. "That's because expenses have a much greater impact on the fixed-income side, and index funds are the most cost-efficient. We also index a majority of our equity money, especially for the large-cap portion of the portfolio. When you move into small company U.S. stocks, we start to incorporate more managed funds, based in part on our belief that managers have a better chance of beating the averages in these less-efficient markets. It's also hard to find good indexes in this area."

When he does use active management, Osborn looks for four primary characteristics: consistency of performance, cost structure, low turnover, and depth of management. "We're not necessarily looking for the best-performing fund over recent time periods," he explains. "We're looking for funds which have shown an ability to consistently give above-market returns over a number of market cycles. We want below-average expense ratios. Turnover is also important, because the trading spread among stocks, especially for smaller companies, can run as high as 6 percent. And we look for organizations with a consistent philosophy and the ability to manage a wide range of funds effectively through different managers. That way we're not reliant on any one star manager."

Looking ahead, Osborn says stocks are still the place to be, although he expects prices to be driven primarily by earnings, since interest rates aren't fluctuating much any more. "That means you won't see spectacular returns in either direction, like you have in the past. Instead, the market should be insulated against big moves, although it will remain volatile on a day-to-day basis."

Occupation: Partner, Bingham, Osborn & Scarborough
San Francisco, California
Birth Date: April 5, 1948
Education: BA, Amherst College, 1970
JD, Hastings College of Law, 1975
Biggest Mistake Investors Make: "Going after the hot deal and being overwhelmed by performance numbers, both for stocks and mutual funds; they buy the fund that's up 70 percent without understanding why."
Best Investment: Buying S&P 500 index funds in 1995 and holding on.
Worst Investment: Several real estate limited partnerships he purchased in the 1980s, in which he lost 80 percent of his money.
Advice: "Look for consistency. Worry about the fund that's gone up much more than the market, as well as the one that's gone down much more."
Market Outlook: Cautiously optimistic. "I expect returns to approximate earnings growth rates, which means maybe 10 percent annually going forward."

JAMES O'SHAUGHNESSY

O'Shaughnessy Capital Management

Jim O'Shaughnessy's new book reveals the secret everyone wants to know: *How to Retire Rich*. So what's the answer? "First, you've got to start saving money," he says. "Then you must invest it in the stock market, think long-term, and use a proven strategy."

O'Shaugnessy is famous for backtesting various investment techniques to see which ones make the most money over time. "There is underlying empirical evidence that shows there are certain ways that work very well, and others that perform poorly," he says. "For example, every strategy that bought high-priced stocks, in terms of what you had to pay for sales and earnings, underperformed during the period I examined."

Why is it so important to stick with a strategy? For the same reason doctors tell their patients not to smoke, O'Shaughnessy explains. "They know there is underlying empirical evidence that proves smoking is bad for your health. The same is true for investing. If you don't stick with a strategy, and just go with the hunch of the moment, you're going to be an accidental investor thinking with your heart rather than your head."

O'Shaughnessy should know. He first learned the perils of investing by using his heart after graduating from college. He had some money in the bank and decided to make a living by trading options, which was a disaster. "I realized how difficult it was to trade well over long periods of time," he shares. "I started doing some research and it indicated that the people who made piles of money were investors, not traders. After coming out whole, I changed my focus and became an investor."

He started his own money management firm in 1988 and recently launched a series of mutual funds that follow the various strategies he has uncovered doing countless studies with various computerized databases. One strategy follows a version of the popular "Dogs of the Dow" technique, which calls for buying the ten highest yielding stocks in the Dow Jones Industrial Average and holding them for exactly one year. A more sophisticated technique is what he calls his "price momentum strategy." "Stick with low price-to-sales ratios and high relative strength," he advises. "In other words, buy cheap stocks that have done well on a price appreciation basis. Limit yourself to the stocks in your database with a price-to-sales ratio below 1, PE under 20, or price-to-book ratio below 1, which are all indications a stock is cheap. You then marry that to strong price performance over the previous year. What you're doing is buying a stock the market may have hated, but is starting to change its mind about." This strategy turned a $10,000 investment in 1951 into $14 million by the end of 1994. During that same period, a similar investment in the S&P 500 only grew to $1 million. O'Shaughnessy also emphasizes the importance of diversification. For him, this means owning at least 50 different stocks from various industries, although he says individuals with smaller portfolios can do well with around 25 names.

His most conservative strategy is perfect for people in retirement, he says. "It focuses on using the Value Line data base," O'Shaughnessy explains. "You take the stocks with the highest safety ranking, which is one, and from that list of about 100, you buy the ten with the highest dividend yield. You'll find they're almost always utility companies, yet the capital appreciation component blows bonds out of the water."

Specific company fundamentals, like management and the current business environment, are worthless to O'Shaughnessy. "Study after study proves that when you put too much emphasis on that stuff, you end up doing worse in the end," he insists. "There are two ways to invest: the proud way and the humble way. The proud way is how most of us invest. We think we're smarter and better than everyone else and can make selections on a stock-by-stock basis. That doesn't work, and 80 percent of all managers can't even beat the S&P 500. The humble way recognizes that no one of us is as smart as all of us. So it searches for empirical evidence and sticks with what works. The human forecaster always loses, but models never vary. Of course, the same types of events are not going to occur again exactly in the future. But until such time as they stop letting human beings price securities, I think the people who use disciplined quantitative approaches based on well-tested and empiricially supported methods are going to do much better with their investments than everyone else."

Occupation: President, O'Shaughnessy Capital Management
Greenwich, Connecticut
Birth Date: March 24, 1960
Education: BA, University of Minnesota, 1985
Biggest Mistake Investors Make: "Listening to their hearts, not their heads."
Best Investment: Dell Computer (Bought for $3.50 in 1995 and still owns it.)
Worst Investment: Purchasing an insurance company stock at age 22 because of a takeover rumor. (He lost more than 30 percent of his money in a short time.)
Advice: "Find a strategy that is right for you and stick with it through hell or high water."
Market Outlook: "I'm a fully invested bear," he says.

L. ROY PAPP

L. Roy Papp & Associates

Even though Roy Papp has lived and traveled all around the world, he's most comfortable here at home. After serving in the military, Papp studied economics at Brown University. He went on to get an MBA at the Wharton School before being recruited by the Chicago investment firm Stein, Roe & Farnham. "I started out as an accounting man in training working specifically for Wells Farnham," Papp says. "I was really a glorified clerk. But I worked my way up to becoming a senior partner in the firm."

Along the way, Papp was also involved in politics, which led to an appointment on the Fannie Mae board in 1969. A few years later, he got a personal invitation from President Ford, asking him to become the U.S. ambassador to the Asian Development Bank in Manila. "My wife and I decided to accept, and I resigned from both Fannie Mae and Stein Roe."

As a bank director, Papp helped to decide which countries got loans. While he didn't do any investing as part of this role, he still played the market with his own personal money. "Since I was in Manila, I was never awake when the New York Stock Exchange was open, and I got the *New York Times* about two weeks late," he says. "It was clear to me I could not buy stocks that required quick judgments. So I focused on companies that I felt comfortable owning for three or four years. This was in 1975. Stocks were so cheap at that point, it wasn't hard to find things that were attractive. I learned to just sit with my investments and hold on. As it turned out, I made more money being on the other side of the world using that philosophy than I did actively managing my accounts at Stein Roe."

After his term on the Bank ended, Papp and his wife headed for Phoenix, where he started up his own investment shop. At first he managed money for friends out of his home. Once his business grew, he recruited son Harry and Harry's wife Rose to come join him in the firm. Today, L. Roy Papp & Associates manages some $1 billion in both private accounts and three mutual funds.

Papp's a big believer in the enormous economic growth that continues to take place around the globe, so much so that he started a fund in 1991 called America-Abroad. But he exploits this potential through buying U.S. multi-nationals, instead of foreign stocks. "I think you're a lot safer that way," he maintains. "You don't expose yourself to currency risk, you avoid having to deal with varying accounting standards, you save on operating expenses, and you don't have to worry about the political instability inherent in some countries. Most importantly you have SEC protection. You don't get this when you buy foreign stocks. There's a new financial scandal in Japan almost every month. We've had very few financial scandals in the U.S. over the last 50 years. That's an enormous plus."

Sticking with American companies, according to Papp, also lets you invest in the future instead of the past. "The big businesses in smaller countries are involved in steel, cement, and infrastructure," he observes. "You can't export this stuff. They're behind the rest of the world, not in front of it like we are in the U.S. Our economy is based on technology, which is the future. That's worth a much higher premium."

As for the argument that owning foreign stocks helps to increase the diversification of your portfolio, Papp counters that's nonsense. "World markets tend to move in the same direction," he insists. "There is one major difference. If we catch cold, everyone else gets pneumonia. Conversely, if others catch cold, we usually aren't affected. For example, everyone said that when Japan got into trouble in the 1980s we would too. But we didn't."

When Papp searches for investment ideas, in addition to a globalized business plan, he looks for companies growing at a good rate. "I don't want them doubling every year, because that can't be maintained," he notes. "The ideal rate for me is 20 or 25 percent a year, but a good rate is 12 percent. And I want to buy stocks at a multiple at or near that of the overall market." He also prefers monopolies, but admits they're hard to find. "On the other hand, I'm happy with companies that are either leaders or number two in their industry," he adds.

He'll let go of a holding once it trades for a 50 percent premium over its intrinsic value. "Because that number changes every day, I don't think you're wise setting a specific price," he says. "There are really three good reasons to sell a stock: if you screw up, the industry changes, or if the company is so successful that it becomes overpriced."

Occupation: Managing Partner, L. Roy Papp & Associates
             Phoenix, Arizona
Birth Date: March 18, 1927
Education: AB, Brown University, 1951
             MBA, University of Pennsylvania, Wharton School, 1955
Biggest Mistake Investors Make: "Trying to get a high yield or return; you always wind up buying poor quality, because high return equals high risk."
Best Investment: Richard Irwin (Bought in 1975 for $10.50 a share, and Dow Jones acquired the company a month later for $26.)
Worst Investment: A north sea oil stock he purchased in the 1960s, which he lost most of his money on.
Advice: "Most people feel at risk when they own stocks. They've got it backwards. I'm nervous when I'm sitting in cash, because stocks are where you should be at all times."
Market Outlook: Bullish.

MARGARITA PEREZ

Fortaleza Asset Management

Being female and Puerto Rican is an unusual combination in the world of finance. However, Margarita Perez maintains it hasn't been much of a factor in her successful career. "It's investment returns that really drive this business," she insists. "If you are doing a good job, I don't think anyone is going to worry about your gender or race. After all, when it comes to money, the only color people see is green." Perez makes money for her mostly institutional clients by investing in the securities of small-cap growth companies. "I find that they are growing very fast and are a lot of fun to follow," she says. "I also have access to top management. I can talk to them, look them in the eye, and really get a sense of the direction they're taking."

Perez moved from her native Puerto Rico to Chicago at the age of 14. She was always good with numbers and figured she'd become a math teacher. "At DePaul University, I was introduced to accounting and finance for the first time and thought it was great," she recalls. "I realized I could do something other than just teach math to someone. So I decided to pursue accounting for a while and eventually became a CPA." She took a job with Borg-Warner's treasury department, while going to school at night to get an MBA in international marketing. "At Borg-Warner, I was given a chance to join their in-house pension investment group," she recalls. "Once I tasted that side of finance, I was hooked." When the corporation became privately held in 1989, her department was downsized, and she decided to start her own investment management firm. As it turned out, Borg-Warner was one of her first clients.

Perez gets her investment ideas from many channels, including regional brokers, screening through computer databases, attending investment conferences, and her own in-house research. "I'm not a quant," she maintains. "I really practice fundamental, bottom-up stock picking." She has learned over the years that there are several key factors usually found in successful small-cap stocks. To begin with, even if a company doesn't have a long history of being publicly traded, it must have been around for some time for her to get interested. She further searches for companies with conservative accounting policies. "For example, in the technology area, I like it when companies expense everything up-front and are not capitalizing their software development costs over time," she explains. Perhaps most important of all, she wants her companies to have experienced management. "In real estate, location is everything," she rations. "In small-cap stock investing, I think management is everything. They must have the ability to execute the business plan. Fortunately, most of the time top executives in smaller firms are very accessible. It's easy to get to the CEO."

219

Perez shuns stocks with a lot of leverage on the balance sheet. "Most of my companies have no debt," she insists. To make the final cut, they must register both top and bottom line growth of at least 20 percent. "I often say you've got to have the revenues driving the earnings," she points out. "It can't be just a restructuring story. If the revenues are not rising, eventually the growth won't be there." She prefers to buy these stocks at a reasonable price, but is willing to pay up for strong growth. "Basically, I like to stay at one times the company's growth rate," she says. "If I can get it lower than that, that's ideal. It is essential that you do a real peer comparison. If a company has a big lead over the competition, I'm willing to pay a premium for that."

Before making a purchase, Perez always sets a sell target going in. "It's very easy to fall in love with a fast-growing company," she admits. "If you don't have a sell discipline in place, you can get in trouble." Perez will unload a stock if it meets her target, the fundamentals change, or she uncovers a more attractive opportunity. Her portfolios are highly diversified, holding an average of 65 different names. Turnover can be as high as 150 percent a year. She claims it's simply not possible to be a buy and hold investor when you're dealing with small-caps. "This is an evolving market," she explains. "There are always new entrants. I'm a firm believer that you should take your profits."

Perez still travels back to Puerto Rico, especially now that she has two clients there—a bank and a university. She even had the commonwealth in mind when naming her firm, Fortaleza Asset Management. "It means fortress and fortitude in Spanish," she tells me. "It also has a double meaning, because those of us dealing with the small-cap growth area need all the fortitude we can get."

Occupation: President, Fortaleza Asset Management
Chicago, Illinois
Birth Date: May 14, 1954
Education: BS, DePaul University, 1978
MBA, DePaul University, 1981
Biggest Mistake Investors Make: "Not having a long enough time horizon and being too anxious; people buy stocks expecting to make a million dollars tomorrow. You have to give your investments time to work out."
Best Investment: Hyperion Software (Bought at around $12 several years ago and still owns it.)
Worst Investment: Comptronix (She purchased for $7 in 1994 and it went down to $2.)
Advice: "Develop a plan, know your tolerance for risk and time horizon, and invest accordingly."
Market Outlook: Bullish, especially on small-caps.

MARCUS ROBINS

The Red Chip Review

When it comes to evaluating top executives at smaller companies, Marcus Robins maintains there are five warning signs to watch out for: black shirts, great tans, double breasted suits, hair pieces, and tons of jewelry. "These almost always let you know you're dealing with problem people that you should probably stay away from," says Robins. He publishes *The Red Chip Review*, a newsletter which specializes in analyzing small-cap companies.

Robins has lived in Oregon all of his life. Early on, he knew he was destined to get into medicine. He worked in one hospital or another from the time he was a freshman in high school to the day he graduated from college. But after getting his bachelor's degree, Robins had a change of heart. He decided instead to go on to graduate school, not to become a doctor, but to get into money management. It was quite a change, though not that far-fetched, since he had been fiddling with the stock market since he was in the fifth grade.

Armed with a master's in administration, Robins went to work as a broker at a small investment boutique in Portland. The year was 1979. "It turned out I wasn't very good at sales, but I was good at analyzing companies," he recalls. "So I was the base foundation of what became our research department. Five years later, I went on to help found another local boutique, before moving to the institutional side." In 1988, he got his first shot at money management when he joined Capital Consultants and became primary manager of the WestCap Small-Cap Growth Portfolio. "It was a $100 million western state-based small-cap fund which consisted solely of individually managed accounts," Robins explains. "I wanted to start a public mutual fund, but my boss didn't, so I decided it was time to do something else."

Then two monumental things happened in his life. First, he was about to turn 40 and began rethinking the direction of his career. Then, he made a remarkable killing in a small-cap stock called American Pacific. "It's a specialty chemical company, which drew on my background in medicine and chemistry," he says. "In May of 1988, the company's only facility in Henderson, Nevada blew up, and the stock was crushed down to $2. But American Pacific was an expert at producing ammonium perchlorate, which is used in solid rocket motors to supply oxygen. The U.S. government essentially put them back into business within 18 months. At the end of 1991, the stock was discovered by two major brokerage companies. It went from $2 to $40 when I sold out on February 29, 1992." While Robins won't say how much he made from his investment, he claims to have owned "a ton" of the stock.

He cashed out, quit his job, and made plans to start his own publication geared toward small-cap company research. He taught a finance course at Portland State University at the time and recruited several of his top students to help analyze companies in the basement of his home. The first edition of *The Red Chip Review* was published on August 2, 1993. "The philosophy behind my business was quite straightforward," Robins shares. "At that time, the institutional research and brokerage arena was concentrating more and more on the biggest 500 or 1,000 companies. But the best performance historically has come from small-cap stocks. I wanted to start the Morningstar of small- and micro-cap stocks. It would be a source of unbiased and independent research on these companies, which is something no one else offered."

There are around 11,000 tiny companies trading on the over-the-counter market, although Robins only considers about 4,500 of them to be legitimate. Of that, he's winnowed down the list of most promising candidates to just 300. Those are the ones he covers and assesses for his readers during the course of the year.

For Robins, 20 is a magic number. "My ideal company is one growing earnings by at least 20 percent annually, with a return on equity prospect of 20 percent, insider ownership of at least 20 percent, and institutional ownership of less than 20 percent. If I can find that kind of stock, and then buy it for a multiple of less than 20, it's probably a pretty good bet." Of course, he believes good management is of utmost importance, and avoids what he calls "Slick Willie" executives who own little or none of the company's stock. "I like down to earth managers with a lot of their wealth tied up in the business," he rations.

Contrary to some of the other panelists in this book, Robins insists small-cap stocks should be held for the long haul. "The element of risk declines dramatically with time," he notes. "I tell my subscribers that to make really big money in these stocks, you have to be an investor, not a trader."

Occupation: Publisher and Editor, *The Red Chip Review*
Portland, Oregon
Birth Date: December 8, 1953
Education: BS, Williamette University, 1976
MAd, Williamette University, 1979
Biggest Mistake Investors Make: "Trying to be too cute with a successful story and selling a big winner before it has a chance to really prove its potential."
Best Investment: Synthetec (It went from 34 cents to $15 from 1991 to 1996.)
Worst Investment: Boyd's Wheels (Bought in 1997 for $12, got out at $4, and it ultimately went to zero.)
Advice: "Be more patient and let your winners run longer."
Market Outlook: Bullish, although he expects the small-caps to take market leadership away from the blue chips.

JOHN ROGERS

Ariel Capital Management

John Rogers is on a crusade to get more of his fellow African-Americans to start investing in the stock market. A survey he commissioned in early 1998 shows that only 57 percent of blacks with incomes of $50,000 or more have money invested in equities, compared to 81 percent of all whites. What's more, the average African-American in this category has saved a total of $117,000, almost half as much as their white counterparts. This trend is so troubling to Rogers because, as a kid growing up in Chicago's Hyde Park area, his dad used to give him stock as a present for Christmas and birthdays. The elder Rogers was worried even back then that his peers in the African-American community didn't know enough about the stock market. "It was important to him that his son didn't grow up with that hole in his learning," Rogers says.

At the age of 18, his dad gave him total control over the portfolio he had been building over the years. That's when he began to think about investing as a possible career. He majored in economics at Princeton and started off in the business as a stockbroker with William Blair & Company. But he never liked that job very much. "I was already developing my own investment strategy based on a long-term, patient, value-oriented disciplne," he says. "Being in the brokerage industry didn't really make sense. You had to make transactions happen in order to get paid, which forced you to only think about the short term."

Two years later, he and a friend decided to join forces and start their own investment management firm. "We opened an office on Michigan Avenue in Chicago with dreams of starting a money management and mutual fund company," he remembers. "The thing we had going for us is we were both lifelong Chicagoans, so we knew a lot of people and could get in some doors." The two went to parents, family, friends, and their brokerage clients to raise seed capital before launching the Ariel Fund, which at the time was legally run as a partnership. "It was a way of building a track record," he concedes. "Starting in the summer of 1983, I had about $500,000 under management. Every quarter after that I would go to prospective clients and say, 'I'm 24 years old, but here's how I've done, and this is what you will get if you hire me.'" Today he oversees more than $2.5 billion in private accounts and mutual funds.

"I call myself a contrarian value investor," he says. "There are three things I focus on. First, I want stocks that are cheap and out of favor. I look at the PE and price-to-cash ratios first. Then I try to figure out what a reasonable person would pay for the business if it were to be sold. I like companies selling for no more than 13 times next year's true cash earnings and a 40 percent discount to private market value." His firm concentrates solely on small- and mid-cap companies, with market capitalizations below $5 billion. Rogers claims to find most of his investment ideas through reading. "I read all of the business publications that are out there, as well as mutual fund newsletters and books," he reveals. "I am constantly searching for companies and industries that are doing well." However, some of his best buys come from reading stories about companies that are having trouble. If an article is negative on a stock, Rogers often gets an itch to check it out further

"I spend a lot of time trying to truly understand the management team of every company I consider," he adds. "I want to know all I can about their background, where they were educated, where they worked before, what roots they have in their community, and what they've accomplished. My experience has been that when you encounter any type of disaster down the line, it's usually because of a problem with management."

In addition, Rogers puts each company through a series of social screens. "They revolve around the fact that I stay away from industries I do not think are right for me long term," he reasons. "I avoid tobacco stocks and those that aren't environmentally friendly. I don't think tobacco is a growing industry and am convinced companies that aren't concerned about the environment will have a hard time being successful. I also try to be sure that there's a culture in the companies I invest in that appreciates diversity. But the bottom line is that I believe these social screens lead me to making better investment decisions."

Ariel's motto is "slow and steady wins the race," which alludes to Rogers' aversion to pulling the trigger. "The major reason I'll sell a stock is if I lose confidence in the quality of the product being produced or management's ability to grow the business at above-average rates over the next three to five years," he adds. "I strongly believe that patience is what wins in our business. You find a good company and hold it forever. The message is 'think long term.'"

Occupation: President, Ariel Capital Management
Chicago, Illinois
Birth Date: March 31, 1958
Education: BA, Princeton University, 1980
Biggest Mistake Investors Make: "Buying stocks that are popular; they wind up jumping on the bandwagon after it's too late."
Best Investment: T. Rowe Price (Started buying after the crash of 1987 for $5 per share. The stock has been above $70 since then, and he still owns it.)
Worst Investment: Payless Cashways (Began purchasing it in the spring of 1993 at $13; sold it for $2 in 1996.)
Advice: "If you're going to make individual stock decisions, stick to industries you know well and understand."
Market Outlook: Bearish, expecting a major correction led by the big blue chip companies in the S&P 500.

TRICIA O. ROTHSCHILD

Morningstar Mutual Funds

Tricia Rothschild feels like the world is at her fingers. That's because she spends her time analyzing international mutual funds for Morningstar, the influential fund tracking and rating service. Raised in Wisconsin, Rothschild has a master's degree in Russian and East European economics. She has spent time living in Russia, Poland, and Lithuania. "I first got interested in Russia right around the time Gorbachev came into power," she remembers. "It's such a huge country with a fascinating history."

Armed with her degree, Rothschild came to Chicago planning to work for a company that could put her foreign language and international business skills to use. "I figured I'd get involved with a company that was doing some kind of joint venture in Russia," she says. "I think I was a little too early. Most companies were starting to send their high-level executives overseas to look for possible opportunities, but they weren't looking for someone like me. So I got hooked up with Morningstar, and it has been a great fit ever since."

Rothschild was initially hired to analyze closed-end funds, which are replete with foreign offerings. But when she started, she knew next to nothing about the fund industry. "I understood it was a chance to follow the international markets, while using my research and writing skills," she says. "However, I had to learn everything on the job. The first couple of years, I took some accounting courses and did a lot of reading. We also have internal continuing education at Morningstar from veterans of the mutual fund business. I've since enrolled in the CFA program and am close to completing that."

Two years ago, Rothschild became Morningstar's international funds editor. She spends her time analyzing the dozens of funds in this category. Among other things, she interviews managers and evaluates which stocks they are buying. "The U.S. market is much more developed, and many of these foreign markets are so dynamic," she shares. "Many international funds are brand new. There is so much change and growth taking place in various countries around the world. The investment professionals running foreign funds are just beginning to figure out how many of these markets work. There is plenty of untapped territory to cover."

Rothschild begins her evaluation process by comparing each international fund to its relevant peer group. "It's a mistake to judge a foreign stock fund against the S&P 500," she maintains. "If you did that, you'd say none of them were worth it over the past five years. You also don't want to compare pure international funds to world stock funds, which invest partly in the U.S. That's comparing apples and oranges, too." Once she has evaluated the actual performance results, she then examines them on a risk-adjusted basis. If a fund has great numbers, but subjected investors to tremendous volatility, it may be ranked below a fund with lower numbers and less risk.

When she talks to managers, Rothschild tries to make sure they have a real handle on the stocks in their portfolio. "It's important that they can give me a clear explanation of what they're buying and what their strategy is," she says. "This is particularly important because when you think about it, there are literally thousands of companies they have to choose from around the world. They must have some method for withering down the field. They also have few boundaries, compared to domestic managers. They can choose stocks of almost any style or capitalization."

Because foreign funds have been weak performers over the past decade, some investment pros have suggested that Americans keep their portfolios entirely here at home. Rothschild doesn't buy that argument. "I think you need overseas exposure now more than ever," she maintains. "If you have any kind of contrarian bent at all, the last thing you want to do is load up on a hot market like the U.S. and neglect those areas that have been out of favor. U.S. funds have outperformed in the 1990s. But in the 1980s, foreign funds did better. Frankly, there are just a lot of great companies outside the U.S. that you ignore if you avoid international funds." Although Morningstar doesn't have a recommended allocation, Rothschild says she keeps a good one-third of her portfolio invested overseas.

And while index funds may be the cat's meow these days in the U.S., Rothschild insists they don't work in foreign markets. "For one thing, international index funds force you to overweight the hottest markets just because they're going up," she says. "More importantly the foreign markets aren't as efficient, and there is a lot of room for talented managers to add value."

Occupation: International Funds Editor, *Morningstar Mutual Funds*
Chicago, Illinois
Birth Date: January 3, 1967
Education: BS, Northwestern University, 1989
MA, Indiana University, 1992
Biggest Mistake Investors Make: "Not paying enough attention to fund expense ratios; they make a big difference in down or sideways markets."
Best Investment: Thai Capital Fund (Bought two days before the bhat was devalued in June 1997 for $10 a share; sold out four days later for $20.)
Worst Investment: GT Greater Europe (Purchased in 1993 and finally got out two years later with a big loss and huge tax bill)
Advice: "Know your risk tolerance. You can fool yourself when things are going well by loading up on funds that are volatile, while turning a blind eye toward what could happen in a downturn."
Market Outlook: Bullish, especially on foreign markets.

ROBERT SANBORN

The Oakmark Fund

Although *Barron's* has crowned him the nation's number one fund manager, and various other publications have bestowed similar accolades, Robert Sanborn takes it all in stride. "My mother likes it, and it is an honor," he says. "But it doesn't really change anything for me."

Sanborn is an esteemed value investor who has always had a natural bias toward finding companies on the cheap. The Boston native grew up in a middle-class family and quickly learned the importance of making every dollar count. "I have a younger brother and sister, and my parents never had a lot of money," he reflects. "We did all of our shopping at discount stores like Filene's Basement. We were always looking for a bargain."

While studying at Dartmouth College, Sanborn became interested in economics and contemplated becoming a professor. But shortly after starting graduate school at the University of Chicago, he decided the lifestyle of an academic wasn't for him. "I found I really enjoyed investing and decided to get an MBA instead of a PhD," he says.

Sanborn initially became a securities analyst for the Ohio State Teachers Retirement System pension fund. A few years later, he left to become a portfolio manger at the respected Chicago value investment firm Harris Associates. Back then, Harris only managed private accounts. But, in 1991, Sanborn convinced company brass to let him launch The Oakmark Fund. Talk about a grand entrance! In it's rookie year, Oakmark was up 48 percent, compared to a gain of 9 percent for the S&P 500. Oakmark quickly became the number one fund in the nation, turning Sanborn into a star in the world of personal finance. His star has been rising ever since.

While low PEs, reasonable price-to-book value ratios, and high dividend yields are the gauges most value investors use to define "value," Sanborn follows a different track. "All of these things are meaningless to me, even though I think of myself as a core value investor," he says. "I look at what a business is worth to an owner who owns the whole thing. My view is very eclectic. I can look at a very high-growth company, and if it trades for the right price, I'm interested."

He also wants to make sure every stock he considers is backed by a strong business. "The longer I'm in this field, the more skeptical I am of buying lousy businesses at any price," he says. That's one reason he tends to stick with companies boasting market capitalizations of more than $3 billion, while avoiding small-cap upstarts. "I think that larger companies are better positioned," he insists. "Their outperformance over the past several years has been justified by the fundamentals. I think the current environment still favors them."

To determine how much a company is worth, Sanborn examines a multitude of different factors. "I look at transactions in the marketplace and try to make sense of them and whether they are reasonable," he explains. "I then try to apply those valuations to comparable companies. I like to buy stocks at 60 percent or less of their true value and sell at 90 percent of value. I am constantly monitoring those numbers. It's a hard core thing for me." He also pays much more attention to cash flow than PE ratios. "The 'E' is accounting earnings, which I find is often not reflective of a company's true financial situation," he says. "That's why I like to look at cash flow more closely than reported earnings."

Sanborn follows several guidelines in his investment discipline. First, of course, he pays attention to price and value. Next, he wants companies with owner-oriented management. "I will not invest with a lousy management team, hoping either someone will take them out or that things will somehow get better," he says. "I always assume the current management team is the one I will be dealing with. If I can't find owner-oriented management, I won't buy the stock." He also believes in portfolio concentration. Sanborn hates to sell a stock. He will only pull the trigger if he has misjudged the management team or if the shares approaches that magical number of 90 percent of estimated value. Turnover in the Oakmark Fund averages a meager 20 percent a year.

When he's away from the office, Sanborn loves to be with his four-year-old twins. He also enjoys reading about economic history and politics, and is very involved with the Libertarian political party. "I think the Libertarians are on the cutting edge, and I really respect their message," he says. Sanborn would even like to run for President some day as a Libertarian, although he insists he's not thinking about it seriously at the moment.

Occupation: Portfolio Manager, The Oakmark Fund
            Chicago, Illinois
Birth Date: March 8, 1958
Education: BA, Dartmouth College, 1980
            MBA, University of Chicago, 1983
Biggest Mistake Investors Make: "Not having a long-term program and executing it faithfully; in terms of mutual fund investors, I think they tend to be overly diversified."
Best Investment: Liberty Media (He owned the stock from 1991 to 1994 and saw his money multiply more than ten times.)
Worst Investment: Drypers (Bought the stock in 1992 and lost most of his investment.)
Advice: "Have a long-term program and stick with it. Don't let the inevitable market declines keep you from achieving your investment goals."
Market Outlook: Cautious. "Stocks are fairly valued, but the economic environment remains favorable for equities."

STEPHEN SAVAGE

Value Line Mutual Fund Survey

When it comes to evaluating mutual funds, one thing appears to be certain: You can spot a dog from a mile away. "We've done studies and found this is true about any rating system," observes Stephen Savage, executive director of the *Value Line Mutual Fund Survey*. "You should keep away from those funds that are ranked poorly. It's tough to tell whether a highly-rated fund will stay that way. But the bad ones almost always remain dogs." That information is useful, since if you eliminate all the stinkers from the list of the 9,000 potential funds competing for your money today, you presumably have several thousand fewer names to choose from.

Savage knows a lot about fund ratings. He's devoted most of his career to compiling them. He initially got into the investment area through journalism. In college, Savage was hired by a Canadian newsletter publisher to write for one of its New York-based investment publications. "I got a chance to interview some pretty well-known fund managers," he says. He joined the publisher full time after graduation and convinced his bosses to let him start a mutual fund research publication, called the *Blue Book of Mutual Fund Reports*. It featured single-page research write-ups on each fund, similar to what the *Value Line Investment Survey* does with stocks. "I went out and bought a computer and learned how to set up my own database and generate my own full-page reports," he says. "I put the whole thing together myself."

The service was marginally successful. However, the publisher faced hard times after a postal strike in Canada and decided to shut the publication down after a year. That was in 1986, right about the time when a then unknown firm called Morningstar launched its first fund research publication. Savage left the company to start his own fund newsletter, but had a difficult time building a subscription base. He decided to sell out after just seven months to go work as an editor with Wiesenberger, a company known for its meticulous fund research and performance tracking service. "That job schooled me in the real fine points of mutual fund data and statistics," Savage says.

After being named director of his division, he was charged with modernizing and computerizing Wiesenberger's massive database. "We still had stuff that was being tracked on index cards and hand calculators," Savage notes. "I brought in the resources to build a computerized database and put up a PC network. What used to take 20 hours to calculate now could be done in 30 minutes."

In the winter of 1993, Savage learned that the CEO of Value Line wanted to talk with him about a job. "I called to politely turn her down, and we wound up talking for six hours," he remembers. "What they wanted me to do was very exciting. They wanted to build a mutual fund information division from the ground up, applying the Value Line formula to mutual funds, and competing head-on with Morningstar." Savage was intrigued by the challenge and accepted the offer.

"The day I started, there was nothing more than a drawing on a page of what they wanted to do," he says. "There were no computers or research analysts and I was supposed to get the product together in six months." By working late nights and weekends, Savage's team almost met the deadline, and the *Value Line Mutual Fund Survey* was born in 1993. The company offers both print and online versions of the product. Savage claims there's a clear philosophical difference between his products and those put out by archrival Morningstar. "I would characterize Morningstar as supporting fundamental research on funds, where the effort is put on finding good funds on an individual basis," he explains. "We are much more supportive of the asset allocation approach, where determining an appropriate asset allocation plan is equally as important as the individual funds."

Unlike Morningstar, Value Line also provides subscribers with portfolio allocation recommendations and a list of standout funds. In addition, instead of a star rating, it ranks each fund with a number from one through five, with one being best. Savage and his analysts write individual reports for some 1,600 funds, and like to interview portfolio managers whenever possible.

While Savage personally has a bias toward active management, which is the primary focus of Value Line's effort, he concedes indexing has a place in an overall investment plan. "I own quite a few index funds and consider them to be a good core holding," he says. "But I also like to add actively managed funds to round out the edges. When I find a manager who I believe can legitimately beat the benchmark, I'll include their fund in my portfolio."

Occupation: Executive Director, *Value Line Mutual Fund Survey*
New York, New York
Birth Date: June 23, 1961
Education: BA, Hunter College
Biggest Mistake Investors Make: "Shifting to whatever is hot, getting in when it's too late, and then shifting to the next hot fad, only to get in at the top of that cycle as well."
Best Investment: Mity-Lite (Bought for around $7 in 1995. Today it trades for around $18.)
Worst Investment: Citel (He purchased the stock in 1985 and the company went out of business.)
Advice: "Find a reasonable approach and stick to it no matter what."
Market Outlook: Bullish, but expects the U.S. to trail the returns offered by foreign markets.

MICHAEL STOLPER

Stolper & Company

Although most of Michael Stolper's managed portfolios are fully exposed to equities these days, he admits this is a difficult environment for him to invest in. "If you were a bookie, you would walk up to the table, look at the probabilities, and put your money in your pocket and go home," he insists. "You cannot convince yourself statistically that these prices are sustainable. What you have here is a runaway bull market. There is no new era."

Stolper is the man wealthy folks turn to for advice on choosing managers to take charge of their money. Although he started out in the separate account business, he is increasingly steering his clients toward mutual funds, especially when they are primarily concerned about the bottom line. The reason for this is a function of how investment management firms really work. "They're factories," he reveals. "If your product is large-cap growth, the way you make the most money is by managing separate accounts for individuals, pension funds, endowments, foundations, and by having mutual funds. In all cases, if you run your business properly, it essentially will be the same product with different labels and price points. The overall performance should be similar because you get a blending. But tracking mutual funds is so much easier."

This Oklahoma native has had a lifelong interest in the stock market, although he's not exactly sure why. "I just sort of got the bug," he says. "I thought it was a fascinating business. It looked like easy money without a lot of work." After earning a master's degree in finance, Stolper originally planned to get into investment banking, which he viewed as the most glamorous job on Wall Street. Unfortunately, the big firms weren't impressed by his degree from the University of Oklahoma. He wound up as a retail broker and began using investment advisers to manage money for his clients in the early 1970s. "It became clear to me that it was easier to make judgments about people managing money than individual securities," he concedes. "I was choosing stocks on my own and also had some clients who were being advised. The advisers were doing better. So I had to reluctantly acknowledge that these people were more clever and capable of investing the money." A short time later, he founded a firm specializing in matching the rich with the right people to oversee their portfolios.

Today, Stolper admittedly has his feet on both sides of the mutual fund fence. In addition to analyzing and recommending funds to his clients, he is a director and shareholder of three fund families—Janus, Meridian, and the Pasadena Group. He therefore can empathize with the business concerns they face, including the need to pay for an enormous amount of overhead. That's why a fund's total expense ratio is of little concern to him. "My attitude on fees is that if you don't like it, don't buy it," he argues. "If you think you're buying a Camry and it's priced like a Lexus, go down the street. You're buying intellectual skills. I want the best skills I can get, and I'm perfectly willing to pay up for it." For this reason, he avoids index funds. "I don't use them myself because of my need to handicap," he shares. "I think that once the cyclical part of the S&P 500 begins to crater, just because the economy slows down, this recent reverence for index funds will likely go out the window."

Stolper believes you can have a perfectly diversified portfolio with just five funds. "You certainly don't want any more than that," he insists. "A typical account will have one large-cap growth fund, one small-cap fund, one value-oriented fund, and one broad-based international fund, with each position equally weighted." His goal is to uncover managers who are the best money makers in their respective discipline. "What you're looking for is a pattern of success," Stolper says. "I not only want statistical data, but also to talk with these folks. I interview about 50 or 60 managers a year. One thing you'll find is that the only thing the great managers can talk about is stocks. There's a clear change in conversational pattern and body language when that subject comes up. I happen to think that the biggest problem is overdiversification, not underdiversification."

Deciding when to sell is Stolper's most difficult challenge. "The reality is you sell when you run out of patience," he says. "I'm real slow to add new names. If you run a screen, you'll find that 88 percent of underperformance is style driven. The market doesn't like what the manager is buying, even though they own the same stocks that attracted you to the fund in the first place. If I can't find anything else wrong, I'll stick with the manager."

Occupation: President, Stolper & Company, Inc.
            San Diego, California
Birth Date: August 15, 1945
Education: BA, University of Oklahoma, 1967
            MBA, University of Oklahoma, 1968
Biggest Mistake Investors Make: "Overthinking and then acting on it; most investors overmanage their portfolios."
Best Investment: Investing in three privately held mutual fund companies: Janus, Meridian, and the Pasadena Group.
Worst Investment: An oil limited partnership he bought in the 1980s that became worthless.
Advice: "Never forget that in this business you make most of your money by just showing up. The influence of participation and compound interest is substantially greater than the cleverness of asset allocation."
Market Outlook: Cautious. "I still believe that every once in awhile the gods demand a virgin."

ED WALCZAK

Vontobel USA

As a kid growing up in Norwich, Connecticut, Ed Walczak had dreams of one day becoming a garbage man. "It was neat to see those guys get out there and toss cans into the air," he says. "I thought it was a cool profession as a boy and still do." The only son of a professional baseball player, Walczak decided to study government in college, and thought about going to law school. "Instead I got a graduate degree in international economics before going on for my MBA," he recalls

His first official job was working in the finance department at Ford Motor Company in Ann Arbor, Michigan. "I did that for a little over a year, but it just wasn't as interesting as I thought it would be," he says. Then he met a headhunter who offered him a job in General Motor's treasury department in New York. "The most intriguing thing I did was conduct research on why the Japanese could build cars cheaper than us in the late 1970s," he shares. After less than three years at GM, Walczak considered selling real estate, until another headhunter came calling and offered to bring him to Wall Street.

He eventually landed a job working in institutional sales for Stanford C. Bernstein & Co. in 1982. "I liked the culture there, however I got tired of making the same sales calls over and over again," he admits. "I then decided to switch from sales to becoming a junior portfolio manager at Lazard Freres in late 1984." After a few years there, yet another headhunter approached him with an opportunity he couldn't refuse: the chance to manage money on his own at a company called Vontobel. "I had never heard of them," Walczak concedes. "I did some research and found out they seemed to be a reputable Swiss bank. That was ten years ago."

Walczak now runs $475 million in assets for the firm, including the Vontobel US Value fund. His investment style has evolved over time. At first, he combined both the quantitative and qualitative traits he learned from his first two jobs on Wall Street. "It was more of a Graham & Dodd approach, emphasizing low PE and low price-to-book stocks," he says. "Then I kind of hit the books, and the more I read about Warren Buffett's work, the more I realized how much I agreed with his style." He then proceeded to dig up Buffett's old annual reports and became a self-described "Buffett Moonie."

"Now, just like Buffett, the quality of a company is the most important thing I look for in a potential investment," he says. "I keep my eye on a list of qualitative criteria that Buffett has articulated. They're all mom and apple pie things, such as high returns on capital, shareholder-oriented management, elements of a franchise, predictable earnings, and free cash flow. The company should also be involved in an unregulated industry. Out of all of the stocks out there, I would guess than only 120 or so meet this first test."

After that, he examines whether the company sells for a cheap price. "This involves figuring out its intrinsic value, or what it's really worth," he explains. "I try to go out a number of years in the future and make a reasonable man's guesstimate about whether the current returns can be sustained for several years into the future. If so, I'll come up with some earnings and free cash flow estimates going forward and discount those numbers back to the present using today's level of interest rates. I usually use the 10-year bond. I look for value in stocks the same way I do for bonds. I am really looking at a company's prospective future returns compared to what I could get in a risk-free 10- or 30-year government bond. For me to be seduced out of a risk-free investment, a stock has to offer sufficient increments of return."

Walczak has been having a tough time finding stocks that meet his qualifications in recent years. He was holding 35 percent cash at last check. "If I can't find something that's attractive relative to the risk-free rate, I'll sit on the sidelines," he maintains. "Cash is the residual of my inability to find attractively priced stocks in today's environment."

His sales discipline is equally straight-forward. "I'll get rid of a stock for one of two reason," he notes. "If my thesis for buying has deteriorated, which is a nice way of saying I'm wrong, or if it becomes fully valued."

Incidentally, although Walczak has never shook hands with Buffett, he did get to ask him a question at a Berkshire Hathaway meeting a few years ago. "I asked him about the rate at which he discounted back future cash flow when valuing a stock," Walczak says. "I wanted to make sure I was doing it right."

Occupation: Chief Investment Officer, Vontobel USA
New York, New York
Birth Date: September 17, 1953
Education: BA, Colby College, 1975
MA, Columbia University, 1976
MBA, Columbia University, 1978
Biggest Mistake Investors Make: "Being too momentum oriented. Also, doing what the crowd is doing because it feels good, and because it's so hard to go against them."
Best Investment: Buying regional bank stocks at distressed prices in 1990; many more than doubled in subsequent years.
Worst Investment: Leslie Fay (Bought in 1992 for about $12 per share; finally sold out at around $6. The stock is virtually worthless today.)
Advice: "Be disciplined and, like Buffett says, wait for the pitch. Don't buy unless there's something that's really attractive and undervalued."
Market Outlook: Cautious. "The fact that I'm only 65 percent invested shows I have not been able to find many stocks that meet my criteria," he says.

MARTIN WHITMAN

Third Avenue Funds

When Marty Whitman reads *The Wall Street Journal*, one of the first things he looks for on the stock page is the day's new low list. "I want to buy what's safe and cheap," he says. In fact, Whitman is often referred to as a "vulture investor," a title he's quite comfortable with. "It sure beats being called an asset allocator or academic," he quips. "Those folks don't know what they're talking about. To be a vulture investor means you know what you're doing and can read a document."

Whitman earned his vulture reputation by building a career out of investing in distressed companies that others expect to go out of business. "There's almost nothing I go into where the near-term outlook isn't terrible," he points out. It's a field of expertise he got into almost by accident. "After serving in the Navy, I originally planned to teach economics," he remembers. "But after finishing graduate school, I saw there wasn't much of a future for me as an academic, so I went to work on Wall Street."

He started out in research, before moving into investment banking, managing private money, and ultimately doing control investing. Whitman first began specializing in distressed companies in the early 1970s, when he decided to start his own firm. "I wanted to do corporate finance, but didn't have a lot of money," he says. "There were two fields that were wide open, where I didn't have to compete with big firms like Morgan Stanley and Goldman Sachs. They were bankruptcy and shareholder litigation. I built quite a reputation in both areas." Originally Whitman just gave advice to troubled companies. But he soon realized he could make more money by investing in them instead as a portfolio manager. Today, in addition to managing private accounts and two mutual funds, he teaches a course on control investing at Yale.

Whitman invests in both the stocks and bonds of distressed companies. The instrument he chooses depends on where he sees the most opportunity. "In all cases, the companies I'm buying have cash well in excess of total book liabilities," he points out. "I also won't pay more than a 60 percent premium over book value, and rarely pay more than 12 times what the company's historic net income has been. This is designed to simulate the pricing a first stage venture capitalist would pay if he were financing a private company."

When it comes to investing in severely troubled companies, Whitman almost always prefers secured debt over common stock, since he wants to own the most senior issue available, in case of any potential reorganization. "For credit securities, I always assume there will be a credit default," he notes. "Then I figure out how I will come out in the event that this happens."

Although Whitman describes what he does as a form of value investing, he pays little attention to traditional indicators of value, like dividend yields and PE ratios. "Graham and Dodd (the two noted authorities on value investing) are all screwed up," he maintains. "I analyze companies just like Warren Buffett. I examine the values in the business and stop. The basic analysis of all the amateurs, including Graham and Dodd, is to try and determine at which price a stock will sell. You carry an awful lot of excess baggage with that kind of methodology." He also can care less about the overall market. "That's only important to incompetents who want to make a lot of money by charging fees for stuff like asset allocation," he maintains. "For people who know about the companies they invest in, the market is immaterial. There are always bull and bear markets."

Whitman's portfolio turnover averages less than 15 percent a year. "Most of my companies get taken out through mergers and acquisitions," he says. "If I'm doing everything right, in any six-month or one-year period, there ought to be a lot of takeovers. I will sell a stock on my own if I conclude I've made a mistake or find out the guy in charge is a crook." Two warning signs are when management starts to burn cash or the company has a successive string of bad operating results. Whitman admits that some 20 to 30 percent of his stocks turn out to be total clunkers. However, the gains from his winners more than make up the difference.

As for his own future, despite published reports to the contrary, Whitman insists he has no immediate plans to retire. "I'd become a tennis pro if I could, but I don't think that's likely to happen," he says. "I'll keep doing this as long as I'm competent. This is what I enjoy. Having come out of the distress and stockholder litigation business, mutual fund management is like semi-retirement anyway."

Occupation: CEO and Chief Investment Officer, Third Avenue Funds
New York, New York
Birth Date: September 30, 1924
Education: BS, Syracuse University, 1949
MA, New School of Social Research, 1956
Biggest Mistake Investors Make: "Paying attention to the stock market and reading the stuff put out by Wall Street research departments."
Best Investment: Nabors Industries (Paid 40 cents a share for the stock in 1987, and it's now worth more than $20. He's also a director of the company.)
Worst Investment: Union Federal (Bought for $2 a share in 1993, and it ultimately went to zero.)
Advice: "Buy and hold well-financed companies."
Market Outlook: Cautious. "One thing I'll say is that I would suppose we might be having the same speculative bubble here in the U.S. that Japan had in the late 1980s and early 1990s."

DAVID WILLIAMS

U.S. Trust

David Williams has a record any mutual fund manager would envy. His Excelsior Value and Restructuring is the top performing general equity fund in the nation over the past five years, returning 27.2 percent annually, 6.9 percent ahead of the S&P 500. What's more, he's one of only two managers to beat the S&P in every year since 1993. Yet his fund remained in relative obscurity until recently, when sponsor U.S. Trust finally decided to start marketing it. "Now I get $3 or $4 million a day in new money," he says.

"I don't think this large inflow has hurt my results yet, but I am going to have to use more mid- and large-cap names as we inch toward the $1 billion mark."

Williams has his own theories about why so many of his fellow active managers have been losing out to the indexes in recent years. "For one thing, our fees are higher," he rations. "But more than that, right now the big cap names in the S&P 500 are providing market leadership. It's been that way since 1994. Once the focus turns away from these larger stocks, active money managers will begin to outperform again."

Williams majored in art history at Yale in the 1960s and was a Navy pilot for five years. "After that, I went to Harvard Business School and decided I would like to manage money," he recalls. "My first job was working at T. Rowe Price managing private and pension accounts. For the first six months I was there, the market went down like clockwork every day. It was an unbelievable period to be exposed to investing." It got so bad, the firm brought in a psychologist to help managers deal with belligerent clients who were furious about the negative results. "They kept saying, 'Why should we give money to you when we can get 4 or 5 percent from the bank without taking any risk?' And they were serious," Williams notes. "Now, of course, no one would think of putting their money in a savings account since the market is doing so well."

But Williams isn't apathetic. He has no doubt we'll go through another period like 1974 again. It's just a matter of when. "It all has to do with inflation," he insists. "For the time being, I think inflation's under good control and won't be a problem for the foreseeable future. However, there will come a time when we have higher inflation and the market will take a beating because of it."

Williams spent five years at T. Rowe Price, before starting his own investment firm with a partner in New York. They weren't making enough money, so Williams took a job with Horizon Trust in 1981 as chief investment officer. Six years later, he joined U.S. Trust. "For the first couple of months, I was in charge of a new product which was marketed to smaller accounts of between $250,000 and $2 million," he says. "Most of the proceeds were invested in our mutual funds.

Then they asked me to manage larger accounts. My fund was launched in 1993. Today I run about $2 billion altogether."

Like the quirky name of his fund suggests, Williams looks for companies selling at value prices that often are going through some type of restructuring. "I try to find companies that are under a cloud," he explains. "They've disappointed Wall Street for one reason or another. I really like companies that are in difficulty but have done something to indicate they recognize the problem and are addressing it. Often the companies I invest in sell for relatively cheap prices. By that I mean they have low PE or price-to-cash flow ratios. They also often have new CEOs who are changing what the old management botched up."

Finding companies under a cloud and on the bargain table isn't hard. The challenge is separating those that belong there from those that are unduly being punished and have a lot of promise. Williams concedes you can never be sure about this, although he feels like he improves his chances by scheduling an in-person meeting with management. "It may be psychological, but it does give me more confidence when I hear the story from the horse's mouth, rather than second hand from a Wall Street analyst," he says. "You get a sense of how good they are by how they talk. You also learn whether their plan for the company makes sense. You can evaluate whether it's unrealistic or doomed to failure. If I get a good feel from management, more often than not it turns out to be a successful investment."

In today's market, Williams prefers to buy companies trading for around 15 times earnings, and he sells when that multiple gets up to the 25 range. One way he reduces risk is by maintaining a well-diversified portfolio of some 85 names. "I always have something that's working," he says. "I have both big and small companies, and keep roughly 10 percent overseas."

Occupation: Managing Director, U.S. Trust
New York, New York
Birth Date: July 4, 1942
Education: BA, Yale University, 1965
MBA, Harvard University, 1974
Biggest Mistake Investors Make: "Listening to other people and taking hot tips; you have to do your own work and at least some simple research."
Best Investment: Suiza Foods (Purchased as an IPO for $13 in 1994. Today it trades above $60.)
Worst Investment: Ugly Duckling (This stock lived up to its name. He bought it for $15 in early 1997, and sold out for $10 a few months later.)
Advice: "Think like a contrarian. Buy stocks when no one else wants them, and sell when they're in great demand."
Market Outlook: Bullish, but expecting high volatility with periodic 10 to 15 percent corrections.

U PDATE

on *Wall Street's Picks for 1998*

Those of you who read *Wall Street's Picks for 1998* might be wondering, "What should I do with those stocks and mutual funds now?" Well, wonder no more, because the answer to that pressing question can be found on the following pages. In most cases, I went back to each of last year's panelists and asked, "How do you feel about your pick from last year going into 1999? Do you now consider it to be a buy, sell, or hold?" You'll find the responses on the following pages.

Just so we're clear on definitions, *buy* means the pick is still recommended for purchase in 1999, *hold* suggests you should hang on if you already own the investment, and *sell* is a sign it might be best to take your profits (or losses) and move on to other opportunities.

Some of the experts were sort of on the border, advising a *buy/hold* or *hold/sell* strategy. Buy/hold is a signal they are lukewarm on the pick and aren't strongly advising any new purchases. Hold/sell suggests they consider the stock to be a weak hold and are on the verge of getting rid of it.

THE TOP STOCKS FOR 1998—UPDATE

STOCK	PANELIST	CURRENT ADVICE
Chrysler	Seth Glickenhaus	BUY/HOLD
Cisco Systems	Kevin Landis	HOLD
Cohu	Scott Black	HOLD
Computer Sciences	Elizabeth Bramwell	BUY/HOLD
Crompton & Knowles	John Wallace	BUY
Dell Computer	James Collins	BUY/HOLD
Department 56	Donald Yacktman	BUY
Fannie Mae	David Dreman	BUY
Harding Lawson Associates	William Nasgovitz	HOLD
Herman Miller	Louis Navellier	BUY
International Paper	James O'Shaughnesssy	BUY
Isis Pharmaceuticals	Michael Murphy	BUY
Manpower	Jean-Marie Eveillard	BUY
McDonald's	Elaine Garzarelli	HOLD
Memtec	Vivian Lewis	1
Northern Trust	John Rogers	BUY/HOLD
Philip Morris	Robert Sanborn	BUY
Playtex	Cappy McGarr	BUY
Pre-Paid Legal	Michael DiCarlo	BUY
Q-Entertainment	Andrew Addison	2
Rational Software	Garrett Van Wagoner	BUY
Scientific-Atlanta	Susan Byrne	HOLD
Tokio Marine & Fire Insurance	Martin Whitman	BUY
Wells Fargo	Shelby Davis	BUY
Zoom Telephonics	Al Frank	BUY/HOLD

1–Company acquired by U.S. Filter.
2–Trading Suspended.

THE TOP FUNDS FOR 1998—UPDATE

FUND	PANELIST	CURRENT ADVICE
Artisan International	Bob Markman	SELL
Baron Asset	Robert Bingham	HOLD
Clipper Fund	Catherine Voss Sanders	BUY
Dreyfus Aggressive Value	Thurman Smith	SELL
Harbor Capital Appreciation	Harold Evensky	HOLD
Matthews Asian Convertible Sec.	Stephen Savage	HOLD
Oakmark International	Louis Stanasolovich	BUY
T. Rowe Price Dividend Growth	Walter Frank	BUY
T. Rowe Price Equity Income	Michael Hirsch	BUY
Templeton Global Sm. Co.	Eric Roseman	BUY
Yacktman Focused	Michael Stolper	BUY

GLOSSARY

of Investment Terms

American Depositary Receipt (ADR)—Receipt for the shares of a foreign-based stock that are held by a U.S. bank and entitle shareholders to all dividends and capital gains. It's a way for Americans to buy shares in foreign-based companies on a U.S. stock exchange.

annual report—Yearly statement of a corporation's financial condition. It must be distributed to all shareholders of record.

ask or offer price—The lowest amount a seller is willing to take for shares of a stock.

asset allocation—Act of spreading investment funds across various categories of assets, such as stocks, bonds, and cash.

beta—A coefficient measure of a stock's relative volatility in relation to the Standard & Poor's 500 index, which has a beta of 1.

bid price—The highest amount a buyer is willing to pay for shares of a stock.

blue chip—Common stock of a nationally known company with a long record of profit growth, dividend payments and a reputation for quality products and services.

bond—Any interest-bearing or discounted government or corporate obligation that pays a specified sum of money, usually at regular intervals.

book value—What a company would be worth if all assets were sold (assets minus liabilities). Also, the price at which an asset is carried on a balance sheet.

bottom-up investing—The search for outstanding individual stocks with little regard for overall economic trends.

broker—Person who acts as an intermediary between a buyer and a seller.

buy and hold strategy—Technique that calls for accumulating and keeping shares in a company over many years, regardless of price swings.

cash ratio—Ratio of cash and marketable securities to current liabilities. Tells the extent to which liabilities could be immediately liquidated.

chief executive officer (CEO)—Individual responsible for the overall operations of a corporation.

contrarian—Investor who does the opposite of the majority at any particular time.

convertible bond—Security that can be exchanged for other securities of the issuer (under certain conditions), usually from preferred stock or bonds into common stock.

current ratio—Current assets divided by current liabilities. Shows a company's ability to pay current debts from current assets.

debt-to-equity ratio—Long-term debt divided by shareholder's equity. Indicates how highly leveraged a company is. (A figure greater than 1.5 should raise a red flag.)

diversification—Spreading risk by putting assets into several different investment categories, like stocks, bonds, and cash.

dividend—Distribution of earnings to shareholders.

dividend yield—The cash dividend paid per share each year divided by the current share price.

dollar cost averaging—The process of accumulating positions in stocks and mutual funds by investing a set amount of money each month, thus buying more shares when prices are down, less when they are up.

Dow Jones Industrial Average—The oldest and most widely quoted stock market indicator. Represents the price direction of 30 blue chip stocks on the New York Stock Exchange. (Doesn't always give an accurate view of what's happening with the market as a whole.)

fair market value—Price at which an asset or service is or can be passed on from a willing buyer to a willing seller.

Form 10-K—Annual report filed with the Securities and Exchange Commission showing a company's total sales, revenues, and pretax operating income, along with sales figures for each of the firm's different lines or businesses over the past five years.

good-till-canceled order (GTC)—A brokerage order to buy or sell shares of a security at a given price that remains in effect until executed or canceled.

growth stock—Stock of a corporation that shows greater-than-average gains in earnings.

institutional investor—Organization that trades a large volume of securities, like a mutual fund, bank, or insurance company.

intrinsic value—Worth of a company; comparable to the prevailing market price.

limit order—Order to buy or sell a security at a specific price.

market capitalization or market value—Calculated by multiplying the number of shares outstanding by the per share price of a stock. One can also categorize equities into several different classes, including micro-cap, small-cap, mid-cap, and large-cap. The general guidelines for these classifications are as follows:

- micro-cap—Market capitalizations of $0 to $100 million.
- small-cap—Market capitalizations of $100 to $750 million.
- mid-cap—Market capitalizations of $750 million to $2 billion.
- large-cap—Market capitalizations of $2 billion or more.

market order—Order to buy or sell a security at the best available price.

mutual fund—An investment company that raises money from shareholders and puts it to work in stocks, options, bonds or money market securities. Offers investors diversification and professional management.

Nasdaq Composite—An index (formerly the National Association of Securities Dealers Automated Quotation System) weighted by market value and representing domestic companies that are sold over the counter.

net current assets—Calculated by taking current assets minus current liabilities. Also referred to as working capital.

price-earnings ratio (PE)—Price of a stock divided by its earnings per share.

price-to-book value ratio (P/BV)—Calculated by dividing shareholder's equity by the number of outstanding shares. If under 1, it means a stock is selling for less than what the company paid for its assets, though this is not necessarily indicative of a good value.

Standard & Poor's Composite Index of 500 Stocks (S&P 500)—Tracks the performance of 500 stocks, mostly blue chip names, and represents almost two-thirds of the U.S. stock market's total value. It is weighted by market value. (As an equity investor, your goal should be to beat the return of the S&P 500. This is not an easy task, and roughly 75 percent of all mutual fund managers fail to do so.)

stock—Represents ownership in a corporation. Usually listed in terms of shares.

INDEX